The Worth of a Child

The Worth of
a Child

Thomas H. Murray

UNIVERSITY OF CALIFORNIA PRESS

Berkeley / Los Angeles / London

This book is a print-on-demand volume. It is manufactured using toner in place of ink. Type and images may be less sharp than the same material seen in traditionally printed University of California Press editions.

University of California Press
Berkeley and Los Angeles, California

University of California Press
London, England

Library of Congress Cataloging-in-Publication Data

Murray, Thomas H., 1946–
    The worth of a child / Thomas H. Murray.
        p.   cm.
    Includes bibliographical references (p.   ) and index.
    ISBN 0-520-08836-0 (cloth : alk. paper)
        1. Parenthood—Moral and ethical aspects.   2. Childbirth—
Moral and ethical aspects.   3. Parent and child.   4. Children
and adults.   5. Ethics.   I. Title.
HQ755.8.M88   1996
306.874—dc20   95-46977
                                                        CIP

Printed in the United States of America

The paper used in this publication meets the minimum requirements of American National Standard for Information Sciences—Permanence of Paper for Printed Library Materials, ANSI Z39.48-1984 ⊖

To those who have taught me best about the love between parents and children: my mother and father; my children, Kate, Nicky, Pete, and Emily; and my partner in parenthood, Cynthia

Contents

Preface

This book grew from efforts, spanning a dozen years, to make sense of the ethics of adult-child relationships. What are adults morally permitted to do in their quest to have children, biologically related to them or not? What may women do who wish not to bear any child now? Should couples be allowed to accept or reject a particular child because of some characteristic it may have—a genetic disability perhaps, or an undesired gender? What duties do parents have to protect their born children from harm? Are those duties compatible with permitting their children to be the subjects of biomedical research? What duties, if any, do we have to children who are not yet born, but likely to be? How should we weigh the competing claims of genetic and rearing parents against each other and in relation to the well-being of the child in dispute?

I was dissatisfied with many of the discussions of children in bioethics. They were too narrow, from the way the problems were framed to the factors considered and the arguments used to the conclusions reached. It was not difficult to see why this happened: Bioethics had developed hard-won tools for dealing with difficult moral controversies, and it was going to use them wherever it could. If that meant hammering a problem into a shape the available tools could deal with, so be it, even if the problem was distorted in the process. It also meant that questions were often isolated from the contexts in which they arose. This created two problems. First, it led to questions being framed in sometimes peculiar ways, often making them appear less tractable than they were. Second, reservoirs of morally relevant insight were ignored, pushed out of view.

When I began this project—though dubbing it a "project" implies more coherence than was present at that time—I was new to the world of academic ethics in general and bioethics in particular. The discovery that there was such a field as bioethics, in which scholars analyzed just the sort of moral problems that had so perplexed and troubled me, was a revelation. Over the next dozen years, though, I was at first embarrassed and later inspired by an anomaly that I could not deny. The anomaly was this: When I proceeded as orthodox bioethics seemed to declare was correct—by applying a small set of fairly abstract principles—the results were competent, but not terribly illuminating. In stark contrast, when I misbehaved—freed myself from what Stephen Toulmin has called the tyranny of principles and dove headlong into the problem with all its glorious and untidy particulars—the task was more difficult, but the reward, in comprehensive understanding and in persuasive and specific answers, seemed well worth the gamble. Working on a particular problem, I would learn as much or more from history, sociology, or anthropology, or even from careful rumination on commonsense morality, as I would from moral theory. What began as a guilty secret became in time an intriguing phenomenon in its own right. Was there something wrong or incomplete in the orthodox model of how to think about concrete, practical moral questions? With the encouragement of gifted and generous colleagues, I began to take seriously the implications of the gap between the orthodox model and what seemed to yield the greatest results in practice.

This book tries to shed light on a number of perplexing problems in the ethics of adult-child relations. At the same time it asks and tries to answer questions about practical moral reasoning, such as, Why should I believe that this description of a moral problem is better than the alternatives? What sorts of information help answer practical moral questions? What counts as giving a "good" answer to an ethical question? How can I reasonably be assured that this answer is not merely a reflection of local prejudices? In the end it will be up to each reader to judge whether fruitful questions have been asked and convincing answers offered. By making my assumptions visible, I hope to aid readers in their efforts to discern what is valuable and what is not in what follows.

Because the analyses and conclusions in this book depend heavily on the methods I use, and because those methods depart from orthodox bioethics, I felt obliged to give more explicit attention to the process of moral reasoning than is typical of books on practical moral problems. To do otherwise would miss an opportunity to test the power and integrity of these methods. If I ignored or left unanswered criticisms of this approach to moral problems, the analyses and conclusions would be left even more shrouded in tentativeness than they properly should be.

One more word about my intentions: I am not attempting to create a comprehensive moral theory about adult-child relations. As this work will make clear, I doubt that the search for an all-encompassing theory has much chance of success. My intention is more modest and pragmatic: to explore a set of ethical issues about having and raising children with the hope of illuminating what is at stake, to examine critically some important ways of responding to those issues, and to offer some tentative answers.

Throughout this book two interrelated issues remain central. First is the significance of parenthood, and therefore children, in the flourishing of adults. Second is attentiveness to the practices and institutions—families, cultural values, professional norms, social supports—that promote the healthy development of children who themselves are likely to flourish and to raise *their* children well.

This dual concern underlies the ambiguity in the book's title. By "the worth of a child" I mean both the significance of a child to its parents and the child's own value as a creature worthy of moral concern. The title permits a third reading—"worth" as a measure of economic value, whether as one of those amusing calculations of the market value of the raw materials making up a human body (children, being smaller, are worth less than adults by that method) or as the sale of a healthy live child. I intend that reading of the title as ironic. Indeed, why we should reject the reduction of children to their market value is one of the principal issues I take up.

Acknowledgments

Once, at a workshop, I had to describe what I enjoy in my work. I blurted out, "I like having written." I had intended to say that I liked to write, but that was such a blatant lie that the words were edited as they spilled out. The act of writing, besides being a continuous confrontation with your own shortcomings, is also acutely lonely. Yet it is at the same time one of the most intensely social things you can do. Friends and colleagues allow you to try out ideas, they point out holes and identify possible errors.

Many people helped me with this book. First, I want to thank those who offered advice or sent useful information: Miriam Rosenthal, Cynthia Cohen, Lainie Friedman Ross, Laura Rothstein, Stephen Post, Gladys White, Carol Tauer, Jill Korbin, Eric Juengst, Michael Yesley, Grant Gillett, Dewey DuCharme, Christopher Meyer, Michael Kaback, Barbara Bowles Biesecker, Erik Parens, Peter Greco, Bob Lawry, Fred Griffith, and Jackie Barksdale. Thanks to the students who helped me in so many ways in my research, especially Michelle Gerroir and Maggie Feltz. Thanks to those who provided sustained and critical readings of significant portions of the manuscript, including Dena Davis, Roger Crisp, Rebecca Dresser, Albert Jonsen, and Renée Fox. A combination of heartfelt thanks—and sympathy—for those hearty few who have read all or nearly all of the book-in-process: Adrienne Asch, Paul Lauritzen, James Lindemann Nelson, and John Arras. Thanks to Stuart Youngner for his unfailing friendship and sage council. And a special note of thanks to my editors at the UC Press: Stan Holwitz has been a warm and steady supporter, and I cannot find adequate words to thank Elizabeth Knoll for her unflagging encouragement and astute editorial guidance. Why I should have been blessed with such an extraordinary editor is beyond my comprehension. Finally, to my parents, whose abiding love of their children showed us what a child is worth, as well as how to be a good parent; to my children, from whom I have learned more about the worth of a child and the value of a family than from any scholarly text; and to my wife, Cynthia, my coadventurer in parenthood and in life.

1

Why Do Adults
Have Children?

This is a book about the worth of children, which means that it must also be a book about adults and about the values people seek in family life. It is also a book about ethics—the ethics of the adult-child relationship, the scope and limits of parental obligations, the social arrangements and technologies enlisted in conceiving, gestating, and rearing children, and, in another, broader sense, how to think about the issues raised in the scholarly and public debates on bioethics.

The two tasks—exploring the ethics of adult-child relationships and examining what contributes to sound thinking in ethics—are complementary. We will get our clearest and truest ideas about the ethics of adult-child relationships when we have our soundest, most insightful and revealing modes of moral analysis. Likewise, if we want to learn to think creatively about practical moral problems, we must confront them with genuine perplexities, then reflect on where those methods are useful and where they fail us. The two goals are equal and inseparable here.

Perplexities often take the form of specific cases. One that captured the public imagination concerned Mary and Abe Ayala's decision to have another child when one of their children was diagnosed with a life-threatening disease. Early in her adolescence, Anissa Ayala was found to have a lethal cancer of the blood called chronic myelogenous leukemia. The most effective treatment for this disease is a radical one: destroy all of the cancerous cells using a combination of heavy radiation and toxic drugs, then replace them with normal cells. The odds of success are little better than fifty-fifty; but without the treatment, death is virtually certain within a few years.

There is a catch. Unless the bone marrow Anissa received was closely matched to her own immune system—the codes that allow the cells of our body to distinguish friend from foe—the result could be disastrous; the foreign cells might turn against her own body and destroy it, a dreaded phenomenon known as graft versus host reaction. The best match of all would be from a close relative who had the same immune profile as Anissa.

Anissa's parents were tested, as was her older brother, Airon. None of them, unfortunately, was a good match. A search through marrow donor registries was no more fruitful. Now it happens that a brother or a sister has a one in four chance of being a compatible donor. So Mary and Abe Ayala decided to try to have another child who might, if they were fortunate, be a suitable donor.

The Ayalas were in their early forties. Abe had had a vasectomy. It was reversed, and the Ayalas conceived a child. They waited six months before Mary underwent amniocentesis and learned that their child-to-be was another girl (whom they named Marissa) and that she was a compatible donor for Anissa.

Marissa was born on 3 April 1990; the blood from her umbilical cord was preserved in the hope that it might contain the cells Anissa would need to rebuild her depleted marrow. On Tuesday, 4 June 1991, Anissa, after four days in which her entire body was assaulted by lethal doses of radiation and cell-killing drugs, received bone marrow from her little sister. Anissa was nineteen years old; Marissa, fourteen months. Anissa's initial response was excellent. One year and a day after her transplant, Anissa married her high school sweetheart.

None of these facts are in dispute. Yet the case has been the source of an intense controversy about whether what the Ayalas did was morally justifiable. It may be helpful to begin by setting aside issues that were not at the heart of the debate. Putting Anissa through the radical therapy ending with bone marrow transplant was not controversial. Nor was the Ayalas' decision to direct that marrow be taken from one child, even though she was a very young child, in an effort to save the life of her sibling. Although there is still some dispute over its boundaries, the practice of permitting parents to make such decisions about their children is widely accepted. In any case, this was not what the Ayalas' critics fixed upon.

What bothered the critics was that Mary and Abe Ayala were having a child in part because that child might be useful to another person. This, the critics argued, was immoral. One bioethicist was quoted as saying, "The ideal reason for having a child is . . . that child's own welfare—to bring a child into being and to nurture it. One of the fundamental precepts of ethics is that each person is an end in himself or herself, and is never to be used solely as a means to another person's end without the agreement of the person being used."[1] This is a reasonable paraphrase of Immanuel Kant's dictum, "Every rational being exists as an end in himself, not merely as a means for arbitrary use. . . . The practical imperative will therefore be as follows: Act in such a way that you always treat humanity, whether in your own person or in the person of any other, never simply as a means, but always at the same time as an end."[2] Kant's dictum and the contemporary bioethicist's paraphrase of it have a certain intuitive appeal. None of us like to be used; none of us want to be treated solely as an instrument in someone else's design. Good enough so far. But how does this maxim apply in the circumstances of the Ayala case?

One of the problems with great principles is that they do not come with their own rules of interpretation to tell us *when* they apply, and in precisely *what way*. If I hire someone to paint my house, am I treating her as a means only? My interest in her—and hers in me—looks purely instrumental. She is my means to get paint on my house, and I am her means to earn the money to buy food for her family next week. Now Kant's rule allows us to treat each other as means as long as we treat each other as ends also. But what counts as treating someone as an end also when, for example, we are dealing with her only because we want her to paint our house? The dictum does not tell us that. But we ought to be able to rely a bit on common sense here. Means and ends are not always so neatly separable in real life.

What do the Ayalas have to say for themselves? They were troubled and puzzled by the criticism. Abe told a journalist, "Once we decided to have her, we were comfortable, until we found out supposedly it was something we were doing bad."[3] Mary urged her critics "to walk in my shoes and let them feel what I was feeling when we were told that our daughter only had three to five years to live."[4] The Ayalas are frank, then, in admitting that a part of their purpose in having another child was the hope it would save the life of Anissa. But that is not the whole story. Anissa described her family's motives: "We don't even know if she is going to save my life. She's going to be my baby sister. She's coming into our lives. We will love her for what she is, not for what she is going to do for me."[5] The new baby will be loved for herself—treated, that is, as an end—and not only for what she can do for others.

It looks as if Kant and the contemporary bioethicist should be well satisfied.

Anissa's physician, however, gives the family's motives an interesting twist. Dr. Stephen J. Forman says, "The parents see this as a win-win situation. If the bone marrow transplant works, they have saved their daughter. If not, then they have another child." He goes on to add that "throughout history people have conceived children as replacements." [6] Setting aside the imagery of "win-win," which seems more suitable as a description of a business deal than of the profound life-and-death choices facing the Ayalas, Dr. Forman does have a point, or rather two points. First, he tells us that the Ayalas want another child in case Anissa dies, and he appears to approve of this motive. Second, he suggests that having a child to replace one who dies is a common and morally unproblematic act.

Dr. Forman does us a service by reminding us to leave the rarefied air of moral theory and to reflect on why people do in fact have children. To put it in plain language, adults have children for three kinds of reasons relevant to morality: for good reasons, for bad reasons, and for no reason at all. In my experience, I would venture that the last category—no reason at all—describes the births of more children than the other two categories combined. But as nothing in particular hangs on getting exact numbers here, I won't press the point.

Considering the Ayalas' decision to conceive and bear a child in the light of why people in general have children, their decision looks pretty good. They had not one but two good reasons. They wanted to have a child because, from all the evidence, they love children and enjoy raising them. The prospect of losing a daughter prompted them to fill a potential hole in their lives by having another. They hoped as well that this new child would save the life of her sister.

Here we confront a quandary that infects most thinking about adults and children. How should we understand the Ayalas' reasons in terms of the usual contrast between selfishness and altruism? When a couple tells us that they want a child because they like raising children, that seems to describe their motive in terms of the benefit to *them*, the parents, hence as selfish. But, if they are good parents, from the child's point of view this is just great—being born into a loving family. And as those of us who have ventured to be parents know from hard experience, being a good parent requires a great deal of work and sacrifice. Why, then, describe the parents' motive as selfish?

We encounter further perplexities in examining the second reason—

to save Anissa's life. Her parents are willing to undergo vasectomy reversal (Abe) and the risks and discomforts of pregnancy (Mary) and to assume the physical, financial, and emotional burdens of raising another child, all to save someone else's life. These acts are consistent with our usual notions of altruism. But surely they also feel deeply for their ill daughter; they want to avoid their own pain that stems from empathy for Anissa, and they want if possible to avoid the grief and sorrow that would come to them if she died young. Does that make their actions self-serving?

We *can* use the categories of selfishness and altruism here. But it is not clear why we would want to. They do not seem to offer much moral enlightenment about the Ayalas' decision. They do not even seem to be adequate descriptions of the alternatives. Mary and Abe Ayala did this in part for themselves, in part for their children. But perhaps it would be more revealing, and more true to what we regard as good parent-child relations, to say that in doing for themselves they are also doing for their children, and in doing for their children, they are doing for themselves.

The old, familiar moral categories of altruism and selfishness seem to be jumbled up in well-functioning parent-child relationships. Of course, if someone wanted to be a thoroughgoing cynic, he could emphasize what parents get out of it and insist that at heart selfishness was the real explanation. If the cynic were at all clever, we could toss all sorts of typical acts of parental unselfishness at him, but he could always explain them away as serving selfish motives in the end. I stay up all night nursing my sick child: well, if you didn't the child might die and you'd lose all the time and money you've invested, or the child might hate you and make your life miserable later on. A resolute altruist could do similarly, perhaps with a bit more difficulty. But in the end, however impressed we might be at the interpretive imagination displayed, we protest that neither philosophical artiste has described especially well how it really is between parents and children. And we can hardly expect to build sound moral judgments on descriptions that are thin and utterly unsatisfactory. We need a rich description of the moral life of parents and children, one that captures the complexity of motives for having and raising children and the significance of children in the lives of adults—one of the two central meanings of the "worth" of a child.

Whatever framework we choose will have to encompass an assortment of paradoxes: we celebrate individualism, yet we find meaning in family relationships; we cherish freedom, yet we have children whose needs constrain us profoundly; we want the liberty to get up and go whenever it suits us, yet our flourishing depends on lifelong commitments and enduring, steadfast relationships; we exalt choice and control, yet families are built largely on acceptance of people as they are, with all their imperfections; we participate in a vigorous commercial culture, yet we cherish and protect a sphere in which interactions are regulated by values alien to the world of commerce and markets.

The Importance of Context

If forced to declare what I believe is the single greatest problem in scholarly and popular discussions about the ethics of adult-child relationships, I would have to say that it is the failure to place both the questions themselves and the proffered answers in context. This failure manifests itself in many ways. Frequently, discussions about a tough moral problem fail to take into account how the issue in question is related to other issues. In the Ayala case, some bioethics commentators became lost in a wilderness of abstractions and failed to ask why adults have children at all. Sometimes the history of an issue leads people to frame the problem in a way that not only is unhelpful but also makes a sensible answer virtually impossible. For example, the recent history of experimentation with human beings so colored the debate on whether research on children was morally permissible that it led two distinguished ethicists astray—one to a bizarre conclusion, the other to a befuddling rationale.[7]

If we are insensitive to it, we can be blinkered by context. Questions about our moral obligations to fetuses that are not yet born, but whom the pregnant woman chooses to carry to term, have been twice swallowed up: once, by a confusion between public policies and moral judgments; and again by the presumption that these questions are just another manifestation of the abortion debate. Abortion itself, the bête noire of bioethics, has in recent years been framed as a metaphysical dispute over whether and when fetuses are persons. This framing itself has a context and a function. It is not the only way of framing the debate over abortion, and there is good reason to think that it is an extremely unhelpful way of phrasing the question—neat, simple, and irreconcilable—that has allowed both sides to believe in their own moral purity while blocking dialogue and compromise.

Read: Ch 1-3, 5

If context yields insights about why we see things as we do, it is equally helpful in showing us that it is possible to see them in other ways, indicating the factors that disposed people in other places and other times to see them differently than us and suggesting what consequences might flow from those differences. Citizens of the slave-holding Roman Empire, for example, permitted parents who were free to compel the return of a child they had abandoned. The biological parents only had to compensate the people who raised the child for the expenses of child rearing. This policy reflected both the power invested in patriarchy by the Romans and the urgent political need of the free to reinforce blood and birth as the factors that distinguished them from slaves. In a society of many slaves, the free wanted to keep their status from challenge by making the dividing line as clear as possible. In America, ideas about women's and men's roles, the family, and the place of children in the lives of adults have changed dramatically since colonial times. The influence of these ideas on contemporary bioethics is often unacknowledged. Understanding how and why these cultural images evolved yields insight into contemporary disputes.

Facts about social or historical context will not in and of themselves yield particular moral conclusions. Practical moral reasoning, however, falls prey to many snares and traps that a healthy awareness of our environment—that is, our cultural context—can help us identify and avoid. Above all, a concentration on context keeps us grounded in the interests, aspirations, images, and sufferings of real people.

Tapestry and Web

The focus on context suggests a metaphor: a tapestry. Imagine a grand tapestry that portrays a multitude of images of human life, from infancy through childhood, adolescence, then adulthood, old age, and, finally, death. On the tapestry are scenes from every age of life and every important sphere of activity. The sections of the tapestry most important for this book are those that portray children and parents. Of course, the threads that make up the warp and weft of these sections of the tapestry also run through other portions of it. These threads are our culture's conceptions of good—and bad—lives for adults and children. How the various segments of the tapestry relate to one another as the strands weave through is as significant as the portraits depicted in each.

Look for a moment at the parts of the tapestry in which children appear and you will discover a few things. We were all once children. And if we have survived long enough and been educated well enough to read this book, it is because adults provided for us through our many years of dependency, and equipped us with literacy, one of the essential skills for flourishing in our culture.

It has always been so. Every culture that is to survive must make provision for adding new members and giving them the skills needed to participate in the social and economic life of the community. The particular skills needed may have been vastly different among English farmers of the sixteenth century and American suburbanites of the late twentieth century. But unless it succeeds in regenerating both the culture itself and its membership, a community will perish. It is not sufficient merely to produce children. The physical, emotional, and developmental needs of infants, children, and young adults—the group we now call adolescents—must be met.

It is not just the community as an aggregate that needs children and not just children who have needs; so too do adults. Children have helped to meet a variety of adult needs: economic needs, as household workers or as support in old age; emotional needs, for intimacy and affection; and developmental needs, for maturation, for ripening of the virtues appropriate to adult life.

Every culture must have some understanding of how to regulate the relationships between children and adults. Though it is possible to think of these relationships as a set of rules—formal rules codified in the law, or informal rules of moral conduct—this is a very incomplete picture of the relationship between adults and children, a bit like knowing the rules of baseball but having absolutely no appreciation of the subtleties of play or, for that matter, of the point of playing the game. A culture's "rules" for adult-child relationships are merely isolated threads from a much richer tapestry in which its understanding of what constitutes a good and meaningful life for adults forms the warp and its images of children form the weft.

Any discussion of the ethics of adult-child relationships that ignores the tapestry itself, preferring to work only with a few conveniently visible strands, is to that extent impoverished. A culture that relies on such fragmentary understandings faces great intellectual and practical perils. Our intellectual grasp is flawed to the extent that we fail to understand how the visible rules regulating those relationships are an integral part of the much larger, complex fabric a culture weaves out of the lives of its members. The parts of the fabric portraying good lives for adults may be chillingly uniform; there may be utterly distinct pictures for different castes, or classes, or genders. Whether or not we approve of the tapestry in all its detail, we cannot comprehend in more than a superficial way a culture's morality without understanding the images it portrays.

Examining carefully the images of good lives has a critical moral edge as well. Unless the culture in question is exemplary (and probably unknown in human history), its portraits of adult life are highly beneficial to some of its members and less so to others. They may permit, even encourage, the exploitation of some for the benefit of others. We gain moral perspective when we understand how a culture's pictures of good lives lead to actual or potential exploitation.

Children as a group seem especially ripe for exploitation. In their younger years they lack the means to be heard, even for a time the means to speak. They lack the physical power to command a hearing, and usually economic power as well. Yet, in most instances, they receive enough of what they need to become adults. A culture's images of children that explain what children are, why they are worth having and caring for, constitute the other half of the weave and are equally vital to an understanding of the whole tapestry.

The tapestry can also be beautiful. It may contain pictures of families characterized by love and loyalty, in which women and men treat each other with consideration and justice, in which children are valued and nurtured, and in which family life supports the flourishing of all members. However concerned we may be with families that fail to achieve the values people seek in forming families, it is crucial not to lose sight of what those values are—the point of making families and having children. Of all the things I believe are unsatisfactory about the discussion of children in bioethics, the failure to take seriously what we value about children and family life has been the most destructive. I want to bring consideration of those values back into the center of public dialogue.

My strategy is to explore a set of contemporary ethical issues about the relationship of adults and children. By framing the ethical issues, not as clashes of abstract principles, but as disparate views about what gives meaning and worth to the lives of adults and of children, and by acknowledging the social and historical context of these views, my hope is to illuminate what is genuinely at stake in these questions and, where possible, to provide reasonable resolutions to persistent conflicts.

People notice the moral content of decisions or practices when they go awry, or fail to function smoothly, or arouse anger and protest. Our everyday practices, the ones not called into question, are just as full of assumptions about values as those that evoke dissension. But those values remain implicit and hidden since no one, or at least no one we are inclined to listen to, objects to them.

Every society must make provisions for dealing with the failure of its systems, including its systems for regulating the relationships between adults and children and meeting the needs of both groups. Children may be in the care of adults who are unable or unwilling to give them what they need because of poverty, illness, physical or mental incapacity, or a defect of character. Not only good people can become parents.

A child may be in no one's care: orphaned or abandoned. Or a child may need new adults in its life for the reasons just mentioned. To respond to such needs, cultures have devised formal systems such as foster care and adoption, along with a variety of informal practices.

Adults may want and need children but be unable to have them. They might want children for economic reasons, to meet their emotional needs, or to foster their own maturation and development. The same practices meant to meet the needs of children with no or incapable parents—foster care, adoption, and informal methods—can be used to meet these adult needs. More recently, methods for circumventing infertility have emerged as another means of providing for adults who desire children.

Cultures must decide how to weigh the respective claims of children, at various ages, and of adults, with various ties to those children. Cultures must also decide how to weigh claims of different types: economic, physical, emotional, developmental, moral.

All of these interconnected strands form the tapestry. The web comes into play when we try to construct moral responses to those controversies. The web is a metaphor for justification in moral reasoning. It contrasts with the idea, characteristic in moral theory, that we should justify our moral judgments by showing how they are derived from general propositions, much the same way that we prove theorems in geometry.[8] The webs I try to construct are woven from strands borrowed from the tapestry. The challenge is to make a sturdy web with many fibers that blend harmoniously and that are numerous and resilient enough to support a robust ethical judgment.

Organization of the Book

The sequence of topics requires a little explanation. This book is not organized by biological priority: conception followed by gestation, then by issues arising after birth. Instead, this introductory chapter is followed by one entitled "Families, the Marketplace, and Values: New Ways of Making Babies," because these new methods for creating children compel us to ask why people have children, especially what values they seek in making families. I argue here that many adults *need* children for their own flourishing and that what we value about families is distinct from and incompatible with commercialization and the values of the marketplace. My strategy in this chapter is to try to articulate the values at the heart of family life and parenthood, then to see whether new reproductive arrangements, particularly those involving pay for gametes, embryos, or gestational services, are incompatible with those values. Along the way I discuss the idea that moral concepts can be well or ill suited to the institutions and practices being considered.

"Adoption and the Meanings of Parenthood" shows how changing conceptions of parenthood, child nature, and family relationships affect social institutions and practices. Threads from old and ragged tapestries survive in our laws and customs. A particularly influential thread is the one carrying the theme of the child-as-property, especially of its biological father. I also consider two other possible models of the parent-child relationship: the parent as steward and parent-child mutuality. Controversies over adoption pose the question whether flourishing of children and adults has more to do with caring relationships than with biological generation. They also prompt us to ask whether mutuality is a more faithful representation of what is valuable in parent-child relationships than either the child-as-property or the parent-as-steward.

Once parents and children are brought together, new ethical questions arise about what it takes to be a good parent, which is the subject of "Research on Children and the Scope of Responsible Parenthood." This chapter asks when parents are morally permitted to allow their children to be the subjects of scientific research. I argue that particular historical circumstances led scholars to frame this problem in an awkward and unhelpful way. Reframing the problem as a question about the limits of permissible parental discretion offers a more fruitful and

sensible approach. It directs our attention to the scope of parental responsibilities that are powerful and centrally important. It also alerts us
to the dangers of construing those obligations too narrowly either by
focusing excessively on avoiding physical dangers or by ignoring other
legitimate moral considerations.

"Moral Obligations to the Not-Yet-Born Child" takes up the question whether we have moral duties to children prior to birth. This is *not*
a sly way of talking about abortion: "not-yet-born children" are those
whom their mothers have chosen to bring to birth. One of the chapter's
principal arguments is that people make a mistake when they assume
that questions about prenatal obligations are merely a subset of the
ethics of abortion. I argue that we do have significant moral obligations
to not-yet-born children and that those obligations fall not only on
pregnant women but on others as well, especially fathers. Sentimentalized views of pregnancy often act as a kind of spotlight focused on the
pregnant woman's belly. Attending to the all-things-considered nature
of practical moral judgment is a useful antidote to such moral myopia,
as is the analogy with parents'—especially fathers'—obligations to their
born children. The chapter also shows the crucial importance of distinguishing between moral judgments and public policies, a distinction
lamentably often ignored.

"Prenatal Testing and the Quest for the Perfect Child" begins with
an inquiry into the origins of the moral standards governing the practice of prenatal testing—nondirectiveness and value-free counseling. I
try to show the influence of nonmoral factors on the evolution and
acceptance of nondirective prenatal counseling. As a moral guide, nondirectiveness has severe limitations that are being exacerbated by developments that are lowering the barriers to testing and lengthening the
menu of things for which we can test prenatally. I argue that prenatal
testing is a form of perfectibilism, the desire to escape the uncertainties
and contingencies of human relationships. Though some forms of prenatal testing are justifiable, professionals need a sturdier ethic than nondirectiveness, an ethic that enables them to say no to requests for such
things as prenatal sex selection. The quest for the perfect child can create an environment hostile to children—and adults—as they are, with
their many imperfections. Nondirectiveness and the quest for perfection combine to threaten values at the core of human flourishing.

Abortion has become the prototype of an unsettled, perhaps intractable, moral dispute. It comes as the last, rather than the first, issue in
the book because I wanted the reader to decide whether the style of

argument and the emphasis on context were illuminating before I brought them to bear on abortion. In "Abortion and the Place of Motherhood" I explore the use of images in moral rhetoric about abortion and reflect on what transforms apparent disagreements over metaphysical issues, such as when personhood begins, into fierce social battles. Other, equally "fundamental," disagreements exist without undermining social peace. I argue that the energy for the battle is supplied by competing threads in the tapestry—different images of women's flourishing—that are perceived by activists on both sides as incompatible. The struggle over abortion, that is, can be seen as a struggle over what gives shape and meaning to the lives of women, specifically the place of childbearing and motherhood. Moving the focus of debate from intractable metaphysical disagreements to arguments about women's roles might open up lines of dialogue and possibilities for compromise that are unavailable in the abstractions of metaphysics.

Readers who are not particularly interested in questions about methods in practical moral reasoning may stop at the end of chapter 7. The last chapter, "Tapestry and Web," looks briefly at the shortcomings of what has been the regnant methodology in bioethics, which focuses on relatively abstract principles and works from the top down, and contrasts it with an approach that affirms that moral knowledge comes not exclusively from abstract theory, but from considered moral judgments as well. It also looks at the most common criticism of any approach that relies on practical moral judgments—that such judgments are always untrustworthy and hence worthless because they rely on current understandings that might be shrouded with ideology and therefore mistaken. It responds by exploring the sources of moral knowledge, the nature of moral progress, and the role of tradition and contemporary practices in conversations about morality.

It is now time to talk about what children mean to parents.

2

Families, the Marketplace, and Values

New Ways of Making Babies

If collaborative reproduction is viewed positively, reproduction contracts become the instruments of reproductive freedom. . . . In liberal society, the invisible hand of procreative preference must be allowed to flourish, despite the qualms of those who think it debases our humanity.
— John A. Robertson, "Embryos, Families and Procreative Liberty"

Surrogacy is like slavery in the absence of reciprocity, in the fact that one person becomes what Aristotle called an "animated tool" of another, serving simply as a means to another's end.
— David H. Smith, "Wombs for Rent, Selves for Sale?"

There are times when adults hunger for children. *Hunger* is the right word, for it can be felt as a need, a profound longing, not a mere appetite for something pleasant. When we speak of the suffering of people who want to have children but cannot, "suffering" is neither metaphor nor hyperbole: people who crave children to raise and love but cannot have them suffer because, for many of us, our children are a vital part of our own flourishing. The chief moral impetus behind alternative reproductive practices—from medical interventions to surrogacy contracts—is the desire to ease the suffering of infertility.[1]

Despite this worthy purpose, these new arrangements inspire wariness. They are accused of intensifying medical, especially male, control over reproduction; of treating women as nothing more than vehicles for reproduction; of treating children as commodities or products; and of threatening the intimacy of natural reproduction. The uneasiness lingers despite responses that can be given to each of the particular complaints.

Rather than rehearse these arguments, I want to see if it is possible to uncover the root of our discomfort. Could our uneasiness with certain alternative reproductive practices stem from a sense that they threaten to undermine the very values that prompted us to create these alternatives in the first place? In particular, do the values of the marketplace, with their exaltation of individual liberty, control, and choice, endanger what we value in family life?

Suppose the answer to this question is yes. How could such self-defeating practices have emerged? In brief, the story is this: Proponents of alternative reproductive practices defend them as expressions of procreative liberty. This is not surprising. Liberty is a powerful principle with great resonance in our political and moral traditions. We rely heavily on liberty to defend the option *not* to reproduce by using contraception or abortion. If we are free to avoid having children, shouldn't we have equal freedom to pursue parenthood? The fallacy here is a presumption that the choice *to have* a child is morally parallel to the choice *not to have* a child. The former is a choice to initiate a very special human relationship; the latter is a choice to decline such a relationship. The values at the core of the parent-child relationship constrain the former in ways they do not affect the latter.

The story also concerns the tapestry in which negative liberty is such a prominent strand. Negative liberty is freedom *from*, the liberty to do as one wishes without the interference of others. Great principles like liberty do not stand in isolation. They draw their strength from a culture's traditions; those same traditions link liberty so closely with other values that they become a kind of web, each strand supporting and supported by the other strands. In the web of values supporting alternative reproductive practices, liberty is interwoven with an emphasis on the individual who bears rights in sometimes isolated splendor. The web also contains strong threads representing the value we place on choice and control. The model of human relationship favored in this web is the contract, the free agreement of independent, autonomous actors. The social institution that best fits with these strands—liberty, individualism, choice, control, contract—is the market. If you frame your response to the needs of the infertile and childless in terms of procreative liberty, you will find yourself in the web that includes these

other values. Buying and selling reproductive products and services—
sperm, ova, embryos, and gestation—will appear as straightforward expressions of that liberty. It will become difficult to see why we should
be more wary of choice and control here than in other spheres of life.

I want to try to understand the ethics of alternative reproductive
practices by reflecting on what we value about having children and living in families. What we discover there will give us a different perspective on those practices. It will allow us to distinguish morally permissible arrangements from those that threaten to undermine what we value
about families and parent-child relationships. It will also help us to
make sense of our often inchoate fears about the excesses committed in
the pursuit of parenthood.

Infertility and Alternative Reproductive Practices

Infertility is an increasingly common problem for Americans: 7 percent of couples meet the standard medical definition of infertility.[2] There are many sources of infertility, and many offers of assistance, from physicians and lawyers as well as from individuals willing to
sell or donate sperm, eggs, and embryos, or to provide a womb for nine
months. It has been widely noted that a baby can have as many as five
different "parents": a genetic mother and father, a gestating mother,
and a rearing mother and father. We should not forget the other major
actors: the technician who prepared the petri dish in which egg and
sperm joined, the rearing parents' lawyer, the surrogate mother's lawyer, the judge who resolved the dispute between the two lawyers, and,
not least, the banker who approves the loan that pays the technicians,
doctors, gamete vendors, surrogate mother, and attorneys.[3]

Alternative reproductive practices encompass a variety of clinical procedures and social arrangements. Although some esoteric technologies
are employed, many of the new arrangements require no tool more
sophisticated than a turkey baster. What we find morally troubling
about them has less to do with their technological complexity than with
the challenges they pose to our understanding of parenthood and family life.

Take cloning, for example. Cloning entails making identical genetic
copies of an individual. In an experiment to demonstrate that a single

human embryo could be divided into identical copies of itself, scientists took seventeen abnormal embryos and pulled a few cells off of each to see if the individual cells would resume dividing. The seventeen embryos they began with ended up as forty-eight.

Early reports of the experiment created a stir. People were no doubt apprehensive about a technique that might some day be used to create many genetically identical babies. Commentators speculated that some of the clones could be frozen, then offered for sale years later when prospective buyers could see what sort of child grew from their genetically identical siblings. The reaction among bioethicists was interesting. One notable figure was quoted in the *New York Times* as saying he begins "with a presumption of privacy and liberty, that people should be able to live their lives the way they want and to make babies the way they want."[4] He dismissed the fear that if embryos are bought and sold, we might end up with a hundred copies of the same individual. He offers no objection to the principle of a market in human embryos; rather, he claims the specter of identical clones running around is implausible because "environment plays too large a role. You could take 100 Hitler embryos and raise them and never get Hitler again."[5] I suppose that should offer us some comfort.

This prominent bioethicist is not alone in his effort to portray questions about cloning human embryos, along with other novel ways of creating babies, in terms like privacy, liberty, and individual preferences. In the name of procreative liberty, an astonishing variety of arrangements for making and obtaining children have been defended. They are all in the service of creating a family, and so we should welcome them, say their defenders.

Rethinking Procreative Liberty

Alternative reproductive practices challenge our notions of family because they expose what has been at the core of the family—creating and raising children—to values more at home in the marketplace. To some champions of new reproductive arrangements, a set of values fits neatly together. Respecting liberty and privacy means that people in pursuit of their reproductive goals may make agreements with other people to help them reach those goals. In this line of reasoning the fees we pay to purchase gametes or embryos or the services of a gestational mother are no different from the fees we pay physicians and laboratories. Liberty and privacy mesh neatly with concepts of contract and property. Crudely put, in this way of thinking about human reproduction, if people desire to obtain a child, they have a right to pursue that goal, just as they have a right to fulfill their desire for fresh bread by buying a bread machine. We put stricter boundaries on the pursuit of babies than on the pursuit of bread machines. In neither case do we think it is permissible to walk into a place where the desired items lie (respectively, a newborn nursery and an appliance store), slip one under your coat and walk out with it. At a minimum, we insist on a mutually voluntary transfer. The two kinds of goods—bread machines and babies—do differ. We forbid the sale of used versions of the one type (three-year-old children) while feeling completely comfortable with a market in used versions of the other (that is, three-year-old bread machines).

By now, this discussion will strike some readers as utterly bizarre—because it is.[6] Something is out of joint here. Babies are not bread machines. Both can smell very good in the morning (though the baby may need a change and bath first). But the person who supplies the genetic material or gestation for a baby has a different relationship to that infant than the manufacturer or seller of a bread machine has to that appliance.

In the realm of commerce, moral relationships are relatively simple. There are owners and property and prospective buyers. The property has no independent moral significance. Its "worth" is measured fully by the price agreed upon by buyer and seller. The relationship of buyer and seller is governed by contract, an agreement that specifies in often precise detail what each party expects from the other. The relationship between buyer and seller is merely instrumental to the exchange of goods: I give you, the store owner, $150; you give me this bread machine. In the realm of parents and children, of family, the new additions—that is, children—have a more complex moral status than mere property (though children have been so regarded at times). And the relationships among the various parties who may be involved in providing babies—suppliers of gametes, gestational services, and those who wish to rear the children—are more complex as well, to say nothing of the relationships between each of those parties and the children they create. Indeed, it could be said that the main point in having a child is to initiate the relationships that will develop between that child, its siblings, and the adults in its life.

Proponents of strong individual rights in reproductive technology generally acknowledge the great moral importance of children. That importance, for advocates, helps explain why the liberty to pursue parenthood is even more important than the liberty to pursue more prosaic commercial transactions. A fundamental problem remains: We recognize that thinking of children as property, and of family life as essentially a series of commercial transactions, is a grievous distortion. We know of cultures that have treated children as a form of property; indeed, there are practices in our society, in our adoption laws, for example, that appear to be surviving remnants of that idea.[7] It is also possible to analyze family relationships in economic terms. Economic analysis may help us understand how families interact with the larger world of markets. But it remains a fiction, not an insightful description of how families function or, more important, why people live in families. We probably all know families in which relationships have deteriorated so badly that the individuals in them treat each other like untrustworthy business associates. But we recognize those as failed families that could not achieve the abiding relationships of trust, equity, and love to which families aspire, and so had either to split apart or to fall back on relationships based more on contracts than on loyalty and affection. Individual liberty is crucial in setting limits on what we may do to others in the public sphere. However, liberty and the model of the autonomous, self-interested individual so dear to economic theory are a flimsy foundation on which to build an ethic of the family. Our common understanding of liberty as negative liberty is not even especially useful in describing the experience of having and raising children.

As the champions of reproductive liberty proclaim, the freedom to pursue parenthood is one of the most important expressions of individual liberty. (Although it remains one of those things, like having a good conversation, that we cannot do entirely by ourselves.) Acquiring the child is usually as far as they take the story. But having a child has profound consequences for one's liberty. On the one hand, the responsibility of caring for an infant, then a child, then an adolescent, may be the most constraining thing a person can experience. Unless they have arranged for someone else to do it, the parents of an infant are not free to sleep late on weekends (or sleep through the night, for that matter). They are not free to leave their young child home alone while they go out for a movie or a meal. Once you take on the responsibilities of parenthood, many of the freedoms you experienced prior to having a child are altered radically. (When I was a young parent, I would frequently make the mistake of saying that friends of mine were "single" when they were in fact married but had no children. Eventually I realized that my mistake was a reflection of my experience: getting married may alter one's life, but having children changes it radically and enduringly.)

What I have just said takes one notion of liberty—the capacity to do what one wishes—and says that having children diminishes it. I believe this is only being honest. But there is another sense in which having children is profoundly liberating. The kind of liberation I have in mind here is certainly not the liberty of the marketplace. It is, rather, the sort that comes from knowing what genuinely matters, what carries real meaning into my life. This is not just intellectualized self-persuasion, either, like trying to convince yourself that what tastes bad is good for you. No, the experience of knowing what matters and what one should do *feels* as liberating as it is.

One of the most touching ironies in the debate over the ethical limits of reproductive technologies is that ideas about individual liberty and property rights are being advanced in the service of a desire to transcend individualism, constrain liberty (in at least one important sense), and nurture a sphere of human relationship in which property has no place.

Families, Meaning, and Values

Contemporary Americans overwhelmingly identify their family as the primary source of meaning in their lives.[8] In a culture that celebrates autonomy and individualism, this may seem surprising. But our freedom is the liberty to seek or create meaning in our lives; it does not itself provide that meaning. We are deeply sociable creatures who find much of what gives our lives meaning in our enduring, intimate relationships. We share the most intimate and enduring ties within our families.

In his interpretation of development through the human life cycle, Erik Erikson described a period in adult life during which individuals must develop the capacity for generativity—learning to care for people and projects beyond ourselves—or else fall into emotional and moral stagnation.[9] We must learn to care, or we are prone to sink into a narrow and ungratifying preoccupation with our own needs and worries. Liberty in the sense of freedom from intimate, intricate moral ties with other persons turns out—if Erikson is correct—to be antithetical to liberty in the sense of a full development of our humanity, or what Erikson calls a ripening of the vital virtues. Having children—not just genetically, but the experience of responding to their needs and guiding their development—is surely the most common way (but by no means the only way) to meet the challenge of generativity.

Defining "family" is not a trivial matter. The paradigm of a nuclear family remains a woman, a man, and their biological offspring. But if we limited our notion of family only to groups that adhered strictly to this model, then death, divorce, adoption, foster care, remarriage, single parenthood, and some of the new reproductive practices would disqualify most of us who live with or have raised children. We need a more encompassing definition, one that reflects what we value in family life.

In an insightful and compassionate essay on AIDS and the family, Carol Levine suggests three characteristics of human relationships that capture well what we mean when we describe the relationships that typify families. First, the intention, if not always the reality, is that the relationships be lifelong. Second, the relationships embody a commitment to mutual support—social, emotional, and economic. Third, family bonds have an intimacy that distinguishes them from other attachments. Levine's working definition of family is a good starting point: "Family members are individuals who by birth, adoption, marriage, or declared commitment share deep, personal connections and are mutually entitled to receive and obligated to provide support of various kinds to the extent possible, especially in times of need."[10] This notion of family serves two purposes: it emphasizes what distinguishes family bonds from other, less central, human relationships; and it highlights the problem with the punitively narrow concept of family deployed in the rhetoric of "family values."

"Family Values" and the Values Families Serve

It is important to head off one important potential source of misunderstanding. To understand the impact of new reproductive practices on the family, we will need to talk about the values integral to family life and the larger social values served by having families. Here is the problem: the phrase "family values" has become a political slogan, a shorthand for a lengthy catalog of political views, ranging from an affirmation that families are important to advocacy of narrowly limited roles for women, attitudes toward corporal punishment and prayer in school, condemnations of homosexuality, and a host of other moral and political positions.

"Family values" in contemporary American politics has become synonymous with the views of a narrow portion of the political Right. However, both Right and Left in American politics share the blame for the sorry recent history of discussions of values and the family. The Right has promoted its particular roster of positions as *the* only legitimate values associated with family life. At the same time it implied that those who disagree have *no* values worth mentioning. The Left, for its part, did virtually nothing to challenge the Right's claim to a monopoly on values. This was due in part to a greater tolerance for diversity, but also, I believe, to the suspicion that to affirm any set of substantive values was inherently oppressive. The characteristic view seemed to be that we should throw all questions back to what each individual would freely choose, on the assumption that this would be wholly liberating. Individuals, that is, should be free to do anything—except talk seriously about what might be good for themselves and others that people would *not* always freely choose.

Rather than attack the Right for promoting a narrow and occasionally mean-spirited set of values for the family, the Left effectively ceded the entire issue of values and the family to the far Right. The great bulk of the American public, however uncomfortable they might be with portions of the Right's agenda, knew that values and families were important, but got mostly an embarrassed silence from the Left. Other than an espousal of liberty and justice, and a defense of diversity, the Left was reluctant to talk about values. This, I believe, was one of the great failures of American political life in the 1970s and 1980s. The only way I know to reinvigorate that political and moral debate is to call us back to the reasons why people make families—to the crucial values served by families. But to do that requires first taking a closer look at the way the debate over the ethics of new reproductive technologies typically has been framed—as a weighing of fundamental individual rights against an array of vague concerns.

Advocates of alternative reproductive practices tend to dismiss the misgivings people express as misunderstandings, superstitions, or concern about mere "symbolic harm."[11] But I want to take seriously the possibility that the discomfort people feel at a practice such as commercial surrogacy has legitimate concerns at its root. Intellectuals may be overly eager to reject such concerns. When the culture's ideology supports values that exclude, or are incongruous with, the sources of misgiving—when the language of individual rights, property, consent, and contract disguises what is morally significant about families—it becomes difficult to take seriously or to give effective voice to what is genuinely valuable in family life.

We should not overemphasize the distinction between the sphere of the family and the spheres of the market and politics. Family life intersects with these other spheres in countless ways. But it would also be a mistake to collapse the distinction, to see family life as essentially the same as life in these other spheres. Collapsing the distinction ignores what is obvious to anyone who has lived within a modestly well-functioning family: that families serve very important values, values not served at all well by the marketplace or the public forum. For one thing, well-functioning families are the locus for the development of emotionally and physically healthy children. Families are also a principal site for the emotional and moral development of adults. Families provide the setting for nurturing relationships characterized at their best by love, loyalty, and a healthy measure of forgiveness.

Of course, even in the best of families not all things go well. And many families are riven by anger, cruelty, and bitterness. When we think about families we must avoid the temptation to romanticize, to picture only one type of family as the ideal, to deny the ambivalence that infuses even the best of family relationships. Nonetheless, even in troubled families children can experience love, learn that some people are trustworthy, and develop a sense of their own worth and efficacy. We need to be realistic about the many difficulties families encounter or cause, about the rich varieties of ways in which people make families. But we must not allow cynicism, which is sometimes justified, to blind us to what is valuable in families.

Love. Loyalty. Affection. Forgiveness. Trust. Care. Nurturing. Maturation. This is a partial list of the values families serve. But I believe that it will be a recognizable list to most late-twentieth-century Americans. For that matter, it should not have seemed strange to a literate American in the mid-1800s. The ideal of companionate marriage and the view that children are creatures to be nurtured and loved, rather than little demons to be broken, were already a part of American popular culture nearly one hundred fifty years ago.[12] Nor would it surprise me to learn that many of these values were present in far distant times and cultures. John Boswell's study of child abandonment in ancient Rome and medieval Europe suggests that some parents were at least as fond of their children as contemporary Americans fancy themselves to be.[13] A study of eighteenth-century families in the Chesapeake region of Virginia and Maryland likewise found abundant evidence for great affection between parents and children—and great grief when, as often happened, the child died.[14] Thomas Jefferson, probably the best-known resident of that place and time, wrote to his daughter about his hope that his granddaughter "will make us all, and long, happy as the centre of our common love."[15]

Families, although they constitute a distinctive sphere of human life, do not and cannot exist in isolation. Just as children need families and many adults need children, so do families need supportive social institutions and communities. Without a web of support in the wider culture, individual families may collapse under the weight of external blows and the inevitable injuries that even the best of families inflict on themselves.

The values we think of as crucial to family life tend either to be found only in the context of relationships—love, loyalty, affection, trust, care—or, given our social natures, to depend utterly on a foundation of good, enduring relationships—identity, self-confidence, maturation. The centrality of relationships in the values important to families points up another contrast with the spheres of the market and politics. In the market, relationships are secondary to the fair and efficient exchange of goods and services: I deal with you not because I prize the intrinsic value of our relationship but because you have something I want, and vice versa. The relationship exists primarily to promote the exchange of goods.

Likewise in politics, we may form allegiances to pursue short-term or long-term political goals. These allegiances may even, in certain cases, lead to friendships. But there are things I can do to or expect from my political allies that I cannot do to or expect from my friends. I can rapidly shift political coalitions; but I cannot so rapidly shift among friends, certainly not among families, without damaging the values sought in friendship and in family life. I cannot expect my political allies to have abiding concern for my emotional well-being and development. I can and do expect that from friends and family.

Thinking about Values and the Family:
Justice and Individual Rights in Family Life

Values that are fundamental in shaping our relationships in other spheres may play a different role in the family. Take justice, for example. In our relations with strangers in the public sphere and in the marketplace, justice is a crucial value. Perhaps the highest moral compliment we can pay to a social institution is to say that in this institution, justice prevails. In the sphere of politics, we may not need to love one another, but we do need to treat each other justly.

The emphasis is different within families. Justice remains an important virtue in family life, and it is there that we learn our first and most memorable lessons about justice. I have vivid and sometimes painful memories of mediating among the simultaneous, urgent demands of several children. Of struggling with the decision whether to give these couple of hours this evening to playing with my children, talking with my wife, working, or retreating behind the newspaper.

We learn our first lessons about justice as children. Most parents are familiar with the procedure for fairly distributing the last piece of pie between two children: one cuts it; the other gets first pick.[16] Children probably learn their first lessons in ethics from discussions about justice. Countless parents have had conversations like this:

> *Parent to three-year-old child:* "It's time for bed now, Nicky."
> *Three-year-old child:* "But Kate gets to stay up! It's not fair!"
> *Parent:* "Kate is older than you."
> *Child:* "So? It's not fair."
> *Parent:* "Kate doesn't need as much sleep as you do. Unless you go to bed now you'll be miserable in the morning."
> *Child:* "No, I won't. It's not fair. She gets to watch the Muppet Show and I don't!"

How long the conversation continues depends mostly on the parent's patience. (I have never known the child to say, "Oh, I see your point. My older [sister/brother] is relevantly different from me. It *is* fair that [she/he] stay up later than I do, so I will go to bed peacefully.") In my experience, these early lessons in ethics sooner or later end with instruction in the exercise of power—when the parent says, "You are going to bed now because I am the parent and I say so!"

Justice is important in families. Attentiveness to justice is necessary to prevent the wounds that family members habitually inflict on each other from becoming persistent, suppurating sores that drain moral and emotional strength and ultimately sicken the family. Justice is a kind of maintenance value in family life. If you don't keep it fresh and vigorous, then you will find it impossible to achieve the values families make possible. When some members of a family oppress and exploit other members, injustice corrodes that family from within. Families poisoned with injustice are poor soil for the growth of enduring love, loyalty, and intimacy.

In families we learn what it means to be just, and what it means to suffer the sting of injustice. I suspect we also learn, at a deep, nonrational level, that it is important to seek justice and to avoid injustice. Or, sadly, that it is fruitless to be just and that what really matters is becoming the oppressor, not the oppressed.[17]

Insisting, though, that justice be the predominant value in family life is a mistake. It's a very understandable mistake when we consider how readily injustice can seep into our lives as spouse, parent, or offspring, and how pernicious it can be. The mistake is in forgetting why we make families. We enter families not to seek justice but to seek other values— love, learning to care for other people, enjoying the mutual affection and interdependence of parents and children. Justice is not the reason we make families, but it is crucial to any chance we have for achieving those values.

Like justice, the concept of individual rights has shortcomings in this sphere. Individual rights are blunt and clumsy instruments with which to understand the ethics of family life. Suppose you knocked on the doors of all of the houses in your neighborhood with young children in them and asked the parents in each house why they feed their children. What sort of answers would you get? Most parents would think it was a very strange question. But I expect that they would usually mention two sorts of reasons: that children need to be fed and that making certain your child is well nourished is just one of those things that a good parent does. One answer I do not expect to hear is that they feed their children because they have a right to be fed.

Does this mean that these parents believe that their own children, or other parents' children, have no right to be fed? Hardly that. There are times when it seems appropriate—indeed necessary—to assert that a child's right is being ignored. If parents persistently fail to feed their child, then government child welfare agencies may intervene. The state's intrusion becomes necessary because of a grave breakdown within the family, a failure, for whatever reason, to provide one of the essential elements of child nurture. The language of rights, here, serves to justify state intervention into the sphere of the family.

Talk about "rights" works best when it is doing one of two things. First, we invoke rights when we want to erect boundaries against interference by others. The "others" may be the government, an institution or a corporation, or individuals. This sort of claim against interference by others is often called a negative right—for example, the right to be left alone or the right to privacy. Second, we sometimes use the language of rights to state a positive claim—a claim *to* something, such as a claim to be fed by you. One way of thinking is to presume that all cases in which you have a duty to provide me with certain goods or services are best expressed in terms of rights. But there are many circumstances in which the language of rights seems awkward and second best—for example, when talking about why parents feed their children. Perhaps it is more useful to see claims about positive rights as fallbacks—efforts to obtain something that could not be better assured by ties of affection or loyalty or by moral duties deeply ingrained into complex social practices, like parenting.

Understanding the moral intricacies of family relationships through a concept like individual rights is like opening a beautifully carved front door with an ax. It is undeniably effective; it thrusts the state into the middle of family life; it leaves a heavy toll of destruction in its path; and it is justified only by an emergency such as a fire. A fireman's ax, of course, is not the preferred way of opening your front door. Similarly, asserting that someone's rights are being violated within a family may be necessary; it inflicts its own kind of violence; and it is wise to limit it to occasions when great harm would otherwise be caused.

The language of rights is a language most at home in the spheres of public life, government, and commerce. I have a right to keep you from trespassing on my land; I have rights of free speech and freedom from governmental interference into my political and religious activities; I have a right to go to court to ask that you fulfill the terms of the contract we both signed. In these spheres, the concept of a right is powerful and important and represents a great moral and political advance. The concept of universal human rights is a growing bulwark against oppression by governments that succumb to the temptation to abuse their own citizens.

Even outside the sphere of the family, however, talk about rights expresses only a small part of what is important in our moral relationships with one another. We do many things out of friendship, kindness, sympathy, and solidarity—not because you have a "right" to our friendship, kindness, sympathy, or solidarity. Indeed, these sound like oxymorons: a "right" to my friendship? to my sympathy? If someone insisted that she or he had a right to my friendship, I might feel pity or annoyance; I would certainly feel that they failed to grasp something very important about the nature of friendship. The same is true of efforts to understand the ethics of family life in terms of rights.

Because the decision whether to make a family, especially whether to have children, may be the most profoundly important life decision most individuals face, we are inclined to the language of rights in thinking about the ethics of such choices. But perhaps a moral concept most helpful for understanding our moral relationships with the state and with strangers in the marketplace is not as helpful in understanding family life. Especially a language that carries with it powerful connotations of property and that elevates choice to a position of near-supreme moral importance. Asserting a right to unlimited choice without regard for its meaning and impact in this sphere could threaten what we value about families. The language of rights with its close affinities for property and contract is an ill-fitting ethic for the family.

What Does It Mean to Have an "Ill-Fitting" Ethic?

Talking of rights as a way of understanding family relationships is not like talking about a "purple idea" or a "repentant toaster," what the philosopher Gilbert Ryle calls a category mistake.[18] It is a different kind of mistake: it is slightly off-center; it misses something important. It is like wearing a tuxedo to a beach party. You might at first think the person in the tuxedo has a wry sense of humor; but when you realize that he is completely serious, that he honestly thinks this is what one wears to the beach, you might feel a little sorry for him. Obviously, he does not understand what beach parties are all about.

Both kinds of mistakes—category mistakes and missing the point—are errors in meaning. In a category mistake, one fails to grasp the meaning of a concept. The result is a linguistic absurdity. When one tries to analyze family ethics with a concept like rights, there is a misfit between the moral concept and the meaning of the social institution and the practices that accompany it. Meaning here signifies the point of the institution and practices, their place in human affairs, the relationships they call forth, the values they support and exemplify. A mistake here results, not in a linguistic, but in a moral absurdity.

An analogy might help make the point. Imagine standing with two companions in front of a great painting, say, one of Vincent van Gogh's intense and vibrant images of sunflowers. One of your companions launches into a learned dissertation on the chemical composition of the pigments in the painting. She seems to know everything about the oxides of this and sulfates of that, which pigments have the greatest luminosity or reflectivity, which become brittle with time, which remain supple. Impressed by your companion's monologue, you ask for her views about the painting. She responds with exactly the same speech. You try again. Does she think it is beautiful? What feelings does it evoke in her? What does she think the artist was attempting to communicate? She stares blankly: she has nothing to say on any of these matters. Her interest in the painting is exhausted by its chemistry.

She has not been talking nonsense. One can speak meaningfully about the chemistry of pigments in old paintings. Experts on such matters are immensely valuable in helping to preserve or restore these great works. But in the practice of appreciating, or understanding, or simply being moved by great art, she has missed the point completely. Her inability to see the painting as anything more than a collection of pigments is likely to evoke our sadness and sympathy. Not so with our other companion in the gallery.

All that he sees is money. "I'll bet that one's worth at least $10 million." "If I could get this one, I'm sure it would appreciate at a good 20 percent a year, minimum." This would-be art dealer clearly is not making a category mistake. Paintings, even great paintings, may be sold; we can describe them in terms of their market value. (The reverse may not be true. It strikes me as a category mistake to talk about a "beautiful" or "awe-inspiring" market.) Our mercenary companion is giving a valid, that is, not incoherent, assessment of each of the paintings. But if that is all he can see in the paintings, he too has missed completely the point of the practice of painting—creating beauty; provoking longing, faith, indignation. Serious works of art create meaning. They can be traded as commodities, and are. But that does not negate the purpose of the practice of painting, nor does it reduce all judgments of the worth of paintings to their market value.

Trying to understand families primarily through concepts such as rights and justice is not incoherent either, but it misses the point of why people make families, the sorts of human relationships people strive to create within families, and the values families serve.

Finding an Ethic that Fits

The values embedded in certain alternative reproductive practices form a constellation that aligns poorly with other values at the heart of family life. Two contrasting images of values and relationships within families illustrate the point.

The champion of procreative liberty celebrates control and choice and portrays decisions about whether and how to acquire children as similar to decisions to acquire other new entities, only more important than most. If choice is valued in selecting a new appliance, all the more should it be valued in selecting a new child. If we are permitted to make voluntary agreements to spend our money to obtain new objects, all the more important to allow us similar freedom of contract and commerce to obtain new children, with one caveat: the children should not be harmed.

The other image is harder to label. It sees a role for values like control and choice within families but insists that these are not the principal values for which we make families; it is aware of the tension between unbridled liberty and control, on the one hand, and the values at the core of family life, on the other. It is vigilant against the encroachment of marketplace values into the family sphere because it recognizes that in commercial relationships the goal is to purchase a good or service, not to deepen the relationship, whereas all that is most valuable in family life centers on nurturing relationships.[19] Potential ways of adding children to the family must be scrutinized to assure that they will not undermine the values sought in family life, now or in the long run.[20]

In a defense of cloning human embryos, John Robertson, an ardent exponent of reproductive liberty, argues that couples wishing to "adopt" (his word) an embryo that is a clone of already living children should know all they want to know about those children. He says, "The right of adoptive parents to receive as full information as possible about the children whom they seek to adopt is increasingly recognized. There is no reason why the same principle should not apply to embryo 'adoptions.' Even though the couple seeking the embryos will be choosing embryos on the basis of expected characteristics, such a choice is neither invalid nor immoral."[21] A couple, that is, may exercise quality control through choice.

The emphasis here on control and choice does not fit well with our understanding of families. Good families are characterized more by acceptance than control. Furthermore, families are the preeminent realm of unchosen obligations. We may choose our spouses (although a persuasive argument could be made that for most of us this choice bears scarce resemblance to the model of rational, autonomous, carefully considered decision making). We may choose to have a child, but—unless we are "adopting" one of Robertson's cloned embryos—we do not choose to have this *particular* child, with its interests, moods, and manners. And as offspring, we certainly did not choose our parents. Yet most of us would agree that we do have moral obligations to our parents, as well as to our spouses and children. An interesting problem for an ethics that enshrines autonomous choice as the fundamental requirement for moral obligation is this: How do you explain the enormously powerful web of moral obligations that supports family life, despite the only partly chosen or wholly unchosen nature of those relationships?

Some of the new reproductive practices require enlisting third parties. Women or men supply gametes, couples provide embryos, and women gestate their own or someone else's fetus. Justifying the involvement of third parties usually builds on the values of choice and control and invokes liberty. The question immediately arises, Why would any third party agree to participate in another couple's effort to have a child? For many people the answer is obvious: money. Robertson states the case bluntly: "If collaborative reproduction is viewed positively, reproduction contracts become the instruments of reproductive freedom."[22] He acknowledges the implication of this view:

Legal liberty allows persons to treat each other as means to reproductive ends, with their negotiating ability and other resources determining the fate of future offspring. The extracorporeal embryo, that potent symbol of human life, becomes subject to the vagaries of a market that drives people to buy or sell reproductive factors and services. Yet such freedom also allows people to determine and satisfy their welfare more efficaciously than by government prescription. In liberal society, the invisible hand of procreative preference must be allowed to flourish, despite the qualms of those who think it debases our humanity.[23]

Freedom equals the right to make a contract, to welcome, in Robertson's memorable paraphrase of Adam Smith, "the invisible hand of procreative preference." The price we pay for that freedom, including a market for human embryos, is the necessary cost of liberty, or so Robertson argues. With admirable tenacity, Robertson leads us down the reproductive path paved by the values of the market—individual liberty, choice, personal preference, contract, and commercialization. We are now in a position to see where we have arrived—and what beautiful, perhaps fragile, shoots have been bulldozed in the rush to build this particular highway.

The difference between the two images is clearest in their responses to surrogate motherhood for pay. How does a paid surrogate child-bearer explain to her other children what has happened? Does she say, "Mommy loves her children so much that she wants to give another woman a chance to have her own children to love"? Does she add, "Oh, by the way, it also lets us buy groceries/pay off the mortgage/go to Disney World/finish the third floor"? What do her children think about their own security? Their relationship with their parents? What have they learned about the nature of the parent-child relationship? Have they learned that it is subject to the same harsh rules of supply and demand as any other commodity? Will such doubts make them more secure, contribute to their emotional development?

What of the surrogate herself? David H. Smith observes that the surrogate contract signed by Mary Beth Whitehead, biological mother of the famous Baby M, gave striking power over Mrs. Whitehead to William Stern, her fetus's biological father. Indeed, the contract gave Mr. Stern "rights Whitehead's husband would not have had if he and Whitehead had engendered a child." Smith grants the appeal of such control to the Sterns, but he worries about the "status they impose upon the surrogate, whose entire life is subordinated to 'the delivery of a product' for another."[24] He considers the analogy of surrogacy to slavery, admitting that there are important dissimilarities but insisting that "surrogacy is like slavery in the absence of reciprocity, in the fact that one person becomes what Aristotle called an 'animated tool' of another, serving simply as a means to another's end."[25]

We need to think not only about the impact on those directly and immediately involved but also about the values, practices, and institutions that affect families now and in the future. Are children likely to flourish in a culture where making children is governed by the same rules that govern the making of automobiles or VCRs? Or is their flourishing more assured in a culture where making children, and matching children with nurturing adults, is treated as a sphere separate from the marketplace, a sphere governed by the ethics of gift and relationship, not contract and commerce?

My claim is not that a market in children, embryos, or gametes violates some abstract principle in the noumenal realm. Rather, it is that given the sort of creatures we humans are, our patterns of psychosocial development, our needs at different stages of our lives—given these facts, certain values, institutions, and practices support our mutual flourishing better than others. Specifically, the values of the marketplace are ill suited for nurturing the values, institutions, and practices that support the flourishing of children and adults within families.

A market in gametes, or even in offspring, might not be a moral and social problem for other sorts of creatures for whom rationality is preeminent. But such a market is a threat for us humans who need affection, trust, and, above all, intimate and enduring relationships in order to flourish.

Note that I did not say that those hypothetical beings for whom a reproductive market might be acceptable were more *rational*—only that for them rationality is preeminent. What would it take for us humans to be most rational in understanding the ethical and policy implications of alternative means of reproduction? It would make no sense whatsoever to ignore what sort of creatures we really are, what circumstances are most conducive to our mutual flourishing. No doubt, there is disagreement about just what institutions and practices are the most likely to support our flourishing. But responsible practical moral reasoning cannot wish such matters away. We cannot honestly pretend to resolve these questions with a strictly moral or legal argument—an appeal to individual autonomy or reproductive liberty, for example. We must take into account factual as well as moral considerations in our practical moral judgments.

Some reproductive alternatives are more troubling than others. For a variety of reasons, a man might produce some normal sperm but not be able to place enough of them in a good position to reach an ovum ready for fertilization. Artificially inseminating a woman with her husband's sperm, for example, strikes most people as eminently acceptable. (The Roman Catholic church is an exception to this general chorus of approval.) Using another man's sperm is more complicated morally.

The usual practice in the United States, known as artificial insemination by donor, or AID, is a misnomer. The "donor" is usually paid for his sperm, making him a sperm vendor. I think this is a serious confusion, not a minor semantic quibble. Calling the supplier of sperm a donor invokes the realm of gifts, and with it the sphere of family and friendship. In commercial sperm banks, the vendors are actually anonymous strangers, paid for their "product" and then sent away, with presumably no more interest in what happens to it subsequently than a seller of office supplies has with what happens to his or her Post-it notes. Some men who sell or donate sperm discover later that they care about what has happened to it.[26] This is evidence that the market is a poor description of what transpires when gametes are transferred from one party to another. Because the market fails as a description, it is unlikely to be a faithful guide to ethical understanding as well.

So far, discussions about the ethics of alternative reproduction in the United States have paid scant attention to the practice of paying for sperm. The prospect of a man sitting in a booth and ejaculating into a container is the source of many jokes. But if I am correct about the dangers of the values of the market intruding on the sphere of the family, then AIV—artificial insemination by vendor—should make us uneasy. Not because of any sexual squeamishness, but because commerce in this realm may threaten what is genuinely valuable within it. Using gametes provided by another man raises other morally relevant difficulties.[27] Even if, as seems likely, those are outweighed by the good of creating new parent-child relationships, we should be concerned about the impact of commercializing the practice.

Suppose we stopped paying for sperm and instead asked men to be genuine donors. Would that create a shortage of sperm? There are reasons to believe that it would not. First, several countries find an adequate number of such volunteers.[28] Second, there is the analogy with blood. In the United States it used to be assumed that you could only obtain an adequate supply of whole blood by paying individuals for it, or by offering them some other advantage. That assumption was false. People give blood because they are convinced other persons need it and they do not have to undergo great inconvenience to make a donation.[29] Like donations of blood, donations of sperm can assuage an important form of human suffering.

Whatever moral difficulties we find in a market for sperm, they are magnified in the market for ova because of the much greater physical risks involved. There are fewer healthy ova available for treating infertility than there are women who want them. Getting healthy ova to use in in vitro fertilization (IVF) and related procedures is a much more elaborate and invasive procedure than what is required to obtain sperm. The woman who will be the source of these eggs typically takes hormones that stimulate her ovaries to ripen multiple eggs, which must then be removed by aspiration or laparoscopy. Why would a woman go through such an ordeal? In many instances, the woman is a genuine donor, providing an egg for a relative or a friend. In other cases, the woman receives money. Compensating the supplier is fine, according to the American Fertility Society's "Guidelines for Gamete Donation: 1993." The guidelines say that "donors should be compensated for the direct and indirect expenses associated with their participation, their inconvenience and time, and to some degree, for the risk and discomfort undertaken."[30] One proposal calculates that with all the interviewing, testing, examinations, the procedure itself, and a full day to recover, an egg donation takes fifty-six hours of a woman's time. Assuming that men are paid $25 an hour for sperm, the authors of this proposal conclude that a woman should "receive $1,400 for her time alone, exclusive of any compensation for travel, risk, or inconvenience."[31] They ask, "Since it is standard to compensate men for sperm donation, shouldn't the policy be equal pay for equal time?"[32] A survey of infertility programs found that women who were paid for their ova received an average of $1,548, with a range from $750 to $3,500.[33]

Market Values and the Values of Family Life

"Equal pay for equal work" sums it up well. Paying individuals for their biological products makes them vendors, not donors. And it places the interactions between the parties squarely in the marketplace. Markets are built on the premise that individuals are rational pursuers of their own satisfaction and that choice and control are preeminent values. Market enthusiasts claim that the more things we allow the market to distribute, the better off we are. In practice, most market proponents recognize that some things should not be bought and sold. But the moral logic of some market advocates encompasses even children.[34] Explanations of why we should not allow children to be bought and sold often rely on two kinds of arguments: either that children have intrinsic moral value or worth and that such things should never be bought, sold, or owned; or that the consequences for children will be bad. I want to suggest a different line of argument.

The key errors in market analyses of the sphere of the family are a faulty set of presuppositions coupled to a dry, shrunken conception of human flourishing. The presuppositions include the notion that people are best understood as rational, isolated individuals in selfish pursuit of their own satisfaction, with the values of choice and control preeminent. There are problems with each piece of this model of human life. The emphasis on the *rational* underestimates the importance of the emotional in human life. The emphasis on the *isolated individual* discounts the great significance of relationships for people's flourishing. The assumption that people's motivations are essentially *selfish* fails to comprehend the complexity of human motivation, especially in the sphere of family life. (Remember the Ayalas.) The celebration of *control* and *choice* fails to acknowledge the very limited role these values play in family life, indeed that a disproportionate emphasis on either can destroy families.

If children flourish best in stable, loving families, then we harm them by promoting a view of human relationship that equates the decision to initiate such a relationship with the decision to buy a wide-screen television or a medium-priced car. If adults flourish best in enduring, warm relationships and if caring for children also contributes to the flourishing of adults, then we should encourage practices and policies that support such relationships. To the extent that the dry view of human flourishing implicit in marketplace values shrinks our perceptions and undermines our support for family life, it threatens not merely children but adults as well.

I am not arguing that marketplace values are linked in some tight logical or mechanistic way so that where one is present the others follow inexorably. Rather, I am claiming that they form a mutually supportive web of compatible considerations. The focus on rational individuals seeking the maximum of satisfaction for themselves supports choice and control as values. The same focus tends to evaluate all things—objects, entertainments, other people—according to how well they satisfy the individual's desires. I like crusty bread, so I chose a bread machine with that feature; you like hazel eyes and curly black hair, so should you choose your children by those characteristics?

What Difference Does It Make?

If we set aside the moral framework of contract and market in favor of one more in tune with what we value about families, how would we regard alternative methods of reproduction? Most significant would be a shift in how we frame the moral question. The currently fashionable way to think about such matters is to place individual liberty and choice on one side of the balance and the harms caused on the other side. Robertson uses this strategy frequently and skillfully. His analysis of surrogacy provides a typical example.[35] Robertson emphasizes the voluntary nature of the agreement between the paying couple and the paid surrogate. He looks at potential harms to the couple and the surrogate as unlikely, not that different from other things we already tolerate, and in any event a consequence of their own free choice.

The child-product of the surrogacy contract is a more difficult story. But not much more difficult. The prospect of harms to such children could be dismissed as implausible or unproved, or as not so different from other practices we tolerate anyway, especially adoption. The parallel with harms to the adults involved in surrogacy ends there. Robertson, like other defenders of commercial surrogacy, cannot use the child's fictitious "consent" to justify any harms that might come to it. But he has another strategy. The child, he argues, benefits because "but for the surrogacy contract, this child would not exist at all. . . . [E]ven if the child does suffer identity problems, as adopted children often do . . . this child has benefited, or at least has not been wronged, for without the surrogate arrangement, she would not have been born at all." [36]

Try now to imagine some novel method of bringing children into the world which this way of framing the issues would condemn, as long as the adults participating did so freely. Cloning human embryos? No problem. Cloning embryos, freezing some and thawing them out later for implantation in someone else? Still no problem. Implanting an aborted fetus's ovary, with its millions of yet-unripe eggs, into a woman's body, so that she might become pregnant with that fetus's ova? It is difficult to see how anyone who frames the argument as Robertson and other enthusiasts do could make a strong objection to the practice. Who is harmed? Not the woman who chose to abort the fetus and gave her consent to using its ovaries. Certainly not the woman or her spouse who wants this supply of healthy ova. As for any children born from these eggs, who could prove they would have been better off never existing?

Would it matter if the reason the woman desired the fetal ovary was her own infertility, or because she is thirty-five and wanted to avoid the increased risk of birth defects that comes from older eggs? Or that she and her spouse wanted children with blue eyes, or some other genetically linked characteristics? I doubt that Robertson or most other supporters of reproductive alternatives would embrace such bizarre practices. But, it is also hard to see how, given the way they structure the ethical balancing, they could argue persuasively against them. You would have to demonstrate harms of such magnitude and certainty to individuals who have not, by their own choice, accepted the risks, that they overwhelm the powerful presumption in favor of liberty. Robertson, for one, looks with favor on doing genetic screening on and then freezing embryos while a woman is young, "until education, career, or relationship goals are worked out. They can then be transferred to the woman when there is a lower risk of a handicapped birth than if fertilization occurred shortly before implantation." [37]

What of healthy fertile women, who want to have their own genetic child, but do not want to go through pregnancy? Robertson believes that "surrogacy for convenience . . . may turn out to be more acceptable if it proves to be an effective way for women to combine work and reproduction. . . . As long as surrogate interests are protected, an optimal situation for all might result from surrogacy for convenience, if one accepts the change in the concept of mother that it would appear to entail." [38] This is precisely the inexorable moral logic of the marketplace, a logic that sweeps everything before it, deterred only by compelling evidence of serious, direct harm to those who have not consented by virtue of their own participation. As for the children thus created, we would have to prove that they would have been better off never being born.

New York State's Task Force on Life and the Law argues that the way the question is framed essentially dictates the answer because it presupposes that the children in question already exist. The task force suggests an alternative framing: whether, given the disadvantages of commercial surrogacy for future children, the practice should be permitted in the first place. [39] We should extend the task force's question and ask if these alternative means of creating children support or interfere with what we value in family and parenthood. Would they, on balance, create not just individual parent-child relationships but the kind of relationships that foster mutuality, loyalty, and love; relationships that endure, that survive the inevitable occasions when the relationship is causing a great deal more pain than pleasure? Beyond individual relationships, would they help build social attitudes and institutions that support the flourishing of children and adults within families?

I am suspicious of practices such as paying gamete suppliers or surrogate child-bearers that thrust the values of the market into the heart of the family. It would be ridiculous to argue that all children born of such arrangements are irreparably damaged, or their relationships with their rearing parents warped. But I do not think it is silly to worry about the effect such practices have on our intimate relationships more generally and on parent-child relationships in particular. Unreflective ideological commitments can and do lead us astray, away from what we genuinely and deeply value. The attitudes and institutions that provide the absolutely necessary cultural support for what we value can be eroded, so gradually that we scarcely notice.

I agree with Robertson and other proponents of new reproductive arrangements about the enormous importance of children in the lives of adults. We both want to promote social practices that match children with nurturing adults. But where he regards contract and commercialization as "the instruments of reproductive freedom," I view them as, at best, threats and, at worst, inimical to the values families are meant to promote. They should be our culture's last resort, if we allow resort to them at all. Cultural meanings are shared creations, and their protection, or change, a shared project.

There is enough reason for concern to throw the burden of proof back onto the shoulders of proponents of marketplace values in reproduction. Show us that the practices you advocate do not threaten what we value about family life and that reasonable alternatives are lacking. Artificial insemination by vendor, for example, would not be justifiable because a nonmarket alternative exists—genuine donors.

To protect the few against the tyranny of the majority, the law may have to permit in the name of liberty some practices that we believe are unwise. But our moral vision must remain clear. If commercializing reproductive practices threatens cultural meanings and institutions, then our respect for political liberty does not require us to welcome such practices. Some commentators argue that procreative liberty is a fundamental constitutional right. Under our constitution, the government must have a compelling purpose to justify interfering with a fundamental constitutional right. But other experts disagree with the claim that our reproductive rights encompass practices such as gestation for pay. Alex Capron and Margaret Radin conclude that the "claim that the right to privacy protects surrogacy may be more plausible for noncommercial than for commercial surrogacy; even if the Constitution should be understood as including a right to bear a child for someone else, it should not be interpreted as including a right to be paid for it."[40] They argue that there is no obstacle in the Constitution to prevent a community from banning commercial surrogacy agencies, brokers, or advertising. I believe that we should prohibit commercial surrogacy.

There is another kind of surrogacy—gift surrogacy. A woman who is willing to bear her sister's or best friend's child out of loyalty and affection is acting in harmony with the values we prize in families. I would urge caution on the part of everyone involved, but I see what she is doing as an act of generosity, an extraordinary gift. Despite the outward physiological similarity between surrogacy-for-love and surrogacy-for-pay, the meanings of the two acts could not be more different. The former builds on a relationship of affection to create new affectionate relationships. The latter transmutes the creation of a child into a commercial transaction—a sort of reverse alchemy, turning gold into dross.

I began this chapter with the vague uneasiness many people feel about some of the new reproductive alternatives, wondering if the qualms were the product of mere habit and superstition or if they sprang from well-founded concerns. I looked at the terms in which the public debate has been conducted, and found them severely wanting. Finally, I tried to recast that debate in terms more faithful to what we value about families and the relationships families make possible, in the hope that this recasting could help us make moral sense out of the proliferation of new ways to make children.

Our concerns, I believe, were well founded. The uncritical celebration of procreative liberty and other marketplace values in reproduction is indeed a threat to what we value about families. Reproductive alternatives need to be examined in the light of those same values.

3

Adoption and the Meanings
of Parenthood

*If adoption were made into a kind of guardianship, children
would not suffer from the lack of honesty and the secrecy in
adoption. They would know who their real parents were and that
they could go back to them at any time.*

—Janet Fenton, President of Concerned
United Birthparents

*Everywhere in Western culture, from religious literature to
secular poetry, parental love is invoked as the ultimate standard
of selfless and untiring devotion, central metaphors of theology
and ethics presuppose this love as a universal point of reference,
and language must devise special terms to characterize persons
wanting in this "natural" affection.*

—John Boswell, *The Kindness of Strangers*

*During the time when our son . . . was away at war, whose was
he? Was it not I who hung from the city walls in suspense? Not I
who seized everyone returning from the battlefield? . . . Who
bandaged his wounds when he returned? Who washed away the
blood? Who took him to the temple and gave thanks?*

—A foster father in ancient Rome

"A Case that Touches the Raw Nerves
of Life's Relationships"

Cara Clausen gave birth to a baby girl on 8 February
1991 in Cedar Rapids, Iowa. Six days later, Roberta and Jan DeBoer,
in Ann Arbor, Michigan, were informed that the baby, whom they had

expected to adopt, was waiting for them; both Clausen and the man identified as the baby's father had surrendered their parental rights. On 25 February, Clausen chose not to appear at the court hearing at which her parental rights were legally severed. The DeBoers took the infant girl, whom they had named Jessica Anne, home to Michigan.

Thus began quietly what eventually became the most publicized adoption case in recent memory. Cara Clausen had lied about the identity of the baby's father. It was not the man who had, apparently in good faith, signed away his parental rights; it was another man, Dan Schmidt, who had learned from Cara only on 27 February that he was the child's biological father. Clausen may have renounced her legal rights to the baby, but the putative biological father had not. It mattered not that he and the baby's biological mother had broken up shortly after she became pregnant and that they were not married. He had never surrendered his legal rights to the child.

The story might have ended there if Clausen had not attended a meeting of a local group called Concerned United Birthparents, or CUB, on 4 March.[1] CUB lobbies in favor of abolishing adoption as it currently exists. Carole Anderson, CUB vice president, prefers a form of foster care in which "there would be no pretending that the guardians who care for and love the child are the real 'parents.' "[2] People who attended that meeting with Clausen implored her to fight to overturn the adoption to which she had just consented. Two days later she filed a motion alleging that the DeBoers' attorney had bullied her into signing away custody and that the termination order was erroneous—specifically, that it was based on false information about the child's biological father, information that Clausen herself had supplied. The lawyer and hospital personnel contradicted Clausen's allegations about whom she had spoken to, whether any pressure had been exerted, and whether she was too befuddled by drugs to know what she was doing. The local juvenile court initially threw out the case, claiming it lacked jurisdiction. But an Iowa district court ruled that a blood test should be performed to determine if Dan Schmidt was in fact the biological father. By 22 July, DNA testing confirmed that Schmidt was in fact the baby's genetic parent.

The child now called Jessica DeBoer was not Dan Schmidt's first child. He had a son, then fourteen, from an earlier marriage whom he had legally abandoned and a daughter, twelve, whom he had never met. He had not voluntarily paid child support for either of his previous offspring. On 27 December 1991, the Iowa district court praised the

DeBoers but ordered them to return the baby to her biological father, Dan Schmidt. At the same time the court ordered Schmidt's fitness as a parent to be investigated.

By early 1992, the DeBoers had decided to continue the legal fight and had begun to talk with the press. The battle over "Baby Jessica," as she became known to the world, continued well into the next year. A hearing in Michigan lasted for eight days, resulting in a 12 February 1993 decision in which Judge William Ager awarded legal custody to the DeBoers and pleaded with the Schmidts (who had married on 11 April 1992) to cease fighting for Jessica's sake. He told them they would be "heroes," that "people all over the United States would say, 'These people have acted in the best interest of their child.' "[3]

The Iowa courts did not agree. Reasoning that since Dan Schmidt had had his parental rights restored, it made no sense to continue to deny them to his spouse and the child's biological mother, the Iowa juvenile court restored Cara Schmidt as the child's legal mother. The Michigan court of appeals deferred to the Iowa Supreme Court on 30 March 1993, ruling that Michigan had no jurisdiction in the case, and ordered that the girl, now two years old, be returned to the Schmidts.[4]

After additional legal maneuvering, including the appointment of a lawyer to represent Baby Jessica, the Michigan Supreme Court on 2 July 1993 agreed with the court of appeals and ordered that she be turned over to Dan and Cara Schmidt within a month. The DeBoers and Jessica's attorney appealed to the U.S. Supreme Court, but their appeal was denied on the thirtieth of July, with Justices Harry Blackmun and Sandra Day O'Connor dissenting.[5] A majority of the justices agreed with Justice John Paul Stevens, who noted that "the Iowa courts determined that the parental rights of the child's biological father had not been terminated . . . and that therefore applicants were not entitled to adopt the child."[6] Justice Blackmun, joined by Justice O'Connor, observed, "This is a case that touches the raw nerves of life's relationships. We have before us, in Jessica, a child of tender years who for her entire life has been nurtured by the DeBoers, a loving couple led to believe through the adoption process and the then-single mother's consent, that Jessica was theirs. Now, the biological father appears, marries the mother, and claims paternal status toward Jessica." Admitting his uncertainty about "where the ultimate legalities or equities lie," Justice Blackmun declared that he is "not willing to wash my hands of this case at this stage, with the personal vulnerability of the child so much at risk" as well as a disagreement between Michigan's decision and a New

Jersey precedent "over the duty and authority of state courts to consider the best interest of a child when rendering a custody decree."[7]

On 2 August, at age two and a half, Baby Jessica was handed over to the Schmidts to return to Iowa where, within a year, her name was changed to Anna Jacquelin and where, the Schmidts and their supporters report, she lives happily with them and her younger sister Chloe.[8]

The law in effect declared that Baby Jessica belonged *with* her biological father, because she belonged *to* her biological father. It did not matter that he had, at first at least, no current relationship with the biological mother. It did not matter that he had never even seen his child until, by the end, she was over two years old. It did not matter that the couple who had cared for her from the first week of her life were acknowledged to be loving and able parents. It did not matter, not enough to make a difference at least, that the child might be harmed by being taken from the only mother and father she had ever known and given to a couple who, no matter how caring and earnest, were complete strangers to her.

One wonders how the courts, and the public, would have reacted if the facts of the case had been a bit different. What if Cara Clausen had waited longer to tell Dan Schmidt? Instead of nineteen days, suppose she had waited three months? Six months? A year? Two years? Ten years? Would the biological father still have a legal claim to his child? A moral claim? When would other considerations—the child's welfare, the emotional commitment of the adoptive parents—outweigh the biological father's claims?

What if Dan Schmidt had waited longer to press his claim after learning that he was the biological father? Suppose he had waited a month? Six months? Five years? Is his "right" to his biological offspring diminished by his delay? Do we take the delay as evidence of something, perhaps his concern for the child, his intentions, his parenting ability? Suppose he had been informed before the child's birth, but had expressed no interest at first? Had made no effort even to learn who was listed as the child's father on the birth certificate? Had waited until well after the birth to press his claim to the child? Would it affect the way we respond to his claim to be the "true" father, to his request to have custody of the child?

The law treats biological parenthood as a kind of property right. Unlike other kinds of property, though, children can be taken away if they are not treated well. Short of serious abuse or neglect, however, their biological parents retain control, unless they surrender it voluntarily. There are good reasons for sustaining a strong presumption in favor of biological parenthood. Imagine that it were otherwise. Imagine that upon the birth of every child, all interested adults could bid to become the rearing parents. Of course, there would have to be some rules for determining who was eligible to enter the bidding and what criteria would determine the winner. There would have to be procedures for appealing decisions that struck a losing party as unfair and mechanisms for minimizing fraud, bribery, and other abuses that inevitably would appear. Like Winston Churchill's description of democracy as the worst of all possible systems of government, except for all the others, the practice of presuming that children belong to their biological parents may have its drawbacks, but it beats the alternatives. Most of the time. But its drawbacks are painful.

Emphasizing biological parenthood undervalues all other forms of parenthood—the many adults, related or unrelated, who raise children. It gives inadequate acknowledgment to the love and loyalty that can develop between rearing adults and the children who flourish under their care. It reflects and reinforces old models of the child-parent relationship that we would otherwise firmly reject—models like the child as property. It has thoroughly repugnant implications, for example, that a rapist has rights with respect to the child created as a result of his assault: the right to block an adoption, to rear the child, or to profit should the child later have good fortune.

Giving such prominence to the biological father's right to his child is far from a novel idea in Western culture. It is a remarkably straightforward application of a model that was dominant in ancient Rome and that remained powerfully influential well into the nineteenth century in America. The current spate of controversies that feature claims by biological fathers is a remnant of the idea that biological parenthood, especially fatherhood, underpins a kind of property right to the child.

Images like this, models of what is natural, fitting, and just, help shape our social institutions, including our laws. They also influence our moral judgments. We can and do at times reject particular images as flawed, false, even iniquitous. Think of the many images that portray groups of people as innately inferior, or the image of women as frail creatures, full of heart but fuzzy in the head, not to be troubled—or trusted—with such masculine enterprises as voting, holding office, or even owning property. Without question, our images of what is right and proper can be stunningly, comically, or tragically mistaken. But they can also be illuminating and powerful beacons calling us to do what is necessary in order for people to be able to make good lives for themselves and those they love, and for societies to fashion institutions that support that quest. What we do not have is the luxury of doing without such images: ideas about the content of good lives, good relationships, good families, good societies.

We can and we must become conscious and critical of such images, especially when they threaten what we value, like enduring love and loyalty between children and the adults who raise them. The child as property of its biological parents is ripe for just such a reconsideration.

Adoption and the Nature of Parenthood

If you searched books and journals in bioethics, you would rarely find any discussions of adoption, except perhaps as an alternative to abortion.[9] There it tends to be treated as an easy and painless way of allowing a birth mother to escape the burden of caring for a child. Such a characterization trivializes adoption, especially the emotional and moral significance for the surrendering biological mother and perhaps for the biological father and other relatives as well. Acknowledging the gravity of the decision to give one's biological child over to others to rear, however, does not thereby establish an unlimited right for biological parents to take back their children whenever they are so inclined. The president of Concerned United Birthparents, Janet Fenton, is quoted as asserting, "If adoption were made into a kind of guardianship, children would not suffer from the lack of honesty and the secrecy in adoption. They would know who their real parents were and that they could go back to them at any time."[10] Many, many people would object to the proposed dissolution of adoption and especially to the characterization of biological parents as "real," consigning all other adults who love and raise children as counterfeit, imitations, unreal—somehow defective and inferior versions of the "real" thing.

Adoption directs our attention to the nature of parenthood, to the different ways in which we link children with adults. It compels us to reflect on what parents are, what they do, and what their relationship is to the child in question. In particular, adoption displays in relatively clear and bold terms the distinction between genetic and rearing parents. Adoption is the most important alternative to biological parenthood for matching up dependent children and rearing adults. Controversies in adoption illuminate the interplay among law, ethics, and changing social conceptions of the roles of women, men, and children and of the family.

The continuities and changes in adoption practices and law embody important alternative conceptions of the parent-child relationship. The two dominant models of that relationship can be characterized as ownership and stewardship. Ownership, as the concept conveys, regards the child as a form of property, over which one or more adults have rights. Stewardship emphasizes the custodial aspect of the parents' role.

The notion that biological parenthood confers a kind of right of ownership over the child is at the same time deeply rooted in our cultural traditions, ingrained in our laws on adoption and child custody, and profoundly offensive to many people. Parenthood as stewardship seems more appealing at first glance. It places the child's interest above the parents, it too has important resonances in our cultural traditions, and it fits neatly with an evolving legal standard favoring the best interest of the child. I will argue, though, that both are defective and ought to be replaced by a third model.

To understand adoption, and the models of the parent-child relationship that underlie adoption practices and law, I want to look now at history. To understand what gives the alternative models their cultural legitimacy and persuasive power, we need to look at the tapestry, at the conceptions of women's, men's, and children's roles that have been woven together into our cultural heritage.

ADOPTION AND
ITS HISTORICAL PRECURSORS

What are the problems adoption is meant to solve? There are children in need of rearing parents. Their biological parents might be dead, or may have fled, leaving the children with no responsible adults to rear them. Then again, the biological parents may have decided that they cannot raise any children, or any more children, or this particular child. Whatever the cause, the result is children in need of adults. On the other side there are adults who were willing to take children into their households. Their reasons for taking in children are as varied as the circumstances that left children in need. They may have wanted the labor children could provide. They may have needed an heir. They may have desired the affection and love of a child.

Adoption as we know it today, with the apparatus that investigates prospective adoptive parents for their suitability and the routine legal awarding of custody to adoptive parents, is a recent development. Nonetheless, social practices meant to solve the problems of children without adults and adults desiring children have existed since at least late antiquity. Informal practices exist here and now—children raised by grandparents, by aunts and uncles, by older siblings, even by neighbors, often without any legal formalities such as custody transfer. If we limit our scope to formalized legal practices that look like contemporary adoption, there would be little to discuss. But if we expand the inquiry to encompass social practices that solved the same problems, we find a rich variety of precedents.

Jean Jacques Rousseau deposited each of his five children in a foundling home. He was an impoverished writer who believed in the importance of his work. Children were a financial drain and a distraction. He defended his actions in his *Confessions:* "This arrangement seemed to me so good, so sensible, so appropriate, that if I did not boast of it publicly it was solely out of regard for their mother."[11] Rousseau's desire—to limit the size of his family—and his solution—to take advantage of the means available in his time for placing one's biological children into the care of others—echo attitudes and practices common in Western Europe since antiquity.

In Rousseau's era, the foundling home was the obvious choice for parents of unwanted children. John Boswell's remarkable history of child abandonment, *The Kindness of Strangers,* presents compelling evidence that parents in earlier times solved similar problems by abandoning children in places frequented by others, where they were likely to be discovered quickly.[12] The practice was so common that its traces are found in language itself. The Latin word *lactaria* was defined by a Roman scholar as "columns in the public market, called the 'nursing columns' because people deposit nursing infants there."[13]

In the absence of effective ways to limit the number of biological children, parents often found themselves with more children than they wanted or were able to rear. With great caution given the paucity of demographic evidence, Boswell estimates that from 20 to 40 percent of Roman children were abandoned in the first three centuries A.D. High rates of abandonment occurred later as well. In Toulouse, France, a conservative estimate is that 10 percent of births resulted in abandonment in the first half of the eighteenth century, rising to more than 25 percent by the end of the 1700s. The rate in Paris was in the same range in the latter part of the century, while in Lyons it was one child in three.

Italy was comparable: the rate in Florence among baptized infants exceeded 40 percent by the early nineteenth century.[14] The rate of abandonment has varied considerably, largely in response to poverty and social chaos; the figures for early modern Europe are probably a high— or from another perspective, a low—point. But the problem of unwanted children is neither new nor uncommon in the history of the West.

Although those who rescued abandoned children were praised, there is no evidence that abandoning one's child was regarded as shameful. The reasons against abandonment given at the time included such things as extolling the virtues of large families, but not that it was wrong. When the biological parents are criticized, it is for demanding a benefit from a child one had previously abandoned.[15] The concept that parents have an obligation to raise all of their biological children had not appeared by the Middle Ages, even though there is ample evidence that rearing parents were expected to provide adequate care for the children accepted into their household.

Boswell cautions us against making anachronistic assumptions about either the fate of abandoned children or the motives of the parents who abandoned them and the adults who took them in. Abandonment was not tantamount to infanticide. Undoubtedly, some children died as a result of being left in a public place, "exposed" as we might say today. But it is likewise beyond question that many such *expositi*, as they were known, were taken up by others to be sheltered and fed. The places where children were left, the tokens of identification often left with them, and a plethora of legal and literary records indicate that such "adopted" children were a regular feature of life in late antiquity and that the children so abandoned were expected often to survive. Rome itself, according to legend, was founded by abandoned children— Romulus and Remus, who were suckled by a wolf and then taken up and raised by a shepherd.

It would likewise be a mistake to think that abandoning a child was an infallible sign that parents were unconcerned about their children's welfare. There were many possible motives for abandoning one's child, including concern for the well-being of one's other children or for the abandoned child itself. It is difficult for us, who might elect to postpone or forgo having children because they would alter our "lifestyle," to imagine the plight of parents whose poverty made it literally impossible to raise a child. Sheer destitution was doubtless the cause of many abandonments. Other motives must have operated as well, including shame (from, for example, an illegitimate birth), concern about dividing property among multiple heirs, along with laziness, selfishness, and others that we would recognize readily today. The Jewish Talmud mentions poverty and hunger, more often than illegitimacy, as reasons why parents abandon their children. Notably, the Talmud's restrictions on foundlings' marriage rights were negated if the abandonment occurred during a time of famine.[16]

Similarly, there were multiple reasons why adults took children in. Children, once past their earliest years, could contribute to the work of the household. In this or other ways they had economic value. Simple sympathy for the plight of infants surely prompted some adults to take them in. And it is also clear from historical evidence that at least some of these adult-child pairings led to the establishment of deeply caring emotional bonds.

The Romans had a concept of *alumni,* which seems generally to have designated an abandoned child raised in another's home.[17] An *alumnus* could be slave or free, or treated as occupying some intermediate category. Numerous inscriptions make it clear that many alumni were cherished as dearly as biological offspring. Indeed, in Roman society a relationship with an alumnus was regarded in some ways as superior to that with one's biological children "because it was voluntary, largely unregulated by law, and drew its strength and force from personal ties of love and kindness. . . . [T]he term *alumnus* became a symbol and expression for a particular type of selfless and loving relationship in Roman society and among its Christian heirs."[18]

There is an interesting puzzle here about the age at which children were abandoned to be recovered and raised by other adults. Though he refers mostly to the abandonment of infants, Boswell does not exclude the likelihood that children were also abandoned at later ages. If adults took children in primarily for their economic value, then older children, who might immediately be put to productive labor, would be most desirable. Infancy, clearly, is the age of least economic productivity. Infants, in fact, could be said to have negative economic value in the short term, because they require the labor of others merely to ensure their survival. Today, infants are most sought after for adoption because, one might say, they have high emotional or affiliative value. Infants appeal to our desires to nurture, and in caring for infants we develop powerful mutual bonds of affection. If, as Boswell contends, Romans picked up abandoned infants in large numbers, and if in many cases they developed bonds of great affection with those children, then emotional or affiliative value seems as likely an explanation of why they did so as does their potential economic value.

Despite the markedly inferior legal status of children (or for that matter, all members of the household save the patriarch), there is abundant evidence that parents in antiquity were capable of sentiments of love toward their children that seem thoroughly contemporary. We have no way of knowing if such attitudes were typical then, but the available evidence indicates that they were by no means uncommon. Boswell notes, "Everywhere in Western culture, from religious literature to secular poetry, parental love is invoked as the ultimate standard of selfless and untiring devotion, central metaphors of theology and ethics presuppose this love as a universal point of reference, and language must devise special terms to characterize persons wanting in this 'natural' affection."[19]

Parental affection was lavished on children taken in after birth as well as biological offspring. Consider this declamation from a foster father: "During the time when our son . . . was away at war, whose was he? Was it not I who hung from the city walls in suspense? Not I who seized everyone returning from the battlefield? . . . Who bandaged his wounds when he returned? Who washed away the blood? Who took him to the temple and gave thanks?"[20] It would make sense to use an argument like this only if the speaker could count on his audience's recognition that worries about your child's safety, ministering to his hurts, and profound gratitude for his safe return were indisputable marks of parental love.

Boswell's monumental study shows how the particular institutions and practices that evolved reflected the cultural predilections of their time. Under Roman law, children—along with all other members of the household including slaves and wives—were the property of the father, under the authority of the *patria potestas,* a broad power over persons and property held by the eldest male in a family. Roman customs and laws regarding abandoned children were shaped by this conception of paternal power and rights. Some of the institutions and practices developed to deal with the problem of unwanted children are appalling by modern standards, for example, selling one's child into slavery or prostitution. In Roman times, abandonment may well have offered the best chance for a child born into dire circumstances. He or she, if Boswell is correct, was likely to be picked up by adults who would at least feed and shelter the infant. If especially lucky, such a child might become an alumnus, possibly even a treasured member of a family.

There were customary places to leave children and laws to settle disputes that might later arise over custody of them. By the Middle Ages, the Christian church had become the most significant social organization. Both the practice of oblation and the foundling home originated and took their form under the authority of the church. Oblation, literally offering, entailed giving one's child to a religious order, often a monastery, to be raised there for a life of religious rigor and devotion.[21] By the thirteenth century, religious orders had established hospices for the poor, the homeless, and the ill. Caring for abandoned children became one of the functions of these institutions. The fourteenth and fifteenth centuries saw the establishment of foundling homes to deal expressly with the problem of unwanted children.[22]

These institutions and practices existed because they solved problems. Abandonment allowed parents to limit the size of their family. Recovery enabled adults who desired children, for whatever reasons, to obtain them. Oblation provided a steady influx of labor for religious orders. Foundling hospitals kept abandoned children from becoming a public nuisance.

That problems were solved for others does not mean that the social devices used to deal with unwanted children kept the interests of those children uppermost. The dismal history of foundling hospitals, with their staggering mortality rates, is sadly consistent with what we know from our contemporary experience with bureaucracies. The children were placed out of public view, where a great many died. As Boswell relates, the civil authorities were concerned mainly with the cost of running the homes: "No records survive from the fourteenth or fifteenth centuries of any civil inquests or accountings of the health, well-being, or prospects of the children—only of squabbles over expenses, budgets, and procedures."[23]

Our contemporary institutions and practices of adoption, like those of ancient Rome or Europe of the Middle Ages, reflect our culture's predilections, solve our problems, and serve a variety of interests, with the welfare of the child not always the leading consideration. Beliefs about the family, paternal authority, the nature of women, and child development were profoundly influential in shaping American law on child custody after the Revolutionary War.[24] It is always easier to see the role such factors played in other times and places than in our own. But we have not been granted any special dispensation from having presuppositions, our bureaucratic institutions are subject to the same pulls of organizational self-preservation and self-enhancement as those of earlier times, and basic human motivations do not appear to have changed markedly.

A look at our distant cultural roots gives us some insight into the origins of our more durable images and practices, for example, the emphasis on paternal authority and property interests that survived in law well into the nineteenth century and continues to exert influence today. It is more than a mere curiosity, I believe, that several recent, widely publicized efforts by biological parents to regain custody of their children are based on claims by the biological *father*, claims supported by the laws of many states, claims that contain powerful echoes of Roman concepts of children as property and of the patria potestas, the power of the patriarch.

From Children-as-Property to Parents-as-Stewards

If contemporary adoption laws tend to treat children as if they were the property of their biological parents, Roman law was unabashedly straightforward about it. The male Roman citizen was head of the family, the paterfamilias, and held near-absolute authority over his children. The power of the patriarch was profound. All the property of everyone in his power, which included his slaves as well as his children and the children of his sons, legally belonged to him. He held the power of life and death over his offspring, no matter how old.[25] Children could also be sold, although the child of a Roman citizen could not be made a slave: such a child became the property of its purchaser but had its full rights as a citizen restored upon being freed, unlike noncitizen slaves.[26] Boswell notes that this protection accorded to Rome's child-citizens probably had more to do with the state's desire to keep a clear boundary between the status of freeborn and slave than with any tender concern for the welfare of its children.[27]

Abandoned children were *res vacantes,* unclaimed objects, who became the property of whoever claimed them.[28] Nevertheless, the biological parents still had certain rights over the child. Diocletian once ruled that an abandoning father could overrule the rearing father and forbid a proposed marriage for his biological daughter—on the condition that he reimburse the foster father for the expenses of raising the daughter.[29] The idea that children, as the property of their biological father, remained in his control held sway for centuries in Roman law, until Constantine declared in 331 that abandoned children should be under the authority of their rearing parents and could be raised as a slave or one's own child, as the father chose.[30]

The children of Rome's citizens were the property of their fathers. Although the specific structures of Roman law, which later had great impact on the legal systems of many Western societies, were less influential in the development of the common law tradition in England and the United States, the underlying concept of children as the property of their fathers was alive and well in colonial America. Michael Grossberg's study of nineteenth-century family law in America, *Governing the Hearth*, begins by sketching the legacy of English law bequeathed to the new country. Children, in this tradition, were "assets of paternal estates in which fathers had vested interests. As dependent, subordinate beings, their services, earnings, and the like became the property of their paternal masters in exchange for life and maintenance."[31] In disputes over custody, fathers could rely on the law for support of "an almost limitless right to the custody of their minor legitimate children."[32]

The American Revolution, with its fierce opposition to patriarchy, began a transformation in our understanding of the family and the place of children within it. The family, rather than an organic whole with the patriarch as its head, gave way to the family as a collectivity of individuals, each with his or her own rights and interests. In nineteenth-century America, the family still had a patriarch at its head; the law still consigned women and children to inferior legal status. But judges could and, over time, increasingly did intervene in family matters to protect the interests of individual members of the family. The patriarch's powers were restrained as new ideas about the nature of marriage, of women, and of children took hold under the sway of convictions about the importance of individual, autonomous choice and the superior significance of accomplishment over that of status inherited by birth.[33]

By 1838, less than two-thirds of a century after the revolution, a judge in Maine could write that "children do not become property of the parents. As soon as a child is born, he becomes a member of the human family, and is invested with all the rights of humanity." In that same decision, the judge declared unambiguously what he believed to be the legal foundation of paternal authority: "If instead of treating his child with tenderness and affection . . . he treats him with such cruelty that he cannot be safely left in his custody . . . [the court] will interpose and deprive him of the exercise of a power, which having been allowed for the benefit of the child is perverted to his injury and perhaps his ruin." [34] The child here is most definitely *not* property. The father's power over his child has its source, not in some form of ownership, but in society's interest in seeing that each of its members is properly raised.

Legal disputes over the custody of children could be every bit as gripping to the American public a century and a half ago as they are today. One such case involved an American woman, Ellen Sears d'Hauteville, who had married Paul Daniel Gonzalve Grand d'Hauteville during a tour of Europe with her family. Unhappy in Europe with her new husband, she returned with his permission to her family in America where she gave birth to a son, Frederick. Gonzalve, as he was called, traveled to America to claim his wife and son, but Ellen refused to return with him or to surrender the custody of her child. Two years later, Ellen and Gonzalve were engaged in a fierce court battle in Philadelphia. [35] Contemporary sources indicate that the case was the talk of the town, much like the battle over Baby Jessica in our time.

Ellen's lawyer argued that Frederick, only two years old, would be best served in the care of his mother and that custody ought to be allocated, not as a property right, but for the good of the child. Gonzalve's lawyers responded: "To whom belongs the custody of this child? The answer is in the human heart, and in the practice of all nations. The father, responsible for its maintenance and education, for its moral standing—his title is indisputable. The legal authorities on this subject are conclusive." [36]

Ellen prevailed. The judges accepted her attorney's argument that the child's welfare ought to be decisive and rejected the notion of paternal ownership. Frederick went home with his mother. Although the case was a blow against the concept of children as the property of their fathers, it was an ambiguous victory at best for women. A woman, such as Ellen Sears d'Hauteville, could persuade judges that a young child should be with its mother, but she did so at the price of invoking a profoundly sentimental notion of maternalism that could equally well be used to limit women's rights in other spheres. The judge who delivered the opinion at the d'Hauteville trial portrayed this view of woman's nature clearly: "[E]very instinct of humanity unerringly proclaims that no *substitute* can supply the place of **HER**, whose watchfulness over the sleeping cradle or waking moments of her offspring, is prompted by deeper and holier feelings than the most liberal allowance of a nurse's wages could possibly stimulate." [37] The concepts of a special maternal sphere and a distinctive women's nature were used to deny women access to public life, including politics and employment. Even science was enlisted in the effort to prove that women had a distinctive nature that rendered them less fit than men for activities outside the home.[38]

By the end of the nineteenth century, the concept of child as property had been replaced in most instances by the concept that parents were stewards, responsible for the well-being of their children. One writer put it thus in 1892: "You have no personal, selfish right at all over your children. You have invited an immortal to come into your temporary keeping; and you have only the right to treat that as a reverent trust committed to you for awhile."[39]

The Roots of Modern Adoption

English common law, from which American law sprang, was initially hostile to adoption. There were other means for taking care of children who needed adults, such as apprenticeships. Adoptions that would affect rights of inheritance were regarded with particular disfavor. In America, however, the appeal of adoption became irresistible by the mid-1800s. If a group of colonies could throw off their own patriarch and form a new political "family," why should not the citizens of the new nation have the right to make their own families by choice and not only by nature?

Adoption was possible in America before the 1850s, but only if one could successfully persuade the state legislature to pass a private act legalizing the particular adoption. By 1900, almost all states had passed laws permitting adoption.[40] The laws typically reflected the courts' and the nation's growing concern for the welfare of the child. Adoption was seen as a way to provide new families to take the place of failed ones. Parents could either voluntarily surrender children or be found unfit and have their children taken away. Biological bonds could be severed and bonds forged by choice and affection put in their place.

Consensus was not as easily forged on the problem of how to treat the inheritance rights of adopted children. In many jurisdictions, adopted children were treated by the law as if they were the children of their adoptive parents in some, but not all, respects. Early adoption laws were often vague or contradictory about inheritance rights of adoptees.

Biological heirs frequently challenged the right of adoptees to inherit from their adopted family's estate. Battles over inheritance, not over custody, were the most common legal disputes in nineteenth-century adoption cases. Adopted children at times fought for a share of their biological parents' estates.[41] American courts continued to treat adopted children as being different from biological children through the end of the nineteenth century. For the sake of the children, and for the protection of the state, adoption was accepted. But the law did not regard it as a complete replacement for biological parenthood.

The Significance of Biological versus Rearing Parenthood

Not until the year 331 did Rome declare that biological parents who abandoned their children lost their rights to those children. The Roman practice of alumni, however, shows that the relations between rearing parents and children could be every bit as valued as the relations between biological parents and children. Through the Middle Ages, biological lineage became increasingly important, and adults who reared foundlings were likely to try to pass them off as their biological children. "By the close of the Middle Ages," Boswell observes, adoptive relations were regarded as "decidedly inferior."[42]

By the late nineteenth century, American courts became willing to give the bonds between rearing parents and their wards enough weight to defeat the claims of biological parents. In an important 1881 case, a man named Chapsky attempted to recover custody of his daughter from the sister of his late wife, with whom she had lived for over five years. The judge observed, "[W]hen new ties have been formed and a certain current given to the child's life and thought, much attention should be paid to the probabilities of a benefit to the child from the change. It is an obvious fact, that ties of blood weaken, and ties of companionship strengthen, by lapse of time; and the prosperity and welfare of the child depend on the ability to do all which the prompting of these ties compel."[43]

The tension between the claims of blood and of companionship remains every bit as strong today. Some advocates for biological parents insist on the supremacy of blood. Recall Carole Anderson of Concerned

United Birthparents, who wanted "no pretending that the guardians who care for and love the child are the real 'parents.' " Yet many rearing parents, whether or not they have formally adopted the child, report bonds of affection indistinguishable from those described by biological parents. And a fierce debate continues about whether adopted children are better off in permanent new homes or should remain tied to their biological parents, even if they must live in temporary foster care arrangements.

When a biological parent says that he or she wants "my" child back, it is difficult to ignore the distinct echoes of earlier concepts of children as the property of their biological progenitors. It would be unforgivably callous to ignore the great emotional pain that surely moves many biological parents to seek a reunion with their missing offspring. The ancients even had a word for such reunions, *anagnorisis;* the quest for reunion was a frequent theme in Greek and Roman literature.[44] It would be unfair also to interpret the longings of contemporary parents as entirely selfish. Surely many biological parents believe that it is in their child's interest to be reunited with their birthparent. It would likewise be a mistake to ignore the significance given to biology—to the implied claim that biological parents have a property right to their offspring. Our culture's history is deeply embedded with the concept of children as property. And however much it has been hedged in by concern for the child's welfare, biology still exerts great force in the law. It helps to explain how a biological father, who has never met or even known about the existence of his offspring, could prevail in a custody battle.

Property, Stewardship, and Mutualism

I am not arguing here that the law should give *no* importance to biology. That would lead to chaos, invite catastrophic abuse of legal discretion in determining who could or could not be a parent, and fail to serve the interests of children or parents. I want instead to use adoption to explore three models of the parent-child relationship. Two of them I have already mentioned: property and stewardship. I want to discuss a third model also, which I will call "mutualism," as it comes in part from Erik Erikson's concept of mutuality. Although mutualism has not received much attention in discussions about parent-child relationships, it offers a better account of those relationships than either the property model or stewardship.

THE CHILD AS PROPERTY

The idea that a child is the property of its biological parents is out of favor, but not dead, either in our laws or our customs. It was starkly visible in the early 1980s in disputes over parents' authority to refuse potentially life-saving treatment for seriously ill newborns. There were those who argued that parents should have virtually limitless discretion to accept or refuse such treatment for their infants. There were others who argued that although parents should make such decisions, their authority was constrained by the best interest of the infant. There were still others who distrusted both parents and health professionals and insisted that any decision to forgo possibly life-prolonging treatment must be overturned.

The first group seemed to view infants as the property of their biological parents, to be saved or allowed to die at their parents' discretion. The third group acted as though parents and children were adversaries and that there could be no such thing as a compassionate decision to allow a severely ill infant to die comfortably. The middle position accepted that the child's best interest was an important standard and that parents usually could be counted on to do what was best for their child, though there had to be means for intervening when decisions clearly went against the child's best interest.

The laws favoring biological parents, particularly fathers, sustain the interests of biological progenitors in their offspring. But the concept of the child as property is based on faulty evidence and truncated ethics. The family in pre-Revolutionary America was viewed as an organic whole, with the patriarch at its head, and the interests of the various family members regarded as inseparable.[45] It does not require a particularly astute knowledge of human psychology to understand that the interests of individual family members do not inevitably coincide and that patriarchs do not invariably comprehend or heed the interests of their spouses and children. Nineteenth-century family law recognized that families, however valuable as collectivities, consisted nevertheless of individual members each with her or his own interests and rights. When the interests or rights of family members were in jeopardy, the courts were permitted, indeed required, to intervene. Treating children as the property of their fathers, or both biological parents, must be based either on a psychological fiction that the parents will always and everywhere act in the child's interest or on a disregard for the child's moral standing as a creature deserving of protection and respect.

The tapestry of history helps illuminate where the concept of the child as the property of its biological parents originates and what functions it served. It also helps us to understand why it was largely swept away over a century ago as American ideas about the nature of children and the goals of marriage and family life were transformed. The thread representing the child as property is loose and dangling; it clashes with other threads representing children, adults, and families in our contemporary tapestry. It hangs on only because it remains connected to a few other threads—like our laws concerning the rights of biological parents in adoption.

THE PARENT AS STEWARD

Stewardship is a more attractive model than property ownership for describing the relation between parent and child. It is the model underlying an 1894 Texas Supreme Court decision keeping a two-year-old child with her foster parents: "The State, as the protector and promoter of the peace and prosperity of organized society, is interested in the proper education and maintenance of the child . . . ; and while as a general rule it recognizes the fact that the interest of the child and society is best promoted by . . . the promptings of paternal affection . . . still it had the right in proper cases to deprive the parent of the custody of the child when demanded by the interests of the child and society."[46] The parent, that is, should manage the upbringing of a child for the good of that child and the good of society.

A good steward manages some entity—a household, farm, portfolio—for someone else's benefit. The first meaning of steward offered in the *Oxford English Dictionary* is "an official who controls the domestic affairs of a household, supervising the service of his master's table, directing the domestics, and regulating household expenditure."[47] The steward's own interests are unimportant; the steward's job is to serve the owner by carefully managing his or her domain. The steward must, in a disinterested way, do what is best for his or her master and the master's property.

Stewardship is superior to property ownership here because it limits sharply what the steward may do with the object of stewardship—in this instance, a child. The owner of property may do anything he wants with it, including destroy it; a steward must manage the child for the benefit of someone other than himself. Stewardship shares with owner- ship the metaphor of the child as property; the difference is in who owns the property—God, the State, the child herself or himself. The notion of property here has lost its most onerous connotations; it is little more than an innocuous metaphor. The parent-as-steward cannot act arbitrarily toward the child, nor can the parent act solely out of self- interest. The parent-as-steward must always do what is best for the child. These are positive features of the model.

But parenthood as stewardship still has its shortcomings as a model for parent-child relations. As a description of a relationship, it connotes disinterestedness, selflessness, a sort of benign but emotionally distant concern for the welfare of the child. This fits poorly with the intensity, love, and intimacy we prize between parents and children. It places no importance on the interests or welfare of the steward who is there, after all, to serve the master by taking care of the master's goods. The model of the parent as steward embodies a conception of the relationship be- tween parent and child that is in a crucial respect the precise opposite of what we most prize. It also discounts the parent's interests, which seems both factually shortsighted—if it leads us toward public policies that are insensitive to parent's needs—and morally erroneous: the inter- ests of parents do count, even if they must often give way to the more urgent interests of their children.

MUTUALISM IN THE
PARENT-CHILD RELATIONSHIP

The child is more than property, and the parent is more than a caretaker. We need a model of the parent-child relationship that acknowledges the immense stake parents and children have in each oth- er's flourishing. We need a model that emphasizes the central impor- tance of the *relationship*, without losing sight of the individuality of the parties. We need a model that reflects relevant facts about parents and children: that the flourishing of parents and children is intertwined; that by doing what is loving for their children, parents experience profound satisfactions and develop virtues that promote their own flourishing as well. Mutualism provides such a model.

Mutualism is a fruitful way to think about parent-child relationships that incorporates both plausible empirical assumptions and widely shared moral judgments. It assumes that enduring ties based on nurturance and loyalty between adults and children do in fact promote healthy physical, psychological, social—and moral—development for both. It also assumes that mutuality is consistent with what we know about human psychology; that there are circumstances in which we can further our own good only by working for the good of another and that there is no psychological inconsistency in being motivated simultaneously to benefit another and oneself by the same pattern of actions. Finally, it assumes that, with the support of appropriate social institutions and practices, relationships characterized by mutuality can and do exist.

The account we give of parents' motivations is particularly important to understanding why mutualism is a better fit than the alternatives. We typically toss all human motivation into one of two bins. The first is labeled selfishness or egoism; the second, altruism. The former is commonly regarded as either morally neutral or bad, but robust and reliable: if you build a system on the presumption that people will behave selfishly, you are unlikely to be disappointed. The latter, altruism, is more morally reputable, but not as robust: if you rely entirely on altruism, you may very well be let down. Mutualism rejects this either-or. There are circumstances—the parent-child relationship being the leading example—in which you cannot honestly describe what motivates the actors—here, the parents—as strictly egoistic or altruistic. It is some inextricable blend of concern for other and concern for self.

Parenthood feels like a very selfless activity at times, when you are doing something you really, really don't want to do, but you do it anyway because it is for the good of your child. But we should not deny the profound joys that parenthood also brings with it, along with the undeniable conviction that by being good parents we foster our own flourishing. It is profoundly misleading to reduce this complex motivation either to egoism or altruism. Mutualism is a more sensitive and honest way to characterize good parent-child relationships. It has the robustness of egoism without its moral taint and the other-directedness of altruism without its fragility.

From the point of view of ethics, mutualism embodies a realistic account of the motivations that support morally desirable parent-child relationships. Those relationships are desirable because they foster the flourishing of individuals and families through the creation of strong, enduring relationships of mutual caring. The fate of those relationships depends itself on creating institutions and practices that support them rather than undermine them, which brings us to the law on adoption.

Adoption: Ethics, Law, and Policy

If we take mutualism as the suitable model for parent-child relationships, certain things fade into the background and others snap into focus. Sliding into the background are claims to possession of a child based solely on biology with no component of relationship—the centerpiece of the child-as-property model. Jumping into the foreground are the caring relationships that grow between rearing adults and the children they nurture.

Existing relationships cannot be the only consideration, or else we would be left with scenarios like this one: a couple steals a baby from a newborn nursery, then raises it faultlessly for six months and claims parental rights. We would not want our laws to reward such a cruel theft by awarding custody to the child thieves. But biological parents, especially fathers with no relation to the children or the children's mothers, would have lesser claims to possess their offspring than under current laws. Relationship is given greater weight, biology less.

The story of Jessica Anne DeBoer, now Anna Jacquelin Schmidt, began this chapter. Recent years have seen many other cases of fathers pursuing custody of their biological offspring by attempting to prevent or overturn adoptions. The Illinois Supreme Court upheld Otakar Kirchner's right to raise his child, Richard, ordering that the child be taken from the couple that adopted him and handed over to Kirchner, who, like Dan Schmidt, had subsequently married the child's mother. Unlike the DeBoer case, however, Baby Richard's adoption had been approved by a lower court. On 30 April 1995, Kirchner and his wife took custody of Baby Richard, by then four years old. The Baby Richard case unsettled many adoptive parents who feared that their children could be taken from them years after their legal adoption.[48]

What would be a decent and sensible public policy for handling custody disputes between adoptive parents and biological parents? Rather than begin with assumptions about the legal rights of the various parties, I want to frame the issue this way: What policies, including laws, would be most supportive of good lives for children and the adults who raise them?

This standard raises at least two kinds of prior questions. First is a question about ethics: What appropriately count as "good lives" for children and parents? We cannot evade this question, although some theorists try to do so by talking about rights and autonomy, property and production. If I have asked the right question, then we must have the courage to answer it as best we can, recognizing always the possibility that we may be mistaken.

The other prior questions have to do with facts: How do children and adults fare under various arrangements for pairing them up? Do children who are adopted as infants develop strong, supportive attachments with their rearing parents? Do they do as well as their peers in school? Are they happy? As adults, are they able to make good marriages, to be good parents? How quickly do children form bonds with their adult caregivers? What happens if those bonds are disrupted after a few weeks? Six months? Two, five, ten years? Do adopted children and their adoptive parents fare better when information about their biological parents is kept secret, or are they better off in open adoptions? Do surrendering biological parents cope with their loss better when they are in regular contact with their biological child, or when they are not? Do individuals vary so greatly in their responses that public policy ought to be highly flexible, able to accommodate a wide variety of relationships between surrendering parents and adoptive families?

The facts are important. They are also, unfortunately but not surprisingly, the subject of dispute. When the stakes are high, in passion or in money, we should expect the parties to hail whatever evidence favors their stance and to disparage whatever weakens it. Do not underestimate the tenacity of a stand in the face of even overwhelming evidence against it: consider the tobacco industry's continued insistence that the connection between tobacco and disease has not been scientifically proven. There is considerably less evidence about the impact of adoption on children, but there is some.

The bulk of the evidence suggests that adopted children do reasonably well. A well-designed Swedish study followed children who were registered by their mothers for adoption and were subsequently either adopted, raised by their biological mothers, or put into permanent foster homes. These children were studied at several ages right into young adulthood and compared to their agemates who had never been registered for possible adoption. Though adopted children showed some early differences, particularly at age eleven, the evidence showed that "the long-term prognosis for adopted children is in no way worse than for children in the general population, provided that the adoptive home is psychologically well prepared for the task of rearing a nonbiological child."[49] In that same study, the children raised by their biological mothers and especially those raised in permanent foster homes showed substantially more problems. The authors speculate that the insecurity of foster arrangements, from which the child could have been abruptly withdrawn at any time, may have been stressful on the child and the rearing parents.

A review of studies on the long-term outcomes of adoption by a leading researcher concludes that although adoptees may be more vulnerable to adjustment difficulties than children living in intact biological families, most of them function quite normally.[50] Adopted children may be likely to attribute problems with their self-esteem or squabbles with parents to the fact that they are not living with their biological parents. Nonetheless, they are very likely to work through such difficulties and become well settled in their communities.[51] Adoption, that is, appears to be neither a panacea nor an awful fate. Most adopted children, in fact, develop relationships with their rearing parents that provide them with the strength and self-confidence to make good lives for themselves.

A recent study of 715 adoptive families confirms the generally positive outlook for children adopted as infants. The study included 881 adopted adolescents in four midwestern states as well as their 78 nonadopted siblings and 1,262 parents. The children in this study were adopted by fifteen months of age and showed good self-esteem, little negative feeling about being adopted, and strong, positive emotional attachments to their adoptive families. Perhaps the most poignant finding was the list of reasons given by the approximately two-thirds who would like to meet their birthparents. The most common reason was to find out what they look like (94%). The next three most cited reasons were "to tell them I'm happy" (80%), "to tell them I'm OK" (76%), and "to tell them I'm glad to be alive" (73%). In fifth place was the desire to know the reason for their adoption (72%).[52]

Our laws on adoption are showing strain. Custody battles that go on for years harm everyone—biological parents, adoptive parents, and, most of all, the child. Our legal system, with its deliberative pace and multiple levels of appeal, may allow justice to be done in many kinds of cases. Where money is the issue, the court can always tack on interest to make up for the time lost. But there is no way to make up for the bonds between adult and child that are forged day by day, yet may be sundered violently by a judge's decision. The point of a child-parent relationship *is* the relationship and all that grows from it. We want to encourage, not discourage, the formation of early, powerful, and confident bonds of love. Drawn out legal procedures leave adoptive parents uncertain whether the child they love today will be taken from them tomorrow. Delays and uncertainties pervert the purpose of adoption. The child's emotional security and healthy development are jeopardized.

Sound adoption policy cannot tolerate prolonged legal disputes or uncertainties about custody. We must have a quick and clear time limit for disputing custody, along with speedy processes to resolve disputes.

We should not abandon the presumption that children belong with their biological parents, as long as those parents participate in rearing and caring for their child. But when other adults have been the primary sources of love and care, for example, adoptive parents, considerable weight ought to be given to their relationship with the child. How long that relationship has existed, what proportion of the child's life has been spent with those adults, along with the quality of the relationship, should be given equal weight to the claims of biology.

As for biological fathers who have had no relationship with their offspring, the law should not reinforce the historical thread of the child-as-property. It may be wise to retain the presumption in favor of biology, even when the biological father's relationship with the child's mother is poor or nonexistent. But the presumption, if not based on property rights, will be easier to rebut with evidence that the biological father is unlikely to provide a good home for the child, or unlikely to form a loving and nurturing relationship with the child. When a child has lived with adoptive parents for months or years, the relationships forged between them should overcome any presumption in favor of biology.

Reconsidering Biological Parenthood

I am urging that we reexamine our legal presumptions that powerfully favor biological over rearing parenthood. If the child is not the property of its biological progenitors, then what reasons support the presumption that children belong in the homes of those parents? The general reason is that it best serves, on the whole, our goal of encouraging strong, positive, and enduring bonds between children and the adults who raise them. At least three considerations support this conclusion.

First, helping a child acquire trust, initiative, self-discipline, self-insight, and the capacities for love, nurturing, and wisdom is a difficult task. For children raised by other than their biological parents, that task appears to be more difficult, even though most such children complete it successfully. When children are reared by their biological parents, they do not have to cope with this additional obstacle to healthy development.

Second, biological ties can reinforce the bonds that grow between parents and children. I have no doubt that powerful, loving relationships develop between children and adults with no biological relationship. But I also know the delight I feel when someone notes how much my child resembles me. I recall an episode many years ago when I took my three oldest children grocery shopping. A woman—a total stranger—approached me and said about my second-oldest daughter, who must have been about two at the time, that "no one would say she was the milkman's child." This struck me as a peculiar compliment, but it was a compliment all the same. Just how biological similarity works its magic is not so clear. Some would probably attribute it to vanity. But I suspect it has as much to do with looking into your child's eyes and beholding there a reflection of your own parents, your brothers or sisters, or your spouse. Your child is not so much an image of yourself as an image of those you love.

The third consideration is to avoid the chaos and injustices that would otherwise occur. If we did *not* presume in favor of biological parents, we would have to find some other policy to put in its place. Should children go to the highest bidders? The couple who promised the best home? Should there be an infant tribunal, whose job it is to allocate every infant born? The absurdity of this is obvious. Subtler injustices may also creep in, the more we permit agencies and courts to intrude into parent-child relationships. With history and human nature as our guides, we can anticipate that parents who differ in culture or class from the officials and judges who intervene in families will be judged more harshly than parents who resemble those same officials and judges. All things considered, we are much better off presuming in favor of biological parents.

But what should be the content of that presumption? Once we reject the idea of child-as-property, we can recast the presumption in terms of relationship. Let me try a tentative formulation: *Our laws about child custody should be based on the presumption that the child's biological parents will act as the rearing parents and will develop an enduring, nurturing relationship with the child. If that presumption proves false in a particular case, the law should favor rejoining, maintaining, or creating such a relationship, even if that entails having the child raised by adults who are not its biological parents.* We should give priority to the relationship. Biological parents should have the initial, unimpeded opportunity to establish such a relationship. If they do not, then our laws should promote the prompt establishment of alternatives.

Once adults have begun raising a child and ties of love created, we should protect those ties. In adoption, once a child has been given to the care of new parents, who in good faith endeavor to raise and love this child, the law should not regard the child as misappropriated property. Biological fathers seeking to reclaim their offspring should be required to demonstrate that the child will be better off in their care than with the adoptive parents. They may appeal to biology, but not as a source of property rights, only as a factor facilitating the development of strong emotional ties.[53]

Suppose that through incompetence or fraud on the part of some private or public agency, biological parents lost their child. Perhaps a new mother was misled about her rights, or was not given appropriate counseling. Perhaps a biological father was not notified that his offspring was being offered for adoption. The mother or father ought to be able to sue the agency for damages. But that right to seek compensation can and should exist independently of policies that favor keeping children with the parents who raise them.

A Hopeful Development

In late summer 1994, the National Conference of Commissioners on Uniform State Laws, a body that drafts model statutes for state legislatures, published a proposed new Uniform Adoption Act. The model statute acknowledges the importance of established adult-child relationships and urges that any challenges to adoption decrees be dealt with expeditiously. It attempts to specify the rights and duties of biological fathers. But it appears that it would still allow biological fathers to make a legal claim for their children for up to six months after an adoption has been finalized, if, as in the DeBoer-Schmidt case, the father had not been properly identified.[54] Otherwise, the burden of proof on biological parents to reverse an adoption decree is stringent:

they must show "by clear and convincing evidence that the decree or order is not in the best interest of the adoptee."[55]

The proposed law probably would not alter the outcome of cases like Baby Jessica and Baby Richard. In each of those cases the biological father had not surrendered his parental rights and initiated his claim for custody before an adoption decree had been issued.[56] If the proposed law had been in place, it might have prevented the cases from being so drawn out, but then again it might not. Although it places a time limit on filing appeals to adoption decrees, it can only urge courts to deal expeditiously with appeals; it sets no time limit on potential legal maneuvering. The law would subject a biological parent who "knowingly misidentifies the minor's other parent with an intent to deceive," to a suggested fine of up to $5,000.[57] What impact such a penalty might have on such parents is difficult to tell. It might have more of an impact on their willingness to admit that they had made such a misrepresentation than on the likelihood of lying in the first place.

It would be unreasonable to demand of a complex new law that it solve all possible problems. A laudable emphasis on adult-child relationships permeates the document. Placement agencies are instructed to give preference to individuals with existing relationships with the child right after those who have previously adopted the child's sibling and those with characteristics requested by the relinquishing parent.[58] Individuals who have physical custody of minors for six months or more, even though they were not initially identified as prospective adoptive parents, would have legal standing to file a petition for adoption.[59] These provisions give a welcome weight to established caring relationships. Whether the new statute can prevent sad and prolonged fights like the one over Baby Jessica remains to be seen.

4

Research on Children
and the Scope of
Responsible Parenthood

What obligations do parents have to their children? On the whole, bioethics has not grappled with the nuances of parental obligations and duties. Sometimes its treatment of issues even seems to lack common sense. Part of the problem has been that bioethicists have considered mostly life-or-death decisions. But sometimes we create our own difficulty by the way we frame the problem. Nowhere has this been more true than in discussions of research on children, in which a history of morally abominable research, mostly on adults, led to the problem— and solution—being framed in terms that were simply irrelevant to children.

When the tools we have at hand are poorly suited for the job, the work is more difficult and the result inferior. We have some useful distinctions for understanding the ethics of research on children. But we have also been stuck with some downright clumsy contraptions. The problems become inescapable when we try to make sense of a morally complex proposal, like one to study the impact of human growth hormone on children with short stature.

A Controversial Study of Growth Hormone

Our bodies produce human growth hormone, or hGH, as part of the normal processes of growth. Children whose bodies cannot produce it do not grow as do other children. Unless they receive hGH somehow, they will become adults with extremely short stature. In a society that values height, those children can suffer severe disadvantages and discrimination.

But not all short children lack hGH. Height is like many other natural characteristics: people vary in how much of it they have. A few are very tall or very short; some are a bit taller or shorter than average; most are near the average. Some of the children who are much shorter than average have no discernible lack of hGH. Nor do they have any of the other signs that often accompany dwarfism caused by the absence of hGH. They are short, in all likelihood, because their parents are short, just as other children are well muscled because their parents are well muscled.

The quandary is this: short stature is a problem for children and adults not merely when it is a disease. In a world constructed for adults of a particular height range, being short enough (or, for that matter, tall enough) to fall outside the range is like having a disability. The world is harder to navigate when you are the "wrong" size. There is nothing intrinsically wrong with being substantially shorter or taller than average; the world could be made to fit a broader range of sizes. But for now at least it is not. And so extreme short stature can be a disability.

For most short children, the problem takes another form. Parents understand that short stature can make life tougher for their child; children can be very cruel to those who look or act "different." Furthermore, the adult world is "heightist." Tall people get many advantages, just by virtue of their height. Most parents want to give their children whatever advantages they can. If they can make a short child taller, why not? Many parents seem to have reasoned this way, because many have sought growth hormone for their children who are not lacking it but who are nonetheless short.

The increasing use of hGH for children who are not hGH-deficient prompted the National Institutes of Health (NIH) to approve a research project to study the effects of hGH injections on such children. The study raised enough questions that NIH asked a special panel to consider its ethical acceptability.

The study was originally planned to include eighty children ages nine through fifteen with normal levels of hGH but well below average height for their age. Each child receives three injections a week for as long as seven years. The study has a control group. Children in that group are treated exactly like the children in the experimental group, except that the injections they receive—600 to 1,100 over the life of the study—contain no hGH. Let me put that another way: None of the children in this study were ill. Some of them will receive as many as one thousand or more injections of a potent hormone; the others will get the same number of shots of salt water.

The special panel concluded that this study was acceptable. The panel's reasoning clung closely to the language of the regulations governing research on children. There are problems with the panel's strategy. A good ethical result is unlikely if the regulations lack a sound moral foundation. When we lack vigorous moral concepts for analyzing problems, we are tempted to take refuge in legalisms. A look at the moral debate at the time the regulations were written reveals that they were built on a flawed effort to understand the ethics of research with children.

The National Commission and the Nuremberg Code

Research on children covers a lot of moral ground. When a child has a grave disease and there is no good standard treatment, the child's only hope may be an experimental therapy. The novel therapy might carry its own substantial risks. But if previous research indicates that the experimental treatment is promising, and there is no solid alternative, then involvement of that child in research makes good moral sense. What makes the case persuasive is the hope that the particular child may benefit.

The ethics of research become more complex as the possibility of benefit to each of the children involved in the research becomes murkier. There are moral complexities, to be sure, when parents are asked to allow an experimental therapy to be used on their child who is suffering from disease. In most relevant respects, though, such a decision is not that different from other choices parents must make about treatment for their ill child. The uncertainty involved in experimental treatments is greater, of course, but we can never eliminate uncertainty. The crucial question in acceding to either standard or experimental treatment is the same: Will this benefit my child?

Another class of research studies has been more controversial: so-called nontherapeutic research, or in plainer language, research intended to gain knowledge but not to benefit its subjects directly. For example, the parents of a healthy, normal newborn might be asked to allow their child to serve as a control subject in a study of the physiology of some awful disease that strikes other babies. Perhaps the researchers want to monitor your baby's blood pressure more carefully than would otherwise be done for a healthy newborn; perhaps they want to draw an extra drop of blood from a heel prick, or a sample of blood from a vein; or perhaps in a study of infant heart disease, they want to insert a catheter through your baby's artery and into the heart, where they can measure changes in pressures and gas concentrations while they administer powerful drugs. It does not require much sophistication in ethics or science to notice great differences between the last experiment and the others. What would moral common sense say about these proposed studies?

If we were assured that there was no risk of harm or discomfort in the first proposed study—more frequent monitoring of blood pressure—indeed that the baby would not even notice it, then we might well agree to allow our newborn to participate in the study. Even if we refused, it is difficult to see what criticisms could be made of parents who did agree. Parents who allow their children to be observed in this manner do not seem to be failing in any important parental duty.

At the other extreme, we would be highly suspicious if parents consented to exposing their healthy babies to the pain and risk of having catheters threaded into their hearts and given powerful drugs, all with no conceivable benefit to their child. We might suspect that the parents did not understand what was to be done to their babies, or were so blinded by awe or gratitude that they were powerless to refuse; or, if they did understand the risks, that they were lousy parents who were not protecting their infant from a completely unnecessary risk of grave harm.

Such were the issues facing the members of the National Commission for the Protection of the Human Subjects of Biomedical and Behavioral Research when they developed their recommendations regarding the ethics of research on children. Should parents be prohibited from consenting to any research that held no hope of benefiting their children? Or should such research be permitted, with restrictions and safeguards?

As with any reasonably complex issue, many morally relevant questions arise. The ones of greatest interest to us are the nature and scope of parents' obligations to their children and in particular whether parents are ever justified in allowing their child to be used to benefit the community. Must we always refuse to expose our children to any risks or discomforts except when they might benefit our child? In the absence of any substantial risk or discomfort, do we wrong our children by allowing them to be used for others' benefit?

What makes this controversy particularly interesting for bioethics is that the most forceful, convincing argument was for banning all nontherapeutic research. Nonetheless, the commission adopted a more moderate stance allowing nontherapeutic research on children if the risks approximated those encountered in daily life and if parents consented. The commission accepted this policy even though the arguments supporting it were notably weaker than the arguments favoring a complete ban on such research. Paul Ramsey, a brilliant, acerbic, and relentless Protestant theologian championed a ban. Richard McCormick, equally brilliant, gave the most thorough defense of the moderate view. Their exchange over this issue illuminates the moral obligations of parents toward their children, even as it exemplifies the dangers of moral reasoning that fails to give full weight to context—in this case, both the historical context that shaped discussions of the ethics of research with human beings and the social context of parent-child relationships.

Ramsey opened his discussion by citing in full a classic text in bioethics, the first article of what has come to be known as the Nuremberg Code. The first sentence of the article is the key: "The voluntary consent of the human subject is absolutely essential." The second sentence is also worth citing in full: "This means that the person involved should have legal capacity to give consent; should be so situated as to be able to exercise free power of choice, without the intervention of any element of force, fraud, deceit, duress, overreaching, or other ulterior form of constraint or coercion; and should have sufficient knowledge and comprehension of the elements of the subject matter as to enable him to make an understanding and enlightened decision."[1] The remainder of the article discusses the sort of information a subject should be given.

If we take the Nuremberg Code seriously—if we accept this first article as a firm moral rule governing research—the implications for research on children are straightforward: there will be none. If the consent of the subject is "absolutely essential" and if this requires that the person "have legal capacity to give consent" and be able to reach "an understanding and enlightened decision," all infants and young children are disqualified along with all youth below the age of legal consent and all adults with significant mental impairments.

Note that this blanket prohibition makes no distinction between research intended to help the child—an innovative therapy, for example—and the nontherapeutic research that troubled the commission. If we followed strictly the Nuremberg Code, all medical experiments on children would be banned, including all studies of promising treatments for children dying from diseases like leukemia and brain cancer. This defies moral common sense. What prompted the drafters of the Nuremberg Code to make such a stark and unqualified declaration?

The Nuremberg Tribunal's task was to try people accused of war crimes. Confronted with overwhelming evidence of astoundingly cruel, almost unimaginable treatment of human beings in the name of science, the tribunal had to articulate a set of standards by which to judge the abominable conduct of the accused who came before it. Grave evil had been done. The catalog of horrors was long and gruesome: prisoners left naked in freezing weather, or immersed in near-freezing water until they lost consciousness or died; wounds inflicted, then exacerbated with glass fragments or dirt to simulate battle injuries; prisoners infected with typhus, some even used as human viral cultures; the list goes on.[2]

Faced with such an unconscionable register of horrors inflicted on people who were captives in the first place and never given any choice whether to participate, there is little wonder why the Nuremberg judges adopted voluntary consent as a clear and ringing first principle. When dealing with unmitigated evil, subtlety and nuance are less important than firmness and clarity. They might have reasoned this way: the Nazi experiments were morally atrocious because they inflicted terrible harms on unconsenting victims; no reasonable person would ever consent to such treatment; insisting that no person be used without his or her voluntary consent prevents the evils of coercion and of excessively risky or harmful experiments; therefore, a policy of voluntary consent will prevent morally monstrous research, like the Nazi experiments, from occurring in the future.

The judges at Nuremberg were not formulating timeless and detailed rules to govern all scientific research. They needed a set of principles for a specific task—trying war criminals for their barbarous treatment of prisoners in what was called, often very loosely, "science." The principles they articulated, the Nuremberg Code, served their purposes very well. In putting it this way, I intend no criticism of the court. To the contrary, I believe they showed admirable wisdom in formulating moral standards for research that would become the starting point for all later efforts. We should not fault them for failing to answer questions they were not asked, questions such as what to do about children or others incapable of giving consent, or whether it makes a morally important difference if the research may or may not be intended to benefit the subject. Later bodies could deal with such questions. The Nuremberg court's emphasis on consent, though, would color all subsequent efforts to understand the ethics of research with human subjects.

By the time the national commission deliberated on the ethics of research with children, a new distinction and a new concept had entered the discussion. The distinction was between research intended to benefit the subject and research with no such intention—what are commonly referred to as therapeutic research and nontherapeutic research. The concept was proxy consent, that is, consent by someone other than the subject who, presumably, knows what the subject would have wanted or has the subject's best interests at heart. Much ink and even a little (symbolic) blood has been spilled by bioethicists arguing over the meanings and significance of these two ideas. I have no desire to add to the deluge of words. What I want to do is to show how readily even the most perceptive thinker can become bewitched by ethical abstractions and how appreciating moral common sense and social context can, in the best sense, dis-enchant. To do that, though, we must revisit the debate in some detail.

Paul Ramsey and the Responsibilities of Parenthood

In his influential book *The Patient as Person,* Paul Ramsey began with a chapter on the ethics of research with children. Contrasting research on humans with research on animals, Ramsey asserts, "Any human being is more than a patient or experimental subject; he is a *personal* subject—every bit as much a man as the physician-investigator." He then links consent to the fidelity that should characterize relationships between persons: "The principle of an informed consent is the cardinal *canon of loyalty* joining men together in medical practice and investigation." Though his language and metaphors are drawn from theology rather than law, his debt to the Nuremberg judges seems clear. Ramsey, though, is fully aware of the quandary created by Nuremberg: how to justify therapeutic research with children. Should children's inability to give a mature and understanding consent deprive them of experimental treatments that might help them? Ramsey articulates a principle that he never abandons: "From consent as a canon of loyalty in medical practice it follows that children, who cannot give a mature and informed consent, . . . should not be made the subjects of medical experimentation unless . . . it is reasonable to believe that [the experimental therapy] may further *the patient's own recovery.*" [3]

Ramsey is suspicious of the idea of "proxy" consent. Certainly, it is necessary at times for someone to decide, on a child's behalf, whether to administer some treatment that might benefit the child. Ramsey is adamant about what such proxy consent could not be: "To attempt to consent for a child to be made an experimental subject is to treat a child as not a child. It is to treat him as if he were an adult person who has consented to become a joint adventurer in the common cause of medical research. If the grounds for this are alleged to be the presumptive or implied consent of the child, that must simply be characterized as a violent and false presumption." The parents' duty is to safeguard their child's welfare, to be their child's protector. But the parent's consent on behalf of the child is not morally equivalent to an adult's consent on his or her own behalf. An adult can consent to participate in a risky experiment, but, Ramsey claims, "no parent is morally competent to consent that his child shall be submitted to hazardous or other experiments having no diagnostic or therapeutic significance for the child himself."[4]

Ramsey is correct that consent has a different moral significance when it comes from the person directly affected, rather than from another presuming to speak for that person. Consent is an extremely powerful moral warrant, particularly in a liberal secular society that gives enormous moral weight to individuals and their preferences. Why are you riding Emily's bike? She said it was OK. What right do you have to demand money from me? Because we have a contract. I paint your house; you pay me $2,000. It is not much of an exaggeration to say that for some persons, including a few moral theorists, consent functions as a universal moral solvent, dissolving all moral dilemmas; as long as there is consent, no further moral justification is needed. Not everyone believes this. Outside of a few doctrinaire libertarians, debates over the appropriate scope and limits of individual liberty are taken very seriously. Are contracts for surrogate motherhood legitimate expressions of individual liberty? Should we be permitted to sell our babies? Our kidneys?

Ramsey's argument is that however potent you think consent is in justifying particular actions, children are incapable of consent. Fictions such as "proxy" consent can only disguise that fact. When consent is a necessary condition for something being morally acceptable—as the Nuremberg Code suggests is true for medical research—it would always be morally wrong to perform that action without genuine consent. Children cannot consent to participate in research. Therefore, without some other compelling moral justification, children cannot be subjects in research. What other justification is possible? Pursuing the child's own welfare. Thus therapeutic research for children can be justified; nontherapeutic research on children cannot.

Ramsey's suspicion of proxy consent contrasts with his enthusiastic embrace of the distinction between research that does and does not benefit the child. He sees this as decisive: "What is at stake here is the covenantal obligations of parents to children—the protection with which a child should be surrounded, and the meaning and duties of parenthood. . . . The issue here is the wrong of making a human being an 'object' and using him in trials not in his behalf as a subject."[5] As always, Ramsey chooses his concepts with care: children made the subject of research with no benefit to themselves are wronged even if no harm comes to them. The analogous concept in law is a battery, an unconsented touching, and Ramsey explicitly pursues the parallel.

Here is where Ramsey runs into difficulties. Because he makes consent a moral fulcrum, he is compelled to defend the proposition that all research on children, however innocuous, that is not done with the hope of benefiting its child-subjects, is immoral and violates "the meaning and duties of parenthood." Our task would be easier if we could consult an authoritative list of parental duties. Lacking such a list, Ramsey employs several strategies to persuade us that parental duties include the obligation to protect our children from nontherapeutic research, even riskless research. He appeals to our ideals of parenthood: "A parent's decisive concern," he writes, "is for the care and protection of the child, to whom he owes the highest fiduciary loyalty, even when he also appreciates the benefits to come to others from the investigation and might submit his own person to experiment in order to obtain them."[6] He expresses skepticism that there could be a scientific experiment that did not exceed "the ordinary risks of daily living."[7] He echoes Kant in stating that "fidelity to a human child also includes never treating him as a means only, but always also as an end."[8] He launches the rhetorical equivalent of a nuclear weapon by suggesting, in a somewhat opaque passage, that research even with "no *discernible* risks . . . imposed on subjects for the sake of supposable or actual good to come" puts us "back with the Nazis."[9] Finally, he acknowledges that the problem is "the *use* of children in research, in which the risks are minimal or 'negligible,' but still not in their behalf medically. It is hard to see how this can be an expression of parental care (or of the state's care *in loco parentis*), or anything other than a violation of the nature and meaning of the responsibilities of parenthood as a covenant among the generations of men."[10]

Is permitting one's child to be a subject in a scientific study where the risks are minimal or negligible "a violation of the nature and meaning of the responsibilities of parenthood"? A frightfully strong and austere conclusion: Could there be some flaw in Ramsey's reasoning? The best contemporary effort to find such a flaw, Richard McCormick's defense of minimally risky research on children, was at best only a partial success.

McCormick = minimal risk to kids OK

Richard McCormick and "Vicarious Consent"

McCormick, a Roman Catholic theologian, agrees with Ramsey that "consent is the heart of the matter."[11] But he points out that we take parents' consent to their children's medical treatment to be morally justifiable: Why cannot parental consent work as well in justifying the involvement of children in research? Saying as Ramsey does that it would amount to treating the child as an object does not provide an answer.

McCormick employs the concept of "vicarious consent" which, he says, is a close relative of proxy consent. Vicarious consent, he argues, "is morally valid precisely insofar as it is a reasonable presumption of the child's wishes, a construction of what the child would wish could he consent for himself." Many children are too young to express their wishes; we are loath to accept a young child's wishes in any event, unless we believe that honoring a particular one would not be opposed to the child's best interest. McCormick asserts that a sound understanding of what a child would wish requires asking, "Why *would* the child so wish?" His answer: "[The child] would choose this if he were capable of choice because he *ought* to do so."[12]

By now McCormick's difficulties are obvious. He has made consent the moral centerpiece of his case and is trying to rescue the moral authority of parental consent by equating what a child *would* want with what it *ought to* want. McCormick is not completely lost for intellectual resources to buttress his case. He calls on natural law theory, a position closely associated with Catholic theology. Focusing on the values and goods that constitute or promote our flourishing as humans, McCormick claims that two assertions account for our willingness to allow parents to consent to therapy for their children: "(a) that there are certain values . . . definitive of our good and flourishing, hence values that we *ought* to choose and support if we want to become and stay human, and that therefore these are good also for the child; and (b) that these 'ought' judgments, at least in their more general formulations, are a common patronage available to all men, and hence form the basis on which policies can be built."[13]

Another big step remains. McCormick needs to make a plausible case that the child—say, an infant whom researchers want to enroll in a study of pulmonary physiology—*ought* to want to volunteer for it. He argues: "To pursue the good that is human life means not only to choose and support this value in one's own case, but also in the case of others when the opportunity arises. . . . [T]he individual *ought* also to take into account, realize, make efforts in behalf of the lives of others also, for we are social beings and the goods that define our growth and invite to it are goods that reside also in others."[14] So infants and children *ought* to want to help others by, for example, participating as research subjects. McCormick tries to clinch the argument thus: "To share in the general effort and burden of health maintenance and disease control is part of our flourishing and growth as humans. To the extent that it is good for all of us to share this burden, we all *ought* to do so. And to the extent that we *ought* to do so, it is a reasonable construction or presumption of our wishes to say that we would do so." He then concludes: "The reasonableness of this presumption validates vicarious consent." [15]

McCormick has traveled a long way from the sort of infants and children of my acquaintance, most of whom recognize a sharp distinction between what they *should* do (in the eyes of their parents at least) and what they would or want to do. I accept that a crucial part of a parent's job is to help their children understand what they ought to do, and to develop a conscience and motivation that helps them want to do what they should do. In other words, bringing *should* and *would* into closer conjunction is one of the principal tasks of parenthood. The move from "ought" to "would" is an interminable battle fought between parents and children as well as within every person's psyche. Far from the "reasonable construction or presumption of our wishes" that McCormick optimistically maintains, presuming that a child *would* want what it *should* want imputes capacities and preferences that most young children flatly lack.

Consent, Parental Duties, and the Ethics of Research

In contrast to this awkward theoretical effort to rescue the concept of consent as a moral justification for nontherapeutic research on children, McCormick's practical conclusions seem eminently reasonable and wise. If the scientific experiments are "well designed," "cannot succeed unless children are used," and "contain no discernible risk or undue discomfort for the child," then McCormick believes "parental consent to this type of invasion can be justified." [16]

Here is our quandary. On the one hand, we have an incisive, comprehensive analysis—Ramsey's—that reaches what seems to be an unreasonable conclusion: that no research on children which does not have direct benefit of its subjects as an aim is ethically justified. Ramsey's analysis would rule out the most innocuous research on children that might be hugely beneficial to other children. On the other hand, we have a nuanced but strained and unconvincing analysis—McCormick's—that reaches what seem to be very sensible conclusions. McCormick would permit nontherapeutic research on children under very strict circumstances, including no discernible risks, with parental consent.

The problem, I believe, is the shared way in which they formulated the problem. For both Ramsey and McCormick, the issue was the ethics of consent. Recall McCormick agreeing with Ramsey that "consent is the heart of the matter." The social and historical context helps us understand why this particular formulation of the ethics of nontherapeutic research with children suggested itself to both scholars. The horrifying history of Nazi experimentation, the primacy and availability of consent as a moral warrant for participating in research, and the focus on medical experimentation with its propensity for dramatic risks and bodily invasions combined to make consent look like *the* moral solution to unethical human experimentation. The fact that consent could be applied to children at best metaphorically did not deter scholars and researchers from trying to beat it into a shape that might justify research with children, as did McCormick, or writing it off—at least for nontherapeutic research—as a "false and violent presumption" as did Ramsey.

Consent, of course, is not the entirety of the ethics of research even with fully competent adult volunteers. The research must be competent, have some reasonable goal, impose no greater risks than are necessary, and protect subjects' confidentiality, among other considerations. In one of the episodes in Woody Allen's movie *Everything You Always Wanted to Know about Sex but Were Afraid to Ask,* a mad scientist appears. He brings Woody and his companion into the laboratory where he shows them his great experiment: he explains that he is exchanging the brains of a lesbian and a telephone repairman. Even if his two subjects had consented to this experiment (a point not clarified in the movie) it would still be unethical because, well, it's nuts. Even a competent experiment that exposed its subjects to more risk than necessary, or to great risk when there was no corresponding benefit to them such as cure of their disease, would be unethical. Consent may be a crucial concept in the ethics of research, but it is not the whole story. It must be a much smaller part of the story when the subjects of the research cannot give consent—children, for example.

If consent is not the entire, perhaps not even the most important, consideration in the ethics of experimentation with children, then Ramsey's and McCormick's formulation of the problem is defective. Rather than try to hammer consent into a shape that accommodates all of our ethical concerns about the involvement of children in research, we can reformulate the question. Let us ask under what circumstances, if any, parents are morally permitted to enroll their children in nontherapeutic research.

We will not expect to find the answer in any reshaped metaphor of consent. And we should not be embarrassed by that. Yes, it would be wrong to impose research on unconsenting adults. It would be wrong even if it caused them no harm; much worse if, like the Nazi experiments, it heartlessly tortured and killed. It is equally wrong to harm children in the name of research. Relying on parental consent is an important, if imperfect, bulwark against abuse; but it does not have the same moral status as an adult volunteer's consent to participate.

Both Ramsey and McCormick saw that the content of parents' obligations to their children was crucial. Ramsey simply failed to go beyond dismissive pronouncements. Recall what he wrote about parents who would permit their children to participate in minimally risky research: "It is hard to see how this can be an expression of parental care . . . or anything other than a violation of the nature and meaning of the responsibilities of parenthood."[17] There have been countless occasions when I have rebuked myself for failing to fulfill my responsibilities as a parent. I cannot say that having any of my children participate in riskless research would rank high among them. McCormick tried to stuff the huge and ungainly octopus of parental obligations into a sack labeled "vicarious consent": it was an awkward fit at best. He became entangled in the metaphor; his effort to cut his way out with natural law theory strained common sense.

If Ramsey and McCormick became prisoners to their framing of the problem, leaving themselves with, respectively, an extreme solution and an ill-fitting one, can our reframing do any better? When a problem does not yield to a head-on confrontation, a useful strategy is to try to capture its crucial features but move them into a different context. If the context of research raises inescapable echoes of Nuremberg, but our problem is what parents may or may not do with their children that is not directly to their child's benefit, let us look for analogous choices that parents face.

Your next door neighbors have been out of work for a year since the factory closed. They are good hardworking people and fine neighbors, but they are in terrible financial trouble at the moment. Their new baby

Crib set ⟨

has been sleeping in a dresser drawer since she came home four weeks ago, but she must move to a crib as soon as possible. They do not have one and cannot afford to buy one. Your two-year-old son will be ready to give up his crib in another six months. It is a bit early to move him into a youth bed: there is always the chance that he might fall out of it in his sleep, or get out of bed at night, wander around the house, and hurt himself. You weigh your neighbors' need and the small risks to your son, and you offer to lend them the crib.

Have you done the right thing?

Your generosity and compassion for your neighbors exposes your child to some slight risks—at the most, probably a small bump on the head. Ramsey's understanding of parenthood, with his exclusive focus on protecting children from any threats to their physical safety, implies that lending the crib would be morally unacceptable, "a violation of the nature and meaning of the responsibilities of parenthood." Surely that is too harsh a judgment. The ethics of neighborliness and charity may not strictly oblige you to lend the crib, but generosity such as this should be valued and is certainly morally permitted. We could jiggle the circumstances of the case to steer judgments toward the obligatory or the prohibited: if the risk to your own child was trivial and the benefit to your neighbors was life-saving or otherwise monumental, we would be more likely to conclude that a genuine moral obligation existed; if the risk to your child became substantial without major benefit to your neighbors (if, for example, the object to be lent was a gate preventing a dangerous tumble down a steep staircase), we would judge it a morally prohibited action, a violation of parental duties to safeguard one's child. The particular factors of the case always do and properly should affect our moral judgments. In the original version it seems fair to say that what those parents did was morally permitted, despite the fact that it added an iota to the risks facing their own child. Under some circumstances, parents are morally permitted to do things that do not take protection of their own child's safety as the preeminent concern. Some people might argue that this case is different from volunteering your child for research. Our relations with our near neighbors are more intimate, the moral obligations more stringent, than those characterizing the relationship between parents and children, on the one hand, and researchers and those who might someday benefit from the research, on the other. Fair enough. Consider another case.

It is 4 P.M. on a Christmas Eve. Your baby has been cranky today, but has finally fallen asleep. You look forward to her and her parents (that is, you and your spouse) having a couple of peaceful hours. The phone rings. It is the director of the Christmas pageant at the church you visited for the first time last Sunday to see if it was the sort of place you and your family would like to attend regularly. One visit was not sufficient for you to make up your mind, but you had left your name and phone number with the friendly usher who had approached you and admired your baby. Back to the phone call: the pageant director (who also happened to be the amiable usher) is desperate and flattering: the infant who was to have played the part of Baby Jesus has chicken pox. (This actually happened to my wife in a pageant she coordinated.) Your lovely baby would be the perfect replacement. All the adults and children attending the pageant would be *sooo* disappointed if they had to substitute a doll for a live infant. Would you be willing to bring your darling to church in half an hour?

Some parents would probably decline, preferring to let their baby sleep and to enjoy the quiet themselves. I cannot see how they can be said to have any moral obligation to do this favor for these strangers. Other parents would accede, some happily, some reluctantly but moved by the prospective disappointment of the pageant's audience. Do the parents who disturb their baby's slumber to benefit these strangers violate their parental duties? The facts, as always, are important. Their baby may be unhappy for a while, but she may find the colors of the costumes interesting. In all likelihood, she will go back to sleep soon afterward, only a little the worse for wear. The pageant will be successful and the audience gratified.

What we must decide is whether the parents are morally permitted to donate their infant's services to the pageant or whether they are morally forbidden to do so. This does not strike me as a terrible moral quandary. Of course, the parents may bring their baby to church that afternoon if they wish. The child suffers no great hardship from it, and some people derive a little good—enjoyment at the spectacle, perhaps a little religious edification, and, most of all, delight in watching the unalloyed joy of the children present. Even though there may be no direct benefit for their child, bringing her to the pageant falls well within the compass of permissible moral discretion. It also reminds us that no impenetrable barricade separates moral relationships within families from the moral world outside. We have special and strong moral obligations to those closest to us; but attending to our familial obligations does not mean ignoring all moral interests and relationships outside the family that might in any way, however insignificantly, affect the interests of those within the family circle. This would not merely put the family first but would put the family above everything else—a dangerously short-sighted view of moral life.

In both of these hypothetical cases parents accept some risk, discomfort, or inconvenience for their child, with no direct benefit for that child. Yet in neither case does it seem that the parents have acted immorally or irresponsibly toward their children. The accusation that they have treated their child as a means rather than an end makes no sense. Neither does any claim that they have violated their sacred parental duty.

Two points about parents' moral obligations to children emerge from these analogies. First, protecting a child's physical safety may be very important but is not the entirety of our moral obligations to our children; risks, especially very small ones, may be accepted in the service of other goods and values. Second, the goods and values that may justify accepting risks to our children can include those of other persons and need not always be limited to our child's immediate well-being.

Turn our conclusions on their head for a moment. Imagine a parent who took Ramsey's comments about parental responsibilities with respect to research and generalized them to the whole of parenthood. This parent would refuse to do anything that did not directly benefit the child, citing all the while a parent's moral duty. We have probably all known overprotective parents, but this case might reach new heights—or, rather, depths. The best description of this parental style is "smothering." Those of us with a more cynical bent might suspect that the parent is using purported parental duties as an excuse for avoiding other moral obligations, perhaps out of miserliness or laziness. At best, we would say that they show a lack of proportion or perspective in their moral judgments, that they suffer from an affliction that might be called moral myopia.

At no point in this discussion of parental duties outside the realm of research have we needed to invoke some fictitious or metaphorical notion of the child's own consent to analyze what the parent is permitted morally to do. If the debate over using children in nontherapeutic research has been bewitched by consent, a little disenchantment can be liberating. Consent *is* crucially important when it is genuinely possible—with competent adults. But different problems call for different analyses more suited to their particular circumstances. Children cannot consent; why try to understand the ethics of research with children through the concept of consent? If parental obligations are central as both Ramsey and McCormick acknowledge, then look directly at those obligations.

The cursory look we have taken suggests that involving children in activities that impose no significant hazards on those children but that may contribute substantially to other goods and values even though the child may not benefit directly is well within the circle of morally permissible parental discretion. Nontherapeutic research, when the risks are truly minimal and the benefits to others potentially substantial, is just that kind of activity.

Whether any particular study satisfies the criterion of minimal risk depends on the particulars of the study. Monitoring a baby's blood pressure, if it involved no invasiveness or discomfort, seems to qualify, as would a quick heel prick for a drop of blood. There might be some disagreement about taking repeated vials of blood by venipuncture: the risks are tiny, but the needle will sting. Threading catheters into the heart and injecting powerful drugs, though, is clearly well beyond what any responsible parent should allow: the pain and discomfort are substantial, the risks real and potentially catastrophic.

Where the risks are minimal and the study is competent and potentially significant, parents are permitted morally, but not obliged, to allow their child to participate: not because the child would consent or should consent—consent being an ill-fitting metaphor in this case—but because such participation does not violate the parents' duties to their offspring and because it enhances other goods and values prized by the community.

Growth Hormone for Short Stature Revisited

Should the National Institutes of Health sponsor a study that gives as many as 1,100 injections to children whose only "deviation" from normal is that they are short? We must consider two separate questions here. First, do parents who enroll their children in this experiment exceed the limits of parental discretion? Second, is it good, morally sound, public policy to encourage such an experiment?

Why would parents permit their children to participate in the study? The only plausible answer is that parents want to protect their children from the cruelty and discrimination experienced by people of short stature. Parents do all sorts of things to try to spare their children from pain or to give them whatever advantages they can provide. A drug that might make their child a little taller could be seen as just another measure parents take to help their children.

When a child's body cannot make a substance necessary for normal growth, development, or function, we say that the child suffers from a disease. Administering a drug that compensates for the missing substance is a benefit for that child, if it does more good than harm. A child who suffers from diabetes cannot make insulin. Responsible parents of such children do their best to promote their children's health by watching their diet, monitoring their blood sugar, and ensuring that they receive appropriate doses of insulin. Children who are short but who have no deficiency of hGH do not have a disease—unless we declare that all those who differ substantially from average on any human characteristic are similarly "diseased." So they are not like children with diabetes, for whom treatment with a drug is justified. A reason that justifies giving a potent drug to your child is that the child has a serious disease for which the drug is an effective treatment. Because short children with normal hGH do not have a disease, we need another good reason for giving them a drug. Perhaps hGH benefits children with short stature.

Unfortunately, the evidence that hGH actually benefits such children is scanty. Growth hormone does appear to accelerate growth, but what matters most to these children and their parents is the child's final adult height. Here the evidence is equivocal: despite the acceleration in growth velocity, the children may stop growing sooner and end up no taller as adults. Let us say that several years worth of hGH injections did add two or three inches to adult height. What sort of benefit is that?

If growth hormone does in fact increase the adult height of children with short stature, then the benefit is far different from the benefit a child with diabetes derives from insulin. A diabetic child's health and life are threatened by the inability to make insulin. A short child who makes normal hGH is not ill and does not suffer from any dire physiological imbalance. Short children with normal hGH are not in any special danger from disease. Growth hormone for such children is not a treatment for any physiological disease, and there is no particular medical benefit from it. But, it is true, being a bit taller for such children could mean that they will suffer fewer cruelties at the hands of other children and less discrimination as adults.

The benefit is entirely social. If it works at all, growth hormone in such cases works by blunting the impact of social prejudice against short people, not by dealing with the roots of prejudice. Those roots are left untouched. Instead, the use of growth hormone for children of short stature tacitly accepts heightism. Parents who seek it for their children understandably want to spare them from discrimination. But as their children benefit, other children, whose parents perhaps cannot afford the tens of thousands of dollars a year needed to pay for hGH, continue to bear the burden of discrimination. Indeed, as those who are fortunate enough to be able to afford hGH climb closer to average height, those left behind will stand out as even more "different."

Imagine that we discovered a possible "treatment" for another form of social prejudice—a hormone that reduces the amount of melanin in the skin. If it worked, giving it to children would cause them to have a lighter hue. It might diminish the amount of racial discrimination they will face by making them appear less different from the light-skinned majority. Does it make sense to deal with racial prejudice by trying to obliterate physical differences? Should we encourage biomedical fixes for complex social problems? Or would be we wiser to deal with the roots of prejudice? [10]

Even if we were able to lay aside our concerns about justice and the sources of discrimination, to defend this research we need to consider the risks to the children involved and weigh them against the potential benefits. We can divide both risks and benefits into two categories: physical and psychological. The most obvious physical harms are the 600 to 1,100 injections each child in the study will receive. Half of the children will get hGH in their shots, half will receive nothing more than sterile salt water.

Consider first the children receiving the saltwater placebo. Other than the pain of the shots and the very remote chance of infection or other complications, the study exposes them to no other significant physical risks. But a thousand-plus injections is not a trivial matter. Anyone who can recall how as a child you regarded the prospect of a *single* injection will not dismiss lightly an experiment designed to give as many as 1,100 to each participant.

The physical benefits to such children are much less clear. They will receive a three-day workup by the researchers and regular follow-up by experts. This intensive medical scrutiny might uncover subtleties that normal health care did not. If that happened—and no one can say how likely it is—then children in the placebo group might benefit. Another possible benefit for the children receiving growth hormone is a so-called placebo effect. Sometimes people who receive a presumed inactive treatment nonetheless do better than those who receive nothing at all. In this study, finding a placebo effect would mean that the children injected with saline solution grew taller than they otherwise would have. The possibility of such a placebo effect was the primary reason offered by the experimenters for injecting salt water into half of the children. I know that the mind and body interact in often mysterious ways. But I must say that the likelihood that saline injections will make kids grow taller seems about as likely as pixie dust allowing them to fly.[19] In any event, it seems fair to say that the likelihood of children in the control group benefiting by an increase in their adult height is remote. On purely physical grounds, then, the study brings more harms than benefits to the children in the control group.

To be fair, we should also look at the balance of psychological benefits and risks. The committee convened by the NIH identified two kinds of potential psychological benefits: "the possible gratification of participating in an important study" and "information that may later be useful to one as a parent."[20] I don't mean to downplay the satisfaction gained by doing something important that can aid others in distress. But these hypothetical psychological benefits are awfully insubstantial compared to the psychological risks.

Children learn what is important about them according to how we treat them. They can learn that their short stature is just one, relatively insignificant, aspect of who they are that pales in importance compared to their wit or expressiveness, the warmth of their smile, or any of hundreds of other details of character and appearance. Or children can learn that their short stature is such a grievous deficiency that it justifies hundreds of injections, regular visits to the doctor, great worry, and, for many, tens of thousands of dollars. Children, that is, can learn that their short stature is a central defining characteristic of their identity—one in which they will assuredly, even with hGH, come up short. The children who receive placebo injections will get this message just as surely as the children getting the drug. Unless salt water *is* a kind of pixie dust, these children will be no taller for all of the hundreds of injections they endure. But they will have learned that their short stature is a severe and crucial deficiency.

The children who receive hGH face a slightly different array of risks and benefits. A leading authority on pediatric endocrinology lists several possible hazards, including diabetes, hypertension, and abnormal growth of both soft and bony tissues, and reports that some children developed leukemia after treatment with hGH.[21] Nevertheless, most experts appear to believe that hGH is reasonably safe. The significant hazards are either rare or unproved. The physical benefit, of course, would be an increase in adult height. But in what sense is increased height a benefit? Being short is not a physical illness, and being taller is not its cure. The point of trying to make children taller is to diminish psychological distress and social discrimination. Increasing height is the means, not the end. The important balance will be between the psychological and social risks and benefits.

If children who receive hGH gain a few inches in adult height, and if that gain diminishes the discrimination they experience at the hands of others, and if the intense focus on their short stature is more than offset by their pride at being less short than anticipated, then they may benefit on the whole. Of course, some, perhaps most, of the children who receive hGH will be no taller for their trouble. Even when the treatment is effective, the increase in height in unlikely to be dramatic. For a boy of 5'3" or a girl of 4'10½" a gain of even three inches will not bring them up to average height for their sex.[22] Previous studies found that children with demonstrable hGH deficiency expected greater height gains than hGH treatment could deliver. The children, as well as their parents, experienced disappointment and a sense of failure. Nor were they any happier about themselves.[23] At best, the evidence that a child would benefit significantly from hGH treatment is equivocal. We do not know whether there will be any increase in final height. Even children who gain a few inches may find little comfort. They will still be shorter than average. Their self-confidence may be blighted by their failure to grow as tall as they and their parents thought was so vitally important.

Under the circumstances, do parents who enroll their children in this experiment exceed the limits of parental discretion? The most likely motive for a parent is the hope that his or her child might indeed be one of the fortunate few who would benefit from participating. I say "fortunate few" because the children would have to be lucky in three ways. They would have to be among those participants randomly assigned to receive hGH rather than saline solution. They would have to be one of the as yet unknown proportion of those receiving hGH who become significantly taller. And they would have to experience less discrimination and develop a more robust sense of self by virtue of that gain in height. The odds are not favorable. But then neither are the odds that any particular child will benefit significantly from music lessons. I suspect that most parents who enroll their children in music lessons hope that the child's latent musical gifts will blossom, that he or she will learn habits of dedication and lessons about the relationship of hard work and success that will last a lifetime, and that their perfected talent will provoke respect, if not awe, among their peers. I have no idea what the actual numbers are of children who reap such marvelous fruits from their musical experience compared to those for whom it becomes mainly an exercise in parent-child conflict. But it would not surprise me if the ratio of success to failure was roughly comparable to the ratio for children enrolled in this experiment—substantially less than half.

If we take the optimistic view about physical risks—that the serious ones are fanciful and the pain of the injections tolerable—and an equally optimistic view about the likelihood of social and psychological benefit, then we can draw a rough analogy between enrolling one's child in this experiment or in music lessons. The psychological risks are probably much greater in the experiment, but then so is the concern to spare your child from discrimination and damage to self-esteem.

I do not believe we can say that parents who enroll their children in this experiment clearly violate their obligations to their children. They hope that their children will benefit from participating, even if the benefit does not so clearly fall into the realm of the "therapeutic." I would have to say the same about the parents of dark-skinned children who wanted to spare them from discrimination by placing them in a (nonexistent and hypothetical) study of a skin-lightening hormone that was no more physically risky than hGH. On the other side, parents who choose not to use hGH for their short-stature children also act as responsible parents. They may look at the pain and risks involved and decide that it is more important to stress their child's strengths. (I would say exactly the same about parents who chose to emphasize their children's abilities and accomplishments as well as pride in their ethnic history rather than attempting to change the color of their skin.)[24]

Deciding that parents do not choose wrongly by choosing either way is not the end of the story. We need to address the second question: Is it good, morally sound, public policy to encourage such an experiment? There are many reasons to say no. First, at least half and probably more than half of the children in the study are likely to be harmed more than helped by it. Second, if the study showed that some non-hGH-deficient children grew a few more inches, parents of other short children would have an additional incentive to seek growth hormone for their kids. Since their children are not ill, insurers would resist paying for such an expensive treatment, just as they oppose paying for certain kinds of cosmetic surgery. If insurers resisted successfully but hGH was still available to those who could afford it, then savvy, wealthy parents could get it for their children as just another of the advantages that money can buy. Nor would there be any reason to limit it to short children. If you can buy a few inches, and height confers a competitive advantage, then parents of average and tall children might also want to give their kids a leg up, so to speak. To the advantages of wealth would be added one more—enhanced height.

We do have options. We could adopt the egalitarian approach and make hGH available to all children at public expense. Unfortunately, this would do nothing to defeat heightism. Although average height would rise, there would still be a wide range with plenty of children at the lower end of the curve. Indeed, with a premium placed on height, discrimination against the relatively shorter might intensify. A few groups would benefit. Pediatric endocrinologists would be kept very busy. Investors in the drug companies that manufacture hGH would become wealthy. And a few others would profit, for example, fabric makers, because everyone would need larger sizes. On the whole, though, we would be worse off. Many more children would get hundreds of shots, more of our national resources would go into making hGH, and discrimination against the relatively shorter would be reinforced rather than diminished. Not a pretty picture.

Perhaps the best result would be proof that growth hormone does nothing for short children who are not hGH-deficient. Parents would then have no reason to give it to their children, and the ugly scenarios would not have to be played out.

There are, and have been, other possibilities for controlling the non-therapeutic use of human growth hormone. The companies that make hGH could require that it be given only to children with medically demonstrable hGH deficiency. That is unlikely to happen. Companies want to sell more, not less, of their products. Indeed, the NIH experiment has corporate sponsorship. More plausibly, pediatricians could take a professional stand that firmly opposes hGH treatment for children not clearly suffering from disease or at great risk of disability. To their credit, pediatric professional societies have urged caution in the use of hGH.[25] Nonetheless, persistent parents can usually find a physician willing to prescribe hGH for their child (who will, incidentally, probably be male, as were approximately 90 percent of the children enrolled in the NIH study). Firmer stands with tighter professional self-regulation is probably our best strategy for now.

Honoring the Worth of a Child in Research

How should we honor the worth of children in research? We should, of course, protect them from needless harm. We do that in at least two ways: by requiring researchers to demonstrate that the research is important and the risks minimal and by respecting parents' authority to protect and guide their children. We also honor children's moral worth by acknowledging that young children are not just tiny adults when it comes to the moral weight we should give to their consent. Young children's consent does not protect them from harm as well as an adult's consent. To say that a young child consented to participate in an extremely risky nontherapeutic study would never excuse our subjecting them to such unjustified risks.

A better acknowledgment of children's moral worth would be to see participation in nontherapeutic research as one of a class of activities in which parents and children are asked to contribute to the community's well-being and that involve minimal risks to the children. We honor children's worth here by protecting them from overzealous researchers and awestruck or uncaring parents and by recognizing that good rearing of children does not mean a phobic shielding from all imaginable dangers, but rather a sense of proportion that includes acting responsibly toward one's community.

Perhaps because the moral foundation for research on children has been so vague, even well-intentioned people trying to make sense of a proposal like the NIH study of growth hormone for children of short stature may take refuge in tenuous readings of regulations rather than ask the two questions I believe we need to ask: Do parents who enroll their children in this experiment exceed the moral limits of parental discretion? Is it good, morally sound, public policy to encourage such an experiment?[26]

A preliminary look at the limits of parental discretion suggests that parents act within the bounds of good parenting when they consent to a wide range of research protocols for their children, including research likely to benefit their child but also research that might benefit others without being unduly risky to their children. Parents who enroll their children in the NIH growth hormone study are probing the boundaries of parental discretion. Many people might feel that they have stepped over that boundary. Even with a tentative yes to the question whether parents are morally permitted to enroll their children in such a study, the second question remains.

What may be permissible for individual parents may not be wise for us as a community. Encouraging hormonal treatment for social discrimination muddies the line between disease and disadvantage and prompts us to look for medical solutions for social problems. If hGH works in children with normal growth hormone levels, then we must make hard choices. If we permit parents to obtain hGH for their nondeficient children, we would face two equally unpalatable scenarios. We could either heap another, physically distinctive, inequality on top of the other inequalities wealth can buy. Or we could engage in a futile and expensive orgy of competition after which there would be the same number of winners and losers as before.

The most sensible course is to restrict this powerful drug to occasions when it treats disease. Professionals could accomplish this by self-regulation, bolstered, if needed, by laws to discourage the proliferation of hGH treatment for nontherapeutic uses. We should not thwart parents who want to do what is right for their children. But as a community we must recognize that there are situations, like arms races, when the effect of each individual party pursuing self-advantage makes everyone, collectively, worse off. We do not need an experiment on growth hormone for healthy children to show us that.

5

Moral Obligations to the Not-Yet-Born Child

Decisions about the welfare of future children must be left to the parents who conceive, bear, support, and raise them rather than to the employers who hire those parents.
—Decision of the U.S. Supreme Court in *Automobile Workers v. Johnson Controls*

Mrs. Jessie Mae Jefferson became famous in a way no one would envy. Just days before she was to give birth, Mrs. Jefferson's physician diagnosed her as having placenta previa, a condition in which the placenta blocks the birth canal, preventing normal delivery. Treatment for placenta previa is straightforward: perform a cesarean section. Mrs. Jefferson, whose husband was minister of the Shiloh Sanctified Holiness Baptist Church, refused, saying that God would heal her. Her doctor disagreed; he predicted a 99 percent likelihood that her baby would die if she did not have a cesarean section. Mrs. Jefferson herself had only a fifty-fifty chance of surviving a vaginal delivery, the doctor claimed. The local court authorized Griffin Spalding County Hospital to perform a cesarean section with or without Mrs. Jefferson's permission. When the Jeffersons appealed to the Georgia Supreme Court, they were turned down.[1] A few days later, Mrs. Jefferson gave birth vaginally to a healthy baby.[2]

In *Automobile Workers v. Johnson Controls,* a company had enforced a "fetal protection policy" that banned fertile women from workplaces in which lead, a substance dangerous to both adults and fetuses, was present. The case of Mrs. Jessie Mae Jefferson and the *Johnson Controls* case, which was decided by the U.S. Supreme Court on 20 March 1991, raise questions concerning the moral and legal circumstances of pregnancy. Should women be denied the choice whether or not to accept risks to their own health and to the health of any child they might bear? Would a woman who chose to continue working at Johnson Controls despite such risks be making a morally defensible or indefensible decision?[3]

There are many questions that arise in the arena of ethics and public policy concerning the treatment of pregnant women and the children they may bear. They range from the dramatic to the mundane. What can we say and what should we do about women who abuse alcohol or illegal drugs during pregnancy? Should we rely on persuasion? Provide opportunities for rehabilitation? Place them in jail to protect their not-yet-born children? And what about a woman who experiences grave difficulties during labor, when the attending physician or midwife is utterly convinced that a cesarean section is the only way to save the not-yet-quite-born child but the woman steadfastly refuses? About companies that refuse to hire fertile women for certain jobs on the grounds that any fetus brought into the particular work environment might be harmed by exposure to chemicals or radiation? About a pregnant woman who drinks one glass of wine per week? About a woman who smokes occasionally during pregnancy? About a man who smokes frequently in the presence of his pregnant wife? About a woman who fails to seek suitable prenatal care? About a society that makes it difficult for women to get prenatal care?

Discussions about such issues have been blighted by three confusions. The first is the mistaken belief that the crucial issues in such questions are the same as those raised by the abortion debate. The second is a sentimentalism toward pregnancy that often leads to a grievous moral oversimplification. The third is a tendency to conflate judgments about what is morally right and wrong with judgments about what are wise and defensible public policies. We need to dispel these confusions if we are to make nuanced moral judgments and reasonable public policies.

Moral Obligations: Not to be Confused with Abortion

It is assumed that the battle lines drawn in abortion—between those who emphasize the humanity of the fetus and those who stress the rights of women—must be the same lines over which the arguments about forced cesarean sections and workplace reproductive hazards must be fought. But this is mistaken. Even the widely held view that our moral concern for the fetus should grow as the fetus itself grows and develops is for the most part irrelevant to the issues that are the subject of this chapter. The best way to show this is with an analogy.

Imagine what is, unfortunately, only too imaginable these days: that a terrorist pursuing his goals, whatever they may be, conceals a time bomb in a nursery school. Suppose further that he has constructed and planted the bomb in such a way that it will go off when a dozen children will be in the room and that the children will be maimed for life. He has carefully studied the school's patterns and determined a place to hide the bomb where it will not be discovered. Suppose, finally, that he sets it to detonate in one hour.

However urgent the terrorist's cause, it would be difficult—I think impossible—for anyone to justify the intentional maiming of twelve three-year-old children. We might look at mitigating factors: perhaps he is insane, or blinded by grief over the death of his brother or his own children in an attack by the other side. But we judge him harshly. Blowing up young children is a heinous act. To do so intentionally, with the avowed aim of crippling them, is as unambiguous an example of evildoing as we can find.

In the original hypothetical, we had the terrorist setting the bomb to go off in one hour. Suppose instead he set the timer for twenty-four hours, with precisely the same intentions, precisely the same expected results, and no increased likelihood of detection and prevention. Would his action be any less morally wrong because an additional twenty-three hours intervened between the events he initiated and the harm he caused? I can find no good reason to think so. All of the circumstances relevant to our judgment of him remain the same; the increased interval does not seem important.

Imagine instead that a week has elapsed between planting the bomb and its explosion. Does the fact that more time has passed affect our moral evaluation of his actions? Again, assume that all other circumstances remain the same. Make the interval a month. Does that affect our judgments? A year. What about three and a half years?

At this point credibility is strained, no doubt. Why would a terrorist want so long a delay between secreting and detonating his bomb? Isn't it more likely that the bomb would be discovered in such a long interval, or that it would malfunction? As the terrorist's motives are inexplicable to me in any case, I have little hope of explaining why he would choose such a long fuse. And yes, discovery or malfunction seems more likely as the time increases. But if he has planned it well, he might be very confident of the result even with several years' delay. It is worth noting that in the world of terrorism, it is not so odd to find a substantial lag between an action and its consequences. It might be years before a would-be terrorist undergoing training in explosives actually gets to use that training; but if his teachers knew the likely consequences of their efforts and intended that they be brought about, their culpability does not fade with time.

My point is this: that even with a prolonged interval between the action and its results, our moral judgments of the action remain clear. Furthermore, to the extent that the terrorist's culpability is at all diminished, this diminishment has nothing to do with time itself, but rather with other factors that are a consequence of the passage of time. These are the same sort of factors that generally figure in our moral judgments; the interval between an action that intends evil and its results is not, by itself, relevant. The terrorist who hides a bomb set to explode in three and a half years, with every intention of maiming twelve three-year-old children and with every reason to believe that his intention will be fulfilled, does something just as evil as the terrorist who uses a shorter fuse.

This is true even though, in the case of the three-and-a-half-year timer, the children who will be maimed have not yet been born. It would be equally true for a four-year fuse, in which case the children to be injured were not even conceived.[4] (This is important in distinguishing these cases from abortion, since even the most fervent abortion opponent does not equate unfertilized gametes with born children.)

Our concern with harm prior to birth does not extend to all embryos and fetuses. The argument here is relevant only to those embryos and fetuses (and gametes) that will become children. We do not need to settle here the question of when an embryo or fetus becomes a person. As long as we can agree on some age at which the moral significance of a human being seems unequivocal—birth is as good a marker as any for now—we can address a host of questions about moral obligations prior to birth.

There is another advantage to seeing fetuses this way: it helps us locate an upper limit to our moral concerns. Whatever our obligations to fetuses might be, they can be no more stringent than our obligations to other persons, most relevant, our born children.

We are concerned with a fetus or embryo that a pregnant woman has opted to carry to birth. This approach has nothing to say about abortion, in which the moral status of fetuses or embryos, or as some would have it, the sacredness of life per se, is thought to be crucial to the moral permissibility of abortion.[5] To discuss moral obligations to the not-yet-born child—the embryo or fetus intended to be brought to the point where its status as a person is uncontroversial—requires only that we recognize that the timing of a harm is unimportant in judging whether some moral responsibility was violated.

Despite an unpromising earlier history, the law increasingly seems to agree. Before 1946 lawsuits on behalf of children injured prenatally rarely found a sympathetic court. The legal issue was whether there could be a duty to a not-yet-born child. But that year began "a rather spectacular reversal of the no-duty rule. The child, if he is born alive, is now permitted in every jurisdiction to maintain an action for the consequences of prenatal injuries, and if he dies of such injuries after birth an action will lie for his wrongful death," according to W. L. Prosser's authoritative text on tort law.[6]

Is viability, "quickening," or some other index of fetal maturation a relevant criterion for the courts to use in distinguishing legitimate from illegitimate suits? Courts have certainly used such a criterion, but is it valid? Dawn Johnsen, who strenuously opposes the concept of "fetal rights," asserts that "viability is a meaningless distinction in the fetal rights context because the state's interest in the health of its future citizens is equally strong throughout pregnancy."[7] Prosser agrees that viability is not important, at least in tort law: "Certainly the infant may be no less injured; and logic is in favor of ignoring the stage at which the injury occurs." Prosser acknowledges that it could be difficult to link early prenatal events to the particular injuries suffered by a child. But he concludes, "With recent advances in embryology and medical technology, medical proof of causation in these cases has become increasingly reliable, which argues for eliminating the viability or other arbitrary developmental requirement altogether."[8]

Johnsen predicts horrendous consequences for women if the concept of fetal rights were to be widely accepted in the law. But we are not concerned here with generalized rights for the fetus, only with harms done to children when they were yet fetuses. The fear of such consequences has had its own unfortunate consequence: unyielding opposition to any notion that people might bear moral responsibility not to harm a fetus that will later be a child. Such a stance dismisses very firm and sensible moral intuitions, for example, that a lifetime injury done to a fetus one minute before birth, versus one minute after, must bear some moral resemblance to one another. Most people, I suspect, recognize the moral untenability of such a position. By not taking seriously the possibility of moral duties to not-yet-born children, commentators brand themselves as unreasonable and morally insensitive, and thereby cut themselves off from potentially broad public support. There is a better path, through consideration of the prerogatives and duties of parenthood and through a scrupulous disentangling of moral judgment from public policy.

Thinking about Parents and Children: An Antidote to Sentimentalization

If it makes sense to talk about moral obligations to fetuses intended to be brought to birth, what is the extent and what are the limits of those obligations? The prospect that such obligations could dominate the lives of pregnant women energizes opposition to the very concept of moral obligations to the not-yet-born child. Certainly the history of our treatment of pregnant women gives good reason for concern. We have tended to treat the relationship between pregnant woman and fetus as one without parallel in human relations. In a certain, biological sense, it would be difficult to do otherwise. Men cannot have the same intimate connection to new life as a woman carrying a not-yet-born child. Our concern, however, is not with the biology of pregnancy but with what that relationship requires morally. Pregnancy does have some moral parallels. An essential feature of carrying a not-yet-born child is that another human is highly dependent on one's actions and choices for its own welfare. But this, of course, is also the essential feature of parenthood. What mothers *and* fathers do affects their born children. The list of actions and their effects will not be identical between pregnant women and their not-yet-born children, on the one hand, and parents and their born children, on the other. Actions that may be harmful in one set of circumstances may be quite harmless in another. But there is no big news in this: sound ethics always pays close attention to particulars. Nonetheless, the moral duties are essentially the same: parents of born children, just like parents of not-yet-born children, are obliged morally to act responsibly toward their charges, take reasonable steps to advance their welfare, and avoid unnecessary risks of serious harm to them.

We have tended to shroud pregnant women and their not-yet-born children in a mist of sentimentality, often to the detriment of women. It has been used to justify excluding women from education, professions, and factories. There is no doubt that such a sentimentalized view infects our moral judgments and our public policies. It would be useful to have a way to see the moral obligations of pregnant women to their not-yet-born children that could help us pierce the mists of sentimentality. Fortunately, there is such a way available.

The first step is to recognize that, however stringent our obligations might be to not-yet-born children, they cannot be more stringent than our obligations toward born children. It is crucial here to avoid a confusion: we are inclined to think that a pregnant woman is in a special relationship with her not-yet-born child because so many of her actions may have a direct effect on the fetus within her and because it seems that no other party can have nearly so immediate an impact on that fetus. Pregnant women do have many opportunities to benefit or harm their not-yet-born children; this is indisputable. But parents of born children also have a multitude of opportunities to do good or ill for their offspring. Pregnant women may have more occasions to harm or help their not-yet-born children, but that does not indicate that the underlying moral obligations that guide all such decisions are different in kind or intensity.

A particular action may have similar or very different consequences on a child depending on whether it is done before or after birth. Abusing alcohol during pregnancy can result in the permanent physical damage to a child known as fetal alcohol syndrome. Of course, alcohol abuse by the parent—mother or father—of a grown child can also result in considerable harm, ranging from emotional damage, neglect, and physical abuse to death from an automobile accident caused by the alcohol-impaired parent. Not all actions prior to birth are more dangerous to not-yet-born children than to born children. Some things parents do with born children would be harmless or nearly so to the not-yet-born child. For example, parents who take their five-year-old child to neo-Nazi rallies afflict that child with a warped and hateful political consciousness. Bringing the same child to the same rallies in utero has none of those effects.

That a greater proportion of a pregnant woman's actions may have a substantial impact on her not-yet-born child's well-being than a parent's actions on his or her born child does not alter the moral considerations that go into each decision how to act. If we have a duty to take reasonable care not to harm our born child and to take reasonable measures to ensure his or her healthy development and preparation for adult life, that duty is not of a totally different kind for the pregnant woman and her not-yet-born-child, even if it applies to a greater proportion of her actions.

Emphasizing the parallel between parents' duties to born children and pregnant women's duties to their not-yet-born children lifts the mist of sentimentality in two ways. First, it removes the temptation to treat pregnancy as a morally unique state. Pregnancy is distinctive in many respects, to be sure. But we should not abandon the useful means we have for thinking about the nature and extent of moral obligations and prerogatives just because someone is pregnant. Second, emphasizing the similarity with parents' moral relationship with their born children prompts us to look at the moral obligations men have to their children.

A Father-Child Analogy

Until recently in the United States, companies were permitted to exclude women from workplaces on the grounds that hazards there placed fetuses at risk. Some companies cast their nets widely, over all women from their teens until their fifties, unless they could prove they were surgically sterilized. A decade of infertility was not sufficient, nor was evidence that birth control was used and that no child was wanted.

One case involved the American Cyanamid plant in Willow Island, West Virginia. Women had been banned from a section of the plant in which lead, toxic to fetuses and adults, was used. Finally they were admitted, but only upon proof that they were sterile. Several women underwent surgical sterilization in order to get these desirable jobs; nonetheless, that section of the plant was closed down shortly afterward.

Postpone for a little while consideration of the public policy issues, and focus on the moral one. Should a woman who might become—or is—pregnant take a job in which she may be exposed to substances that might harm her fetus? Now turn that question into an analogous one about a father and his born children.

Suppose a man worked in the oil fields of West Texas in the early 1980s and found himself thrown out of work when the price of oil plummeted. He has been the principal wage earner for his household, comprised of himself, his wife (now pregnant), and two children. A friend who moved years ago to Texas City, a complex of oil refineries and petrochemical plants on the Houston Ship Channel, calls with good news: there is a job for him in Texas City if he wants it.

Our protagonist is no stereotype of the oil field roughneck. He is well read, thoughtful, and determined to make the best ethical choice for himself and his family. He knows, for example, that Texas City is in a "cancer corridor," an area with a higher than expected incidence of cancer. This is not such a surprise, given the heavy concentration of petrochemical facilities emitting who knows what into the air and water. (The citizens of that community awoke one morning to discover that overnight the paint had peeled off several cars, presumably as a result of some noxious belch from a nearby company.) If he moves there, he is exposing his children, his wife, his not-yet-born child, and himself to a small but undeniable increased risk of cancer in their lifetimes.

Of course, staying in West Texas has its disadvantages as well. Without a salary, he is thrown onto the ungenerous social welfare system of that state. He will lose his health insurance, and with it the relatively easy access to care, including prenatal care. In a few months he will lose his house. Brought up to believe that he should be the breadwinner, he feels himself a failure, and though he is home most of the time now, he finds that his anger and frustration make him a sullen parent and spouse.

If he moves his family to Texas City, he will be able to feel pride in himself once again and return to being a good parent and partner. There will be money for decent housing and food and good health insurance. His wife would be able to receive the prenatal care she wants and needs.

If such a man, balancing all of the considerations involved and with his wife's full agreement and support, chose to take the job and move his family to Texas City, it would be arrogant to say that his choice was morally indefensible, even though it increased his family's and his chance of dying of cancer. He balanced—appropriately—that risk of potential grave harm, with its very low probability, against the advantages of moving there to take a good job with good benefits. Putting it another way, he made an all-things-considered decision that, in the light of his available options, is eminently sensible.

A woman who chooses to take a job in which her not-yet-born—or perhaps not even yet conceived—child is at some risk of harm from workplace exposures makes a decision analogous to that made by our former roughneck. A person, woman or man, is justified in taking into account a variety of factors: obligations to your family; the consequences for your spouse, your children, and yourself; your own interests and legitimate desires. In fact, a failure to give all relevant factors their due weight would be evidence of moral myopia.

Moral Myopia

Moral myopia in these cases—treating pregnant women as if the fact that they were pregnant was the exclusive or predominant morally relevant fact about them—is the mistake into which sentimentalism about the pregnant woman–fetus relationship leads. Pregnancy becomes a kind of moral trump card, carrying the trick no matter how strong the other cards on the table. A woman who becomes pregnant and chooses to carry that fetus to birth does not become a moral hermit, stripped of all other relationships, forbidden to consider even her own welfare except as it concerns the fetus she carries. She remains a full-fledged moral agent, with a complex variety of moral relationships, and with the right to consider her own well-being.

The United States Supreme Court reached a similar conclusion in *Automobile Workers v. Johnson Controls*. The company had barred women from battery manufacture until 1977. In that year they had women sign a statement explaining that there was some, but not conclusive, evidence that a fetus might be harmed if its mother were exposed to modest levels of lead. In 1982, Johnson Controls adopted a fetal protection policy that excluded women from jobs where they would be exposed to lead, as well as jobs from which they might be promoted into positions involving lead exposure.[9]

Employees sued in 1984, claiming that the fetal protection policy constituted sex discrimination that violated the Civil Rights Act of 1964. One of the plaintiffs had been sterilized in order to keep her job; a divorced fifty-year-old woman took a pay cut when she was transferred; and a man protested because he was denied a leave of absence that he wanted in order to reduce his lead levels in anticipation of becoming a father.[10]

The Court, with Justice Blackmun writing the majority opinion, declared that the company's fetal protection policy violated federal law. It noted the obvious bias in the policy: "Fertile men, but not fertile women, are given a choice as to whether they wish to risk their reproductive health for a particular job."[11] Johnson Controls also failed to set reasonable limits on its policy: the company "has chosen to treat all its female employees as potentially pregnant; that choice evinces discrimination on the basis of sex."[12] The Court addressed, at least implicitly, the moral dimensions of the case as well when it asserted that "decisions about the welfare of future children must be left to the parents who conceive, bear, support, and raise them rather than to the employers who hire those parents."[13] The Court's majority opinion concludes by declining to impose its own views in place of a woman's judgment about whether to take a job that might pose some risk to her not-yet-born or not-yet-conceived child: "It is no more appropriate for the courts than it is for individual employers to decide whether a woman's reproductive role is more important to herself and her family than her economic role. Congress has left this choice to the woman as hers to make."[14] These choices are now protected by law. They are also morally defensible to the extent that protecting our children from risks of harm is not the only thing we must consider, however important it is.

The Scope of Parental Responsibility

Exploring the scope and limits of parental obligations to born children gives a little perspective to discussions about our moral obligations to not-yet-born children. Avoiding harm is certainly important, but are parents obliged to elevate avoiding harm to their children above all other ends? Suppose that you are a parent with young children who want to play outside. Does the possibility—small but not zero—that harm might come to them from, say, a rabid dog, or neighborhood toughs, or a runaway car, impose on you a moral duty to build concrete barricades around the perimeter of your yard with electrified barbed wire on top? In the typical American suburb, this would be, to put it mildly, an overreaction. Even if you could afford such fortifications, your obligation as a parent to prevent harm to your children surely does not extend this far. You could justify your decision to forgo such protections (not that anyone would insist on a justification) by saying that you would use the money instead for your children's education. But you need not cite their interest at all. It would be enough to say that you prefer a border of flowers, or good relations with your neighbors.

Parents are not expected to sacrifice all other considerations in order to protect their children from every conceivable harm. That is too strenuous a requirement, and too narrow a view of the moral life of parents.

Am I ever permitted to expose my child to risks for someone else's benefit? My family and I have lived in Cleveland since 1987; the weather is much better than is generally supposed. But there are occasional nasty storms in winter. Suppose a father was home with his six-month-old infant in one of the western suburbs, when his mother, who lives in the snow belt to the east, called in desperation. A wicked snow and ice storm had pelted the area, and the power had gone out at her house. It was getting dark, the house was growing colder by the minute, and she was terrified. The neighbors she knew have all gone away for the holidays, and the police were too busy dealing with accidents to come to her assistance. "Please come get me," she begs.

None of your neighbors is home and no other baby-sitters are available. You have only two alternatives: let your terrified parent sit in her darkened and chilled house; or bundle up your baby, strap her in a car seat, toss blankets, flashlight, diapers, and formula in the car, and set out across the now-treacherous roads that link east and west sides.

The appropriate question here is not, what would you do? but does the father who shrugs and, with all reasonable precautions, sets out on the journey to his mother's house, infant in tow, make a morally justified choice? Like all such practical moral judgments, the actual facts, the specific circumstances, are very important. But suppose that his assessment of the risks was reasonably accurate—that his mother was in greater danger than he and the baby would be even while driving and that in any case her terror was excruciating. His assessment of his moral responsibilities might have looked like this: my duty to keep my child from harm is stronger than my duty to help anyone else. But surely I have an obligation to help my parent, even if that means exposing my child to some degree of risk. Besides, I love my mother and would feel terrible if I could not help her, and maintaining my self-respect as a good son counts for something.

A father who made such a judgment, even though it meant placing his child at risk, makes a morally defensible choice. There are much less dramatic, mundane instances of this same principle. We leave our child with a sitter because we want to see a play; we take our baby on an airplane because her aunts and uncles want to see her—and us. In such instances, a good moral decision maker weighs the morally relevant considerations and makes an all-things-considered judgment. Indeed, sound moral judgment consists of just such a roundup and weighing of relevant matters.

I have tried to make three points so far about ethical decisions concerning the not-yet-born child. The first we can call the "child-as-maximum" principle: whatever moral obligations we have to not-yet-born children, they cannot be more weighty than our obligations to our born children. Second, as a way of avoiding the trap of sentimentalization, we can look to the father-child relationship as an analogy with the relationship between pregnant women and not-yet-born children. Under comparable circumstances of burden and benefit, duty and interest, we should ask no more of a pregnant woman for her not-yet-born child than we would ask of a father for his born child. Third, once we recognize the all-things-considered nature of sound practical moral judgment, we can avoid moral myopia—treating the fact that a woman is pregnant as a moral trump, obliterating all other relevant moral considerations. Our remaining source of confusion is the failure to see the difference between moral judgments and public policies.

Distinguishing Ethics from Public Policy

Anyone who has given it a few seconds thought understands that public policy does not follow straightforwardly and without remainder from moral judgment. Breaking a promise is wrong, but our laws do not treat all broken promises as equivalent. If I agree to pay you $500 to repave my driveway, you do as agreed, but if I renege on my promise and refuse to pay, you may take me to court and the court can order me to pay up. But if a brilliant and attractive woman meets the same paver at a party, charms him to the point of infatuation, promises to call him next Saturday and never does, the paver will find no solace in the law. That would be true even if the harm done to him by dashing his dreams of a wonderful life with such an intelligent and beautiful woman was much, much greater than an everyday quarrel over an unpaid invoice.

Though societies often like to buttress their moral convictions with the force of law, determining that something is unethical is neither a necessary nor a sufficient reason to make it unlawful. I know of no moral code that declares it a grave wrong to park for more than thirty minutes on a downtown street, but many communities adopt such prohibitions. And there are a multitude of moral offenses—lies, broken promises, failures to fulfill familial obligations—that escape the law's attention.

We may choose, for a variety of reasons, not to use the power of the state and its laws to compel people to do what we are convinced is ethically right, or to punish what we are equally certain is morally wrong. Other values might be compromised because enforcement would be intolerably intrusive or erratic. Or enforcing the law might require a disproportionate share of community resources for the good it would do. Imagine a world in which everyone who broke a date could be sued for emotional distress; or where every parent who did not fulfill the community's standard of ideal parenting could be accused of neglect. Communities have concluded sensibly that many moral failings are best left to other means of social sanction than the law.

Public discussion about moral obligations to not-yet-born children has a habit of forgetting this crucial distinction between morality and public policy. It is one thing to say that parents who raise their children to be racists are doing something terribly wrong, both for their children and for those who will suffer from their distorted hatreds in the future. It is quite another thing to say that we should use the power of the state to forbid parents from teaching these beliefs to their offspring, or that we should take their children away.

We do in fact remove children from parents, but only when we have reasonably clear evidence of abuse or neglect. Teaching a repugnant ideology, as long as the children are fed, clothed, housed, and not beaten, is not the sort of abuse or neglect for which our laws permit intervention. Filling a child with hatred and fear is an awful thing to do, and a profound moral wrong. But we do not permit the state to judge which beliefs parents may and may not teach their children. The potential that the state could misuse that discretionary power is just too great. The system by which abuse and neglect are uncovered, adjudicated, and such children provided for may be cumbersome and profoundly flawed. And without a doubt there are parents who are doing morally repugnant things to their children—like teaching them to hate—whom our laws leave untouched. The distinction between morality and public policy, nonetheless, is a crucial one both in principle and in practice.

It is possible, and consistent with other realms of human affairs, to make a moral judgment that, for example, a woman is not fulfilling her moral obligations to her not-yet-born child and yet to refrain from using the law's power to compel her to do what we are convinced is right. Suppose that the experimental procedure of fetal surgery for diaphragmatic hernia became established practice. Perhaps 50 percent of infants undergoing the surgery had the defect fully corrected; without the surgery, all would die within a year or so of birth. Suppose a fetus was found to have such a hernia; the woman carrying the fetus fully intends to bring it to birth. But when she is told of the procedure required—cutting into the womb, partially removing the fetus, repairing the defect, putting the fetus back, and reclosing the womb—she refuses, saying she is terrified of anesthesia and does not want anyone cutting on her uterus. She will have the baby; it will be born alive; but it will rapidly waste and die because its underdeveloped lungs cannot wring the oxygen it needs from the air.

We need to ask two kinds of questions about this case. First, does she have a moral obligation to undergo the surgery? Second, and separately, if she does have such a moral obligation, should our laws force her to have the procedure?

Before trying to answer these questions, let's try an analogy. Consider the case of a child suffering from a lymphoma. All treatments have been exhausted except for irradiation to kill the cancerous cells, followed by a bone marrow transplant. A successful marrow transplant requires an excellent match. If such a match can be found, there is a 50 percent chance of a full recovery; if not, the child will waste and die. Unfortunately, the available marrow registries have no good matches. But all members of the immediate family are typed and, lo, there is one perfect match—the child's father. Upon being informed that he is the only and ideal donor, the father shivers and refuses. He declares that he is terrified of anesthesia and cannot bear the thought of having the marrow sucked from his bones.

Again, there are two kinds of questions. First, does this father have a moral obligation to donate his marrow to his child? People may differ here, but let us put this in context. As a parent, I have done many things for my children that are more unpleasant, painful, and dangerous than a marrow donation. I have taken my children to carnivals in the summer and watched them drop to the ground, crying that they couldn't walk another step. (This could happen within 30 yards of the entrance, on the way *in*.) The choices are either to go home and disappoint them or their brother and sisters or to carry them. I have very distinct memories of the pain in my back and neck and shoulders as I carried them around while they wiped their candy-covered fingers in my hair. Now contrast that with a nice, clean, cool hospital bed, with people coming by regularly to offer me water and ask whether they could do anything to make me more comfortable. Furthermore, if what was at stake was not just an interesting experience for my child but my child's very life, I would say that if I had an obligation to endure discomfort for my child's benefit at a carnival, I surely have a moral obligation to endure some discomfort to try to save my child's life. Perhaps the father in this case has done as much or more. The chance that I could save my child's life at the price of a far-fetched risk of serious harm and an assurance of moderate discomfort to myself strikes me as something I not only would do, but should do. To put it concisely, I think a father who had a fair chance of saving his child's life under such circumstances has a moral obligation to do so. The burdens to him are far, far outweighed by the potential benefits to his child; and his duty to promote his child's well-being clearly encompasses accepting such burdens.

Whether you agree with my weighing of burden and benefit in the context of parental duties is less important than seeing that this is an appropriate way to approach the moral question. But now comes the second question, the one about public policy: If for whatever reason the father continues to refuse, should we strap him down and forcibly take his marrow? We may be convinced that a good father would consent to donate his marrow; we may be angry at this man for refusing; we may think he is failing his duty as a parent. We may think and feel all these things and yet, without being inconsistent, we may stop short of compelling him to surrender his marrow.[15] Moral judgment is one thing, public policy another.

Recall now the woman who refuses surgery to correct her not-yet-born child's diaphragmatic hernia. Let us assume that the burdens on her and the prospective benefits to her not-yet-born child are comparable to that of the potential marrow donor father and his child. Her duty to protect her not-yet-born child from harm is also comparable to his. Without any inconsistency we can say that she is not fulfilling her moral obligations to her not-yet-born child (just as the father failed his duty) without forcing the operation on her against her will (just as we refrained in the case of the father). Indeed if the burdens, benefits, and duties were more or less comparable, and we reached different conclusions about the man and the woman on either morality or public policy, our judgments would be inconsistent and therefore suspect.

Coerced Cesarean Sections:
The Father-Child Analogy

A case such as Jessie Mae Jefferson's increases the temptation to use the power of the medical profession and the courts to force a woman to do what others—here her doctors—believe is best for her not-yet-born child. The doctors, as it turned out, were wrong in their predictions for Mrs. Jefferson and her baby. But there are other cases in which doctors make accurate diagnoses of conditions like placenta previa. The Jefferson case is complicated by another fact: Mrs. Jefferson's refusal was based on religious grounds. Courts in the United States give special deference to religious beliefs. Suppose we confronted a case like the one reported many years ago by four Israeli physicians. A woman, forty weeks pregnant, refused cesarean section for her fetus, which was delivered stillborn. Afterward she told a nurse that the death solved personal problems for her.[16]

What can we say about moral obligations and public policy in such cases?[17] We need an analogy closer to the facts of a genuine placenta previa. The benefits to the not-yet-born child are much more clear-cut than in the marrow donor/fetal diaphragmatic hernia case: nearly 100 percent healthy survival with a cesarean section against virtually certain death without it. It would be useful also to find a procedure in which the burdens on the father parallel even more closely the burdens of cesarean section.

One possible analogy is the case of a father who is an outstanding match as a donor for his child who needs a liver. A procedure now used takes a lobe of liver from the parent donor and transplants it into the body of the child. Under normal circumstances, the donor's liver will regenerate. If all goes well, the child's new liver will function and grow. The burdens on the father donor are roughly comparable to the burdens of cesarean section. The transplant, however, falls short of successful cesarean section in the benefits it provides the child. Transplanted organs can be rejected; preventing rejection typically requires suppressing the recipient's immune system with potent drugs that have undesirable side effects.

Despite the less than perfect fit, we can use the analogy to explore the boundaries of both moral obligation and public policy for cesarean section cases. If we concluded that the father has a moral obligation to donate a lobe of his liver, then certainly the pregnant woman has a moral obligation to consent to cesarean section to save the life of her not-yet-born child. The burdens are comparable, but the benefits are even greater in the latter case. Likewise, if we concluded that coercive public policies are justified to make fathers give up pieces of their liver to benefit their children, then consistency suggests that we should be willing to force pregnant women to undergo cesarean sections when the benefits to their not-yet-born children are more certain.

Consider the father. Does he have a moral obligation to donate a lobe of his liver to his child if it is the only available treatment, and is very likely to save his child's life? The risks of surgery are not trivial, but neither are they grave. Major complications are uncommon and in the great majority of cases part-liver donors recover uneventfully with good regeneration of their liver. The invasiveness, risk, discomfort, and recovery time are greater in this case than in the marrow donor one. But so is the likelihood of benefit. There is room for disagreement, to be sure, but I would argue that parents ought to make such sacrifices for their children, that this father has a moral obligation to donate a lobe of his liver to save his child's life. Most parents, I suspect, would need little persuading to become a donor, just as most pregnant women readily agree to a cesarean section when told that the procedure will benefit their not-yet-born child.

But suppose this father, for whatever reason, refused. Should our public policy compel him to submit to anesthesia and surgery against his will? As in the marrow donor case, I think most people would say no. The prospect of forcibly restraining a man in order to take out a piece of a vital organ for someone else's benefit—even his own child's—

gives us pause, for the same reasons we were reluctant to take the other father's marrow.

The problem with the analogy is that the certainty of benefit to the child is less than with the not-yet-born child case. What if the father were a superb match for his child? And what if new antirejection techniques were developed that virtually assured the liver would function normally in the child with no significant side effects? What if, that is, the benefits were essentially identical to the cesarean section for placenta previa case? The argument for a moral obligation to donate becomes even stronger. But it still seems unlikely that we would force a father to undergo surgery without his consent. We might think he was irresponsible or unreasonably fearful. We might try every strategy we could think of to persuade him to donate. But in all likelihood we would stop short of physical force.

The pregnant woman in labor, with a condition such as placenta previa that puts her not-quite-born fetus in grave jeopardy, under comparable circumstances of burdens and benefits to the liver donor father, has a moral obligation to consent to cesarean section. But if, like our hypothetical father, she refuses to consent to the procedure, then we may try our best to change her mind. If her consent is not forthcoming, though, as with the father, we should not force the procedure on her.[18]

It will not always be easy to find a good father-child analogy for the range of moral quandaries and policy decisions found in the nexus between pregnant women and not-yet-born children. But looking for such analogies helps us guard against sentimentalizing the ethics of that relationship. It also leads us to the more familiar and well-explored terrain of parent-child relationships, in which we may find examples and principles that may help guide us through the less-explored moral terrain of pregnant women and not-yet-born children. Finally, insisting that good public policy follows no more immediately from moral judgments on these questions than on any other allows us to discuss temperately and sensitively what specific moral obligations do exist here, and their limits.

6

Prenatal Testing and the
Quest for the Perfect Child

*What you have to do is this, Bosk. When you get up in the
morning, pretend your car is a spaceship. Tell yourself you are
going to visit another planet. You say "On that planet terrible
things happen, but they don't happen on my planet. They only
happen on that planet I take my spaceship to each morning."*
> —A medical geneticist describing to sociologist
> Charles Bosk how he copes with his work

*If we believed that the world was a problem to the child and not
the child a problem to the world, we might be better able to
imagine how raising a child with a disability could give much
the same gratifications as raising another child who did not start
life with a disabling condition.*
> —Adrienne Asch, "Reproductive Technology
> and Disability"

Beware of absurd hypothetical examples; they are likely to be true.

At a national conference of geneticists and genetic counselors, the discussion turned to sex selection, using prenatal testing to learn the sex of a fetus and then aborting it if it was not the desired sex. I wanted the audience to think about this practice as a misuse of their clinical skills and a sophisticated technology to abort healthy fetuses, so I offered them a hypothetical case. A couple comes to you for prenatal testing saying that *unless* their fetus has major problems, they will end the pregnancy. Anybody, they tell you, can love a healthy child. But this couple believes that they are capable of much greater love than the average couple, and they want one who will be a real challenge, whose need for love and care exceeds the capacities of most adults.

I got mostly the reaction I was hoping for, except for one older man who leaped up and hurried to a microphone on the floor. "I've *had* that request!" he announced—from deaf parents, who wanted assurance that their child would also be deaf, like them. If the fetus would be able to hear, they planned to abort it. I remember nothing else about that session.

The Quest for the Perfect Child and the Human Genome Project

People have worried for years about the possible uses of technologies such as prenatal testing in pursuit of the "perfect child." The preference of at least some deaf parents for similarly deaf children reminds us that "perfection" may have different meanings for different people. The concern, I believe, is well founded: not because of disagreements about what constitutes perfection in one's child, but because of what the quest for perfection bodes for the meaning of parenthood.

The concern is rapidly gaining urgency because of two developments. First, some of the most important barriers to obtaining information about one's fetus are crumbling. Ever since the first successful attempt at prenatal diagnosis in 1960 (by drawing a sample of fluid, containing fetal cells, from a woman's uterus),[1] two major hurdles have been the harm to the woman because of the invasive nature of the techniques by which fetal genetic material was obtained and the risk of inducing a spontaneous abortion. Those barriers may soon be eliminated if a promising new technique known as fetal cell sorting reaches maturity. It turns out that fetal cells are present not only within the womb; a few make it into the mother's circulatory system. With a technique no more invasive than drawing a little blood from a woman's arm, we can get samples of her fetus's genes and chromosomes. Of course, we need a technique to separate the relatively few fetal cells from the many cells of its mother—the "sorting" in the procedure's name. If fetal cell sorting can be made to work and its cost brought into line with amnio-centesis and chorionic villus sampling (CVS), the current methods of obtaining fetal cells, it will effectively obliterate the barriers posed by invasiveness and risk.

Second, the sheer amount of raw genetic information that could be provided by prenatal testing is expanding at a dizzying pace. The Human Genome Project, a fifteen-year scientific undertaking that will identify all of the estimated one hundred thousand genes in the human body, is well under way. Already genes that increase a person's risk for breast cancer and for colorectal cancer have been identified. Other genes related to heart disease and stroke are also being tracked, and several genes possibly linked to Alzheimer's dementia have been found. These discoveries are merely the first droplets of an advancing wave of genetic information about to engulf us.

Genes affect more than disease. Our eye color is inherited, as is the color and texture of our hair (as well as whether or not we lose it). As the example of sex selection shows, people may want to use prenatal testing and abortion not merely to avoid grave diseases but to avoid other characteristics as well. Suppose someone had a very unhappy ado-lescence and blamed it on the fact that she had red hair. (I admit a bias here. Both my youngest child and my wife have more than a trace of red in their hair and, to my eyes, their hair is beautiful.) When this disgruntled person learns that the gene or genes responsible for red hair are discovered, she hurries to her neighborhood geneticist. She wants her fetus tested to see if it too carries the cursed trait. If it does . . .

Prenatal testing was created as a means for adults to avoid the birth of children with problems ranging from significant to absolutely devas-tating. In practice, the barriers of invasiveness and risk were too high to tempt prospective parents to use prenatal testing to detect anything less than severe health problems with their fetuses. As the risks decreased, the preference for males in certain cultures led some couples to judge the risks worth accepting in order to avoid the birth of a girl.[2] Now that the barriers are on the verge of crumbling and the menu of genetic information about to grow exceedingly long, the time has come to take a hard look at the moral foundations of prenatal testing. Can the cur-rent understanding of the ethics of prenatal testing guide us through the thicket of increased demand for prenatal testing for a potentially massive list of human genes, many of which may have nothing to do with disease or disability? The answer, I fear, is no.

Unilateral Moral Disarmament

The quest for the perfect child is now poised to enlist in its service the ever-growing power of genetic technology. In the face of this onslaught, genetic counseling maintains a position akin to unilateral moral disarmament. Genetic counseling claims to be based on an ethic of value neutrality and a nondirective counseling style. Together, these components of genetic counseling's ideology provide no defense against even the most outrageous requests by prospective parents. The ideology of nondirectiveness offers no means by which to distinguish parents who want to avoid the birth of a profoundly impaired child who will die soon in any event from parents who want a child without attributes that they regard, perhaps idiosyncratically, as undesirable. Genetic counselors do not invariably give in to such requests. Many refuse to collaborate in sex selection, and many more would surely refuse to help a couple who wanted to use the power of modern human genetics to design the child of their fantasies—or at least dispose of any fetus who deviated more than a little from their requirements.

The problem is that by their own professional moral standards, genetic counselors are compelled to view most value judgments on their part as deviant, as failures to live up to the norms of the profession. Some values are considered legitimate in the counseling setting: compassion and patience, for example, along with commitment to informed, autonomous decision making by prospective parents. But on other crucial matters, the ideology that is supposed to underpin genetic counseling has nothing useful to offer. Value neutrality and nondirectiveness provide no vantage point from which to treat parental requests with a healthy dose of moral skepticism, or to preserve the counselor's own personal moral integrity. I have no doubt that counselors find ways to preserve their integrity. But that success is in spite of, not because of, the ideology of nondirective, value-free counseling.

I believe there is something at stake here that goes well beyond the usual concerns about eugenics, even eugenics by the "back door."[3] The power of prenatal testing threatens to change fundamentally the meaning of parenthood. In concert with some of the values implicit in alternative reproductive technologies, prenatal testing makes children increasingly the product of explicit adult choices. Prenatal testing involves the choice whether or not to have *this particular child,* rather than the choice whether to have *a child*.[4] We need to examine the origins of contemporary genetic counseling in order to understand how we have arrived at this pass, and what route may guide us out of it.

The Ideology of Nondirectiveness

Sheldon C. Reed popularized the phrase "genetic counseling." In his influential 1955 book on the subject, he offered this advice to counselors: "The parents often ask us directly whether they should have more children. This question is one that we do not answer because we cannot. The counselor has not experienced the emotional impact of their problem, nor is he intimately acquainted with their environment. We try to explain thoroughly what the genetic situation is, but the decision must be a personal one between the husband and wife, and theirs alone."[5] The genetic counselor's job, in other words, is simply to help his or her clients to understand the facts of the case. What is the probability of inheriting the disease that killed the prospective father's father? How likely is a woman the age of this prospective mother to have a child with Down's syndrome? What are the risks of amniocentesis? The genetic counselor is *not* in the business of telling people what to do about this information. Strict value neutrality requires that the counselor should not impose her or his values on clients.

Genetic counselors strove to be nondirective. That is, they did not want to tell their clients what direction to take. They learned how to fend off tactfully requests from their clients for advice about what they should do. By 1974, the concept if not the term "nondirectiveness" was so well accepted that it permeated the definition of genetic counseling offered by a committee of the leading professional organization in human genetics, the American Society of Human Genetics. The definition reads in part: "Genetic counseling is a communication process which deals with the human problems associated with the occurrence, or risk of occurrence, of a genetic disorder in a family." The definition goes on to stress the counselor's obligation "to help the individual or family . . . comprehend the medical facts . . . , understand the options . . . , choose the course of action which seems appropriate to them in view of their risk and the family goals" and "make the best possible adjustment."[6]

To see how drastically this departs from the usual physician-patient interaction, imagine your doctor explaining that she has diagnosed you as having lymphoma, a cancer of the blood. When you ask what you should do, all your doctor will give you is a list of your treatment options, with various probabilities. You ask for advice: Doctor, which is the most sensible? But your physician adamantly refuses to give a clinical judgment. Her job, she insists, is to give you the facts, not to express any values.

It was certainly true in the not-so-distant past that doctors were all too likely to ignore their patients' values and preferences. In many cases physicians would not even inform their patients of options other than the one the doctor favored, or would present the alternatives in misleadingly gloomy terms. We should not become nostalgic for those days. But we want our doctors' advice. We want the benefit of their clinical experience to help us decide which among the options makes the most sense. In some instances, our particular values might lead us to reject the doctor's first choice, and our doctor must respect that decision. But we expect more from our physicians than noncommittal nondirectiveness.

The first genetic counselors tended to be Ph.D.'s—scientists, not clinicians. James R. Sorenson claims that this cohort "practiced genetic counseling, one might say, almost by accident. . . . [W]hen reproductive problems involving suspected genetic actors occurred they were about the only ones available who could provide some information."[7] The first M.D.'s to act as genetic counselors tended to be academic physicians who, like their genetically expert Ph.D. counterparts, probably were drawn into genetic counseling more by circumstance than design. They also may have seen their roles as providing expert but neutral interpretations of complex facts and probabilities, not offering practical clinical wisdom. Nondirectiveness served them well in their role as neutral expert.

In 1969 the first graduate program in genetic counseling, a master's degree program, was established at Sarah Lawrence College.[8] Many genetic counseling professionals in the United States have a master's degree in genetic counseling or come from the field of nursing or social work. Almost all of these counselors are women. Of those with M.D.'s and Ph.D.'s, an international study found that 35 percent were women.[9]

Nonphysician genetic counselors are in a difficult position. Typically, they depend on physicians or laboratories for patient referrals. They provide genetic services, and physicians act as gatekeepers to those services. Nonphysician counselors do most of the arduous work of dealing with distraught parents. With relatively little power, they have stressed the educational and emotionally supportive aspects of their role. Nondirective, value-free counseling, which is presumed to be the norm governing genetic counseling offered by physician and nonphysician counselors alike, was especially well suited to the role and training of nonphysician counselors.

In a discussion of the "basic tenets of genetic counseling," a leading counselor reports that everyone in her profession is taught to provide counseling that is "1. Educational; 2. Nondirective; 3. Unconditional; 4. Supportive."[10] This sounds much more like the kind of psychotherapy advocated early in his career by the famous therapist Carl Rogers than like the encounter of doctor and patient. Indeed, the term "nondirectiveness" is borrowed directly from Rogerian therapy.

Nondirective genetic counseling was a serviceable answer to the questions posed to the emerging field of clinical genetics. It remains a useful reminder about what should be avoided in encounters between genetic counselors and clients, such as the wholesale imposition of counselors' views. But it was not designed to answer the challenges now being raised by advances in the science of human genetics and the technology of prenatal testing. To understand how an ethical standard like nondirectiveness became accepted and why it survives, we need to look at its social and historical context. We also need to explore the difference between moral justifications and causes.

Moral Justifications versus Causes

Nondirectiveness was the response to a problem: what attitude to take toward the encounter between the genetics expert and the individual or family who had engaged the expert's services. Many factors cooperated to make nondirectiveness appear to be a satisfactory response. From the point of view of ethics, two types of factors need to be distinguished.

First there are the sorts of factors we call *moral justifications*. Justifications provide good moral reasons to support a particular conclusion or course of action. A moral reason for adopting a stance of nondirectiveness in genetic counseling would be that it respects the client's autonomy. Moral reasons respond to moral challenges. They answer such questions as, What justifies this practice?

Then there are *causes*. A cause is a factor that explains why a certain thing happened. A cause might be morally relevant to an accounting of someone's actions. Your best friend failed to keep his promise to meet you after work. He explains that his boss had ordered him to stay late and that you had already left your office so he could not reach you. His boss's command caused him to break his promise to you. Or perhaps you had noticed another person offering to help hungry people on the street, and you were tempted to attribute to him the moral characteristics of generosity and kindness. But then you learned that he was being paid well to do this work. With this explanation of his behavior you no longer see his actions as exhibitions of great moral virtue.

There are cogent moral justifications why nondirectiveness was embraced as the norm for genetic counseling, reasons that help to justify the practice. Then there are causes of this same embrace, causes that help explain why nondirectiveness was adopted, but not how it might be justified. *Reasons that justify; causes that explain:* both types of factors led genetic counseling to take nondirectiveness to its heart. Why bother to make this distinction?

Nondirectiveness became the standard for genetic counseling because of many factors, a few that would count as justifications, more that are explanations, with no justificatory force. Nondirectiveness, that is, was a satisfactory response to a practical problem in a particular historical and social context. It gave good-enough answers to potentially calamitous moral challenges; it permitted a nascent profession to go on with its work in the face of threats that could have undermined it completely; it did not threaten other concentrations of power that might have derailed it; and it felt comfortable to the people in that profession. Over time, practitioners forgot the awkward circumstances attending the birth of nondirective genetic counseling, though, and began to treat it as a self-evident moral truth. But the current support for nondirectiveness is just as much a product of both reasons and causes as was its origin. Holding fast to nondirectiveness, genetic counselors can appeal to our culture's infatuation with autonomy; they can parry accusations of eugenics; and they can live with the often excruciatingly painful consequences of the decisions made on the basis of their conversations with clients. Nondirectiveness will even allow them to avoid responsibility for the increasingly awesome power wielded by prenatal testing. But I believe that the time has come to accept that responsibility.

Why Nondirective Genetic Counseling?

Modern genetic counseling grew into its current form well after World War II, that is, after the idea of eugenics became indelibly linked to National Socialism, death camps, and the murders of those the Nazis considered genetically "inferior."[11] Genetic counseling had to avoid being tarnished by any association with eugenics, whose policies are meant to encourage the birth of genetically fit children and to diminish the number of genetically "defective" offspring. But what does prenatal testing and counseling do if not permit couples to abort such genetically "defective" fetuses?

Genetic counseling found ways to distance itself from past eugenic practices. If one of the evils of eugenics was to declare certain persons unfit to live, then genetic counseling would refrain scrupulously from judging the value of any life. It would dispense only facts. If another of the evils of eugenics was that it was imposed on unwilling victims, then genetic counseling would function only on a strictly voluntary basis. A practice characterized by value-free, nondirective counseling seems as far removed as one could be from judgmental, coercive eugenics. If there is any eugenic taint, it will color the parents' decisions, not the work of the genetics professionals.

By the late 1960s on through the 1970s and 1980s, the idea of patient autonomy became an increasingly resonant battle cry against the professional hegemony of physicians. Doctors may have been accustomed to doling out information as they saw fit and telling patients what to do, but they could no longer do so without being challenged. Patients had the moral, to say nothing of the legal, right to all relevant information about themselves, and to decide what they will do in light of their own values. This is an admittedly simplified version of the tension between patient vulnerability and autonomy, on the one hand, and physician power, sympathy, and temptations to paternalism, on the other. But it is faithful enough to the themes of the debate to make clear the appeal of nondirective genetic counseling. Here were professionals voluntarily surrendering all of their paternalistic power! The patients' values and only the patients' values would rule. Nondirective genetic counseling was the epitome and apotheosis of patient autonomy.

Quite apart from abstract concerns about autonomy, prenatal testing touches on intensely personal matters. People find it difficult to receive news that their fetus is unhealthy without fixing the blame on someone—often themselves. Inherited genetic diseases are a blot on the legacy passed down by our ancestors. Once we have that terrible information, we must then choose whether to continue that pregnancy. A choice like this penetrates to the deepest recesses of our being. How strong am I? How willing am I to accept a life centered around a child who will be more dependent on me, for much longer, than I had ever anticipated in my fantasies and musings about parenthood? Would I be able to love this child in the way that it needs? Am I too shallow? too selfish? Am I deceiving myself into believing that this will be much easier than it will really be? Is this image of myself as a selfless martyr to my child too appealing, and for all the wrong reasons?

Even if none of these questions is raised explicitly, any moderately sensitive person engaged in genetic counseling understands that the interactions they have with clients probe the very depths of identity and character. It seems doubly cruel to follow up the delivery of painful information by imposing on them your judgments about what they must do.

We must also remember that for most of the history of prenatal testing, and still today, most of the disorders being tested for are serious, varying perhaps from significant to grave. When the paradigmatic instances of prenatal diagnosis deal with disorders such as Tay-Sachs disease or other rapidly lethal anomalies, it is easy to see another of the appeals of nondirectiveness. There is a rough but real justice when the parties making a decision bear most of its burden. If parents decided to abort a fetus with Tay-Sachs, then they would have to cope with that decision. Even fervent opponents of abortion would understand, I hope, the gravity of such a decision. Likewise, if parents chose to have a child with Tay-Sachs or some other severe affliction, then the parents were also the most likely parties to bear the responsibility of caring for that child.

Nondirectiveness also permits counselors to maintain at least a little emotional distance from the misery that the news they deliver brings in its wake. Charles Bosk studied the genetic service in a prominent children's hospital. He asked one of the clinical geneticists how he could continue to function among all the misfortune he witnessed. This was the answer:

What you have to do is this, Bosk. When you get up in the morning, pretend your car is a spaceship. Tell yourself you are going to visit another planet. You say "On that planet terrible things happen, but they don't happen on my planet. They only happen on that planet I take my spaceship to each morning." [12]

As valuable as the emotional distance it permits, nondirectiveness also helps the genetic counselor maintain a discreet social distance from the second-trimester abortions that sometimes follow his or her intervention. Bosk observes that physicians who perform abortions are sometimes treated as pariahs. By not expressly recommending abortion, genetic counselors can claim that they are not directly involved, hence not responsible.[13]

Then there is the fact that most genetic counseling today is provided by women. Women more consistently cling to a nondirective stance than do men, and are more likely to defer to patients in the name of autonomy.[14] Why that is so is a matter for speculation. Perhaps women are more protective of other women's reproductive choices. Perhaps women counselors more easily establish good communication with their women clients, and this communicative openness fosters warmth and empathy. Whatever the explanation, the evidence we have suggests that genetic counseling has become largely a woman's profession and that the women who practice it find nondirectiveness congenial.[15]

Taken together, these factors cooperated to shape, and then to sustain, a norm of nondirectiveness in genetic counseling. Some would readily be counted as moral justifications—the desire to respect autonomy, the rough justice of placing the burden on those who make the decision. Most are nonmorally relevant reasons and causes—the urgent need to build a wall between genetic counseling and eugenics; the reluctance to delve more than necessary into this intensely personal realm; the crushing sadness attending genetic disorders (symbolized by the need to fly these heartaches to another planet); protection against the pariah status visited on some physicians who do abortions; and the impact of professional training, roles, and gender.

It would be a mistake to assume that the moral robustness of nondirectiveness is undermined simply because it has its roots in causes that have nothing in particular to do with ethics. But it would likewise be a mistake to rip nondirectiveness out of its social and historical context. After all, it is a practical moral principle. It says that in this realm, for these purposes, people who occupy this role should refrain from making any judgments or conveying any opinions about what their clients should do. In the real world we adopt and cling to principles in part because they offer decent answers to our moral concerns, but also in part because they respond to other nonmoral challenges. When the principle functions reasonably well in practice, I suspect that we remember its moral supports but soon lose sight of the nonmoral factors that may have been more decisive in its adoption in the first place.

Problems with Nondirectiveness in Genetic Counseling

Prenatal testing in the service of sex selection is a harbinger of the technique's future. When parents use prenatal diagnosis to select the sex of a child they almost always prefer a male. If prenatal testing reveals a female fetus, they will abort it. Using prenatal testing for the purpose of sex selection bothers many people, including staunch supporters of prenatal testing and of a public policy that leaves the choice whether to remain pregnant in the hands of the pregnant woman.[16] Moral queasiness about sex selection is not confined merely to the United States or to the West. At a 1990 meeting of physicians, scientists, ethicists, and government officials, under the auspices of the Council of International Organizations for Medical Sciences, sex selection was considered by the Working Group on Genetic Screening and Testing. The conference included representatives from twenty-four countries, including ten delegates from seven nations from the developing world. The Working Group had this to say about genetic techniques and services: "Their use for sex selection (other than to avoid X-linked diseases) is unwise and unethical and should be strongly discouraged."[17]

Dorothy C. Wertz and John C. Fletcher have done the most work on prenatal testing of anyone in bioethics, including a major international survey. They report that in India, the majority of prenatal testing was done for sex selection; indeed, "in the popular mind, prenatal diagnosis has become associated with sex selection rather than the discovery of genetic abnormality."[18] Wertz and Fletcher have been unflagging supporters of prenatal testing and reproductive choice for women. Precisely those commitments prompt them to oppose prenatal testing for sex selection:

It is important that the medical profession take a stand on sex selection, because a laissez-faire attitude could play into the hands of anti-abortion groups in many nations and could lead to restrictive laws preventing abortion, even for fetal malformation. In order to protect women's reproductive choices, and to affirm their equality, the profession will have to abandon its nonjudgmental stance and offer moral guidance. Not to do so would be irresponsible.[19]

This is an interesting argument, or rather two arguments. One is purely pragmatic: unless the profession takes a stand against sex selection, groups that oppose abortion will use public abhorrence at the practice to limit women's access to abortion. This argument says nothing about the ethics of sex selection itself.

The second argument bears more directly on ethics. It says we must oppose sex selection in order to affirm women's equality. Like the first argument, this one does not declare that using prenatal testing for sex selection is wrong per se. It says that in this world, where women often suffer at the hands of more powerful men, and where sex selection is used overwhelmingly to abort female fetuses, the practice of sex selection further degrades the status of women.

Suppose these circumstances were different. Suppose that, in the United States, half of the time people used prenatal sex selection because they wanted a girl rather than a boy. Wertz and Fletcher's moral argument seems to lose its force. In fact, if people used prenatal testing mostly to have daughters, would their argument be turned on its head? Would the logic of their argument then lead us to encourage sex selection as an affirmation of women's value?

I draw two tentative conclusions from this. First, even the most informed and thoughtful advocates of prenatal testing see sex selection as contrary to the goals of the practice. It is enough of a threat to the future of prenatal testing and abortion that the profession must set aside its policy of value neutrality. Second, a more careful exploration of the ethical justifications of prenatal testing is needed. If I am correct in thinking that people would be appalled at prenatal testing and abortion for sex selection whatever the proportion of female to male fetuses who survived, then we need to try to understand the roots of that reaction. We need to see if there are good moral reasons for opposing prenatal testing for sex selection.[20] We need to go beyond the arguments of Wertz and Fletcher, and beyond value neutrality and nondirectiveness as well.

A genetic counseling that insists it will remain staunchly neutral and make no value judgments functioned reasonably well in the past. After all, there were not that many conditions it could detect, and they were generally serious enough that if the prospective parents chose to abort a fetus with that condition, most people could understand the decision, even if they might have chosen otherwise. The clearest exception to the rule of moral gravity was sex selection. We have seen the difficulty that caused.

An ethic of nondirectiveness is wholly unprepared for the coming avalanche of genetic information. The difficulties it has in coping with adults who want to use it to choose the sex of their child will be multiplied, and then multiplied again as it becomes technically feasible to learn your fetus's hair and eye color, perhaps its projected adult height, or its tendency toward obesity. There will be genetic tests for susceptibilities to many diseases, such as heart disease and various cancers. There will be tests for diseases that occur very late in life, such as Alzheimer's. And suppose that people are convinced (with or without good evidence) that certain genes predict a range of behaviors or character traits, such as propensity toward substance abuse, homosexuality, or aggressiveness. What should genetic counselors do when they are asked to help test for such genes?

Jeremy Bentham, the philosopher and proponent of Utilitarianism, once declared that from the standpoint of his philosophy, push-pin (a game that apparently falls short of the intellectual challenge of tic-tac-toe) was as good as poetry. All that mattered was that individuals derived pleasure from it. Nondirectiveness applies a similar logic to children. 'Tis not the genetic counselor's business to judge whether any characteristic is a good enough reason to end a pregnancy, including whether the child would prefer push-pin or poetry. All that matters is that the prospective parents make a free and informed choice.

Nondirectiveness fails not only to provide any good reasons for opposing frivolous uses of prenatal testing, it positively forbids you from raising any moral objections, or making any moral judgments. It is less a moral principle than a principled suspension of morality: When it comes to prospective parents' decisions, we can neither suggest nor make for ourselves judgments of right or wrong. This is, I believe, a morally hazardous situation for genetic counselors and, ultimately, for all of us. Counselors will find it increasingly difficult to maintain their moral integrity without compromising the ideology of nondirectiveness. The rest of us, parents and children, will find the meaning of parenthood and the notion of an "acceptable," let alone a perfect, child changing in ways that we might renounce if we could see them clearly.

Beyond nondirectiveness's helplessness in the face of the coming flood of new genetic information, there are additional problems with it. For one thing, value-neutral nondirective counseling is premised on the claim that we can make a hard and fast distinction between facts, on the one hand, and values, on the other. To be value neutral, we need to know a value when we see it, and we need to know what we can say that is entirely free of values. But there is good reason to doubt that we can make such a neat separation between facts and values in practice, or even in principle.

The philosopher Dan Brock identifies three problems with the fact/ values distinction in the context of physician-patient relationships. First, a division of labor, with physicians concerned merely with supplying facts and patients with values, leaves "physicians' actions fully under the direction of patients."[21] Second is the claim that facts and values can always be distinguished in principle, and sufficiently so in practice that doctors can confine themselves to facts, leaving all value issues to the patients. Third, "the facts/values division of labor . . . assumes that the patient's values or account of the good is correct and so must be accepted and respected by the physician, whatever its content."[22]

Brock criticizes what he aptly dubs the "extreme subjectivity" implicit in the idea that people's values are beyond question or doubt. If we take individuals' notions of their values to be immune to criticisms that they may be false or mistaken in any way, then they can never be rejected as "incorrect, false, or unfounded."[23] Brock points out an often unnoticed implication of the belief in extreme subjectivity of values: if we deny the possibility of any basis for rejecting anyone's values as erroneous in any way, we also must accept that there can be no "basis for accepting them as correct, true, or well founded."[24] This presumption that values are beyond critique and incapable of being corrected— "incorrigible" in the language of moral philosophers—was popular among philosophers in the first half of this century. But it looks less and less plausible in recent years as its implications have been spelled out and its putative foundations undermined.[25] The details of the philosophical arguments are not so important here. What matters is that one of the conceptual underpinnings of nondirective genetic counseling looks exceedingly shaky—the claim that we can neatly divide the facts from the values, with counselors responsible for the facts and clients responsible for the values. Whether or not they *should* divvy up their tasks that way, it is far from certain that they ever *could*.

A strategy of nondirectiveness is naked and unprotected from the cultural whims of the moment. Whatever the current notions of what is desirable and undesirable in one's offspring may be, nondirectiveness has nothing within itself to offer even the feeblest protest. One consequence of increased prenatal diagnosis could be a general devaluation of difference. Congenital disabilities may come to be seen as not merely misfortunes, but eminently avoidable misfortunes. Disabled persons might become increasingly the object of anger and social disapproval.

Advocates for the disabled have been among the sharpest critics of prenatal diagnosis. The technology's principle purpose, after all, is to prevent the birth of people with disabilities. Discussions of prenatal diagnosis and disability commonly understate the enormous diversity of conditions lumped together under the rubric "disability." Champions of prenatal diagnosis highlight devastating genetic diseases such as Lesch-Nyhan and Tay-Sachs. Advocates for disabled persons are more apt to stress the many conditions compatible with happy, warm, and productive lives, including spina bifida, deafness, blindness, and Down's syndrome.

Adrienne Asch's work is a sparkling exception to this trend. Asch reminds us that although biological disability is an undeniable reality, it is only one factor among many that affect disabled persons and their families. Other factors—familial and social resources, attitudes of others, and the presence or absence of physical and social barriers to persons with disabilities—typically exert much greater influence on the person's quality of life. Asch urges us to focus on what we value in becoming parents and on what "frightens, repulses, or distresses us about disability in others, in ourselves, and in those close to us." She writes,

Seeking to avoid the experience of raising disabled children is no crime or callous, selfish statement, as some may claim. It is an honest, understandable, if perhaps misinformed, response to the fears that a disabled child will not fulfill what many women seek in mothering—to give ourselves to a new being who starts out with the best we can give, and who will enrich us, gladden others, contribute to the world, and make us proud.[26]

Asch points us in the direction I believe we must go in order to understand the place of prenatal diagnosis. She urges us to "frame our thinking about prenatal diagnosis and selective abortion in a sincere discussion of what we long for in the experience of having children. Let us then ask how a child's disability will compromise that dream." We need to look at what we value in parenthood and family life—at the worth of a child, and at the impact on those values of the quest for the "perfect" child.

Perfectibilism and Parenthood

At least three kinds of reasons are offered in support of prenatal diagnosis. The first emphasizes the suffering a fetus is likely to endure if it is brought to birth. Sometimes the claim is made that a child would be "better off not being born." This notion draws its strength from a disease such as Lesch-Nyhan, a progressive neurological disorder that leads to death in early childhood, but is preceded by often horrible self-mutilation in which the conscious and self-aware child may destroy his or her own lips and fingers despite the urgent desire not to do so.

The simple reality of prenatal diagnosis, however, is that most of the conditions detectable prenatally are not so bleak as Lesch-Nyhan or Tay-Sachs, another disease with a dismal prospect of early deterioration and death. People with Down's syndrome, for example, may have medical complications and experience learning difficulties. But their lives are not unrelievedly dismal; most people with Down's syndrome can experience joy, growth, and love. As the power of prenatal genetic diagnosis grows, it is likely to extend away from conditions such as Lesch-Nyhan and Tay-Sachs and toward conditions whose impact is diffused by being merely probable rather than certain, by being treatable or preventable, by showing their first symptoms only in midadulthood if not later, or by only a modest or mild degree of impairment, if they can be regarded rightly as an "impairment" at all.

Advocates for the disabled, many of whom wholeheartedly support legal protection for a woman's freedom to decide whether she wants to have a child, argue that the problem is not with that legal right, but with the system within which it is exercised. Adrienne Asch believes that "the whole genetics enterprise is permeated by the medical model of disability—linking every difficulty to the physiological characteristics of the condition and not to any characteristic of the society in which people with the condition live their lives."[27] Living with a disability, advocates claim, is something that genetic counselors may know little or nothing about. Lisa Blumberg points out that counselors are likely to work in medical settings and to know disabled persons only in those settings "where the emphasis is on the person's dysfunction and where the treatment . . . may be unpleasant." She continues, "Counselors have only minimal awareness that people with disabilities have roles other than as patients, and that there are hundreds of thousands of congenitally disabled people who are attending school, going to work, having relationships, and supporting elderly parents."[28] Listing her core beliefs about genetic screening and prenatal diagnosis, Asch includes "that those wishing to use the technology should receive substantially more information about life with disability than they now do" and "that professionals who fail to provide such information conduct their work in a manner that approaches the unprofessional and unethical."[29]

By its very nature, prenatal diagnosis cannot remain neutral about disability. At a minimum it conveys the message that society believes that living with a disability, or raising a child with a disability, is such a grave burden that it is morally permissible and medically appropriate to take expensive measures to ensure that such children are not born. Why else would we train entire professions to do this work, make the technology widely available, and issue official recommendations about when such screening and testing ought to be done? But the claim that prenatal testing and abortion for fetal abnormality can be justified because life with a genetic defect is not worth living is far from self-evident. Indeed, genetic counseling as currently practiced may give a misleadingly bleak view of life with a disability. The conditions for which life might genuinely be a burden to the person living it are relatively few—the exception rather than the rule.[30]

A second reason people might give for using prenatal diagnosis to avoid the birth of a seriously afflicted child is to avert the deleterious impact it might have on themselves as well as on other children in the family. Parents are finite human beings and they possess finite resources—emotional, physical, and financial. An exceptionally needy child might take up so much of the parents' emotional and physical energy, as well as their financial resources, that they would not be able to meet their other children's needs. Nor would they be able to achieve a decently good life for themselves.

Some limitations on this line of argument are immediately apparent. The concern for other children in a family is relevant only if there are now or will be such children. Also, the fact that one of their siblings was needier than they would not be unequivocally bad for them. They could learn a great deal from that brother or sister about love, and about understanding differences. They might acquire experience in caring, in learning how to reach out beyond their own selfish interests. Their parents might provide models of steadfast nurturing. These virtues could serve them—and their family and society—very well as they mature into adulthood. The burdensomeness of a disabled sibling would be a matter of degree, as well as a function of whether the community offered the kinds and intensity of support that would leave parents with sufficient strength to care for all the children in the family.[31] At bottom, the attempt to justify prenatal diagnosis by invoking the harm done to other children or, for that matter, to parents applies only to very severe and demanding conditions, and only in the context of a society unwilling to assist such families adequately.

Preventing the birth of a child who would suffer terribly from a particular genetic abnormality and averting the harm that might befall the siblings of such a child as their parents are strained beyond their limits function best as arguments in favor of prenatal diagnosis for severe afflictions only. They are not compelling and cogent reasons to screen for moderate or mild disorders, and not at all relevant to testing for traits, such as gender, that are not diseases.

If a defense of nondirective counseling is to be found for such conditions and traits, it must lie elsewhere. It lies, I suspect, in one understanding of the meaning of parenthood—an understanding that grants to prospective parents the moral permission to seek a child as near-perfect as possible, leaving it to those prospective parents to make their own definition of "perfection." There is an irony here. This model of selective parenthood seems to reject unconditional acceptance as the proper attitude for prospective parents to have toward their offspring. Yet unconditional acceptance, or as Carl Rogers put it, unconditional positive regard, is at the heart of the same Rogerian psychotherapy that helped spawn nondirective genetic counseling, and indeed gave it its name. It seems that what is appropriate for the goose and the gander does not apply to the goslings.

The quest for perfection in Western culture is an ancient one, with roots in Greek philosophy long before Socrates. The desire to make perfect people and perfect societies already encompassed genetic controls in Plato's imaginary Republic—determining who could and could not have offspring. Through most of Western history, the quest for perfection took the shape of a spiritual or metaphysical striving. More recently, the search for human perfectibility allied itself with the ideas of science and of progress. John Passmore, in his definitive study of perfectibilism in Western culture describes it:

There gradually developed, then, in the eighteenth century a chain of inference which ran thus: Man had until that time been a mere child in respect of knowledge and, in consequence, of virtue; he was now at last in a position, as a result of the development of science, to determine how human nature develops and what is the best thing for human beings to do; this new knowledge could be expressed in a form in which all men would act accordingly and so would constantly improve their moral, political and physical condition. Provided only, then, that "sinister interests" did not prevent the communication of knowledge, the development of science was bound to carry with it the constant improvement of the human condition, to a degree which would be, like the growth of science itself, unlimited.[32]

The quest for perfection was primed and ready to meet modern science in the form of genetics. Indeed, in their hubris, some of the modern champions of genetic progress echo the spiritual nature of the historical quest for human perfectibility. H. J. Muller, an early eugenicist, claimed that "by working in functional alliance with our genes, we may attain to modes of thought and living that today would seem inconceivably godlike."[33]

Does the contemporary quest for the perfect child via prenatal diagnosis bear any resemblance to other forms of perfectibilism? It seems very different in many ways from the ancient philosopher Parmenides' idea of the perfect divine being as eternal, simple, indivisible, and spherelike, or Plato's notion of perfection as the contemplation and knowledge of the ideal forms, of which the things of this world are but imperfect representations. Yet, in other important ways, the desire for the perfect child through genetic technology has much in common with these millennia-old efforts to seek perfection.

The quest for the perfect child is a form of what Passmore calls "immaculate" perfectibilism, the desire to attain something that is wholly without flaw. For modern people, science has replaced pure knowledge and the divine as the means to the end of perfection. Yet what has motivated the quest for perfectibility, and the dangers that come with unquestioning acceptance of perfectibilism, may not have changed all that much. Passmore notes that the perfectibilists "have tried to persuade themselves that they 'lack nothing' by rejecting as worthless all that this world contains. The achievement of perfection has been identified with the development of a capacity for standing aside from life, rising above it."[34] Diogenes Laertius, for example, saw human emotions and relationships as a fundamental threat to equanimity, to peace of mind. He counseled those who aspired to perfection to become passionless and to make "no allowance for anyone."[35] Only in the radical retreat from all human ties and feelings was there any hope for escape from hurt and disappointment.

If one's goal is to disentangle oneself from human ties, having a child is either stupid or perverse. With so much at stake in their children, modern parents, like earlier perfectibilists, might want to protect themselves against the hurt and disappointment that they fear a child with a disability or disfigurement might bring. But is the worth of the parent-child relationship to be judged by how successfully it avoids unpleasantness and totes up its pleasures? If so, and if prospective parents could foretell accurately which attributes in their offspring would yield the optimal sum of pleasures minus unpleasantnesses, then an argument of a kind could be made for permitting a maximum of discretion in prenatal diagnosis. But if the worth of that relationship should be judged on other criteria, then unfettered parental discretion is not so easily justified.

Are we better off if we regard our children as carefully and willfully produced, with just the right characteristics? Or does that nudge the parent-child relationship away from being a relationship between persons united by biology, custom, or law to more of an acquisitionlike relationship? In the former, parents and children create value by their mutual caring and maturation. In the latter, the value is measured by the desirable properties of the object—the child—thus acquired.

The more we come to see our children's characteristics as the product of choice, the more vulnerable we become to the likelihood—indeed, the near-certainty—of disappointment. Life is simply too complex, its dangers too varied, and the wrenches of emotional development, the search for identity, and the need for separation and independence too certain. The desire to prevent hurt and sadness intruding into our relationship with our children is a futile fantasy at its heart. To the extent that prenatal diagnosis reflects the perfectibilist desire to avoid hurt, it is doomed to suffer the fate of other versions of perfectibilism. It fails one of the fundamental tests for any proposed ethic of parent-child relationships—*lucidity*. Any worthwhile account of the meaning of parenthood and the worth of a child must be consistent with what we know about the realities of human psychology, development, and culture as well as the behavior of institutions.

An ethic of parent-child relationships should also be sustainable. That is, it should support institutions and practices that lead to the development of healthy families and individuals, who in turn can raise their own physically vigorous and emotionally sound children, with the cycle of generations continuing on indefinitely. The quest for the perfect child may fail on this count as well. Parents may become less tolerant of children who do not meet whatever standard of perfection is

popular at the moment. Those same parents are likely to feel more responsibility and guilt over their child's imperfections. In many cases,
the guilt will impede further the love and acceptance that is necessary
for a child's emotional maturity and self-confidence. Other people in
turn may become less forgiving of such imperfections, and social institutions may come to reflect those harsher attitudes by diminishing support for children with problems, and their parents. In light of the enduring reality of our lack of control, and the myth of perfectibility, such
changes would diminish, not enhance, social support for families when
they most need it.

The quest for perfection has been spurred by a desire to escape the
limitations and especially the hurts that mark indelibly our existence as
finite, embodied, interdependent beings. The danger in that quest is
that we can become so attracted to some suprahuman idea or entity
that we lose sight of, or even come to have contempt for, the actual,
flawed, and vulnerable human beings with whom we live. Passmore
offers this warning: "often enough . . . men have sought to demonstrate their love for God by loving nothing at all and their love for
humanity by loving nobody whatsoever. These are the men to be feared
above all others—the Robespierres who 'love humanity,' the Inquisi-
tors who 'love God.' " [36]

Passmore urges us to judge a society "on the quality of the loves it
exhibits and fosters." He admits that societies can foster the love of
power, money, or status, but these he calls "low-grade" societies. [37] In
its classical forms, perfectibilism sought to perfect humankind by strip-
ping it of all or nearly all of its human qualities. Modern scientific perfectibilists have had a comparable faith that their methods have the
power either to banish human frailty and evil or at least to put us on
the path of continuous and unending progress. These modern perfecti-
bilisms, like their classical antecedents, often lose sight of the "little
loves" that Passmore believes, as do I, constitute "the highest form of
human activity" we finite beings can achieve. [38] The contemporary
quest for the child without flaw—the immaculate child—is a manifestation of scientific perfectibilism that has elevated science and individual
choice above those not-so-"little loves" that bind parents and children.

Once we reject perfectibilism, we can embrace a conception of parenthood as the sustained effort to work out unmistakably human relationships, that is, relationships devoted to fostering love, dedication,
and mutuality, in the face of ever-present imperfection, ambivalence,
and disappointment. This conception, I think, passes the test of lucidity

at the same time as it promotes the growth of supportive social attitudes and institutions, as well as strong and virtuous individuals.

The desire to avoid "imperfections" in our children is not unambiguously wrong. But it is ambiguous. It has a largely unacknowledged dark side. Beyond that, an ethic of nondirective prenatal counseling, in the service of genetic perfectibilism, surrenders to individual whim the community's shared understandings of the worth of a child, the values to be found in family life, and the meaning of parenthood. What alterations can we make to prenatal diagnosis and counseling that preserve those values?

What Should Be the Future of Prenatal Diagnosis?

The modern conception of parenthood has raised our stake in having children without major flaws. Most of us, especially those of us likely to utilize prenatal diagnosis, will have fewer children than did earlier families. We want each of our children to do well, be happy, and become a source of lifelong satisfaction. We take our moral relationships with each of our children with increasing seriousness. This is mostly to the good, I believe. But it does mean that we may be less willing to have a child whose care may become a burden, or whose life may be marked by more difficulties than we would wish.

Where, then, should we draw the boundaries around prenatal diagnosis? Is it possible to practice this technology without falling prey to the temptations of perfectibilism? I believe that it is, but first we must make a distinction between *what kinds* of genetic information will be offered and the *manner* in which it is offered. To put that another way, we have two problems we need to solve. First, we need to decide what limits, if any, to place on prospective parents' access to genetic information. If parents may inquire about grave disorders such as Tay-Sachs, may they also satisfy their curiosity about late-onset diseases, gender, or eye color? We will need to create a fair process in order to determine what genetic information will and will not be made available. Second and separately, we need to ask how professionals should conduct themselves within the counseling encounter. Should counselors actively press prospective parents to do what they, the counselors, believe is right? Should they encourage them to consider the ethical implications of the choices they make? Or should they fastidiously avoid raising any and all value questions in the effort to remain value-free and nondirective?

Should there be limits on the kinds of genetic information available to prospective parents? There are some afflictions that rapidly darken and ultimately shroud the lives of all children born with them. There are other afflictions that impose severe burdens both on the children born with them and the adults who care for those children. Conditions such as these are more than merely arbitrary matters of distaste: they can profoundly affect the possibility that the child, its parents, or its siblings will have any chance to flourish; that the family into which such a child is born will be unable to achieve the values for which people make families. In these cases, wisdom seems to lie with allowing the prospective parents to decide whether to continue with the pregnancy.

What of conditions or traits that impose serious but not grave burdens? Here the arguments that draw their strength from the suffering of the afflicted child, its siblings, and their parents are less certain and compelling. The specter of perfectibilism raises its head, especially as we approach the less severe end of the continuum. In cases such as these, policy considerations tip the balance in favor of parental discretion. As the burden of raising a child with major disabilities is most likely to fall on the prospective parents, especially the prospective mother, it is most reasonable to err on the side of that likely caregiver and to permit her to make the decisions whether to undergo prenatal diagnosis and whether, in light of the results, to continue the pregnancy. At the same time, we must provide community support for families raising children with disabilities. Perfectibilism will be less of a temptation when we are confident that having a child with a disability will not lead to emotional, physical, or economic ruin.

Where, and on what grounds, can we set limits? Value-free nondirectiveness can give no strong reasons for drawing lines anywhere on the continuum from devastating afflictions to mild or moderate ones or to traits like eye color or gender. But there are compelling reasons for drawing such lines. First, choice is a good in context, not a good in itself. It is certainly not an ultimate good that needs no further justification. It is not sufficient to invoke our cultural predilection for individual choice as a justification for unlimited parental discretion in prenatal diagnosis, especially in the sphere of family life in which choice plays only a limited role.

Second, counselors remain accountable moral agents, even when acting as counselors. They cannot renounce their individual consciences or their obligations as professionals merely by invoking client autonomy. If there is good reason to believe that particular choices are wrong, counselors who abet such choices by providing the information in a manner that implies it is morally neutral are in fact conveying a message about the moral acceptability of the particular action. Counselors who, for example, aid in sex selection declare implicitly that this is within the permissible moral frame.

Third, counselors have good reason to be suspicious of the quest for the immaculately perfect child. The quest is misguided and probably doomed to failure; it is a contemporary variant of a perfectibilism that seeks to escape from the contingency that permeates human existence. It is also at odds with what is genuinely valuable in this sphere, the development of strong, abiding, and loving relationships in the face of our numerous imperfections and disappointments.

In short, we should not offer to provide prenatally information about traits or afflictions that are not substantial burdens on parent and child. We certainly should not assist couples in a misguided quest for the child that embodies their ideal collection of traits, including gender. So how should we draw the line?

It would not be good to allow the line to be drawn according to the whim of each individual genetic counselor. That would be no advance over the whims of prospective parents. The standard to be created is clearly a social standard, not a narrowly professional one. Whatever process we develop to create these standards must respond to the major deficiencies in our current practices, for example, the fact that important voices are excluded—especially the voices of people with disabilities.

We want a process that is well informed and fair. To be informed it must include people who understand what it is like to live with a congenital disability, as well as what it is like to raise a child with a disability. It must take into account the likelihood that genetics professionals may be more familiar with grave disabilities and struggling families than with moderate or mild disabilities or with families that are flourishing with their disabled children. We need, that is, not merely technical and clinical expertise, but the experiences of people with disabilities and their families.[39] To be fair, the process should incorporate the perspectives of those with a significant stake in prenatal diagnosis and its outcomes.

What if a group of persons were brought together who best understood, because they lived it, what it means to be or to have a child with

a disability? Suppose there were a regular meeting of genetic counselors, who could represent the integrity of their profession, with persons
with disabilities, parents raising children with disabilities, and people
who had chosen to end a pregnancy because of a prenatally diagnosed
condition. The conversation within that group would be interesting.
The group would be in a position, based on their respective experiences, to give a realistic account of disability and of prenatal diagnosis
and counseling. We could ask such a group to suggest where the line
might best be drawn. Their deliberations could form the basis of a policy not to offer prenatal testing for traits or conditions below that line.

The Genetic Counseling Encounter

Suppose that professionals such as genetic counselors and
medical geneticists accept something like the proposal I have made.
They will perform prenatal diagnosis, but only for serious or grave conditions, as agreed upon by a lay-professional consensus group. What
impact would such a policy have on the counseling encounter? How
should counselors deal with ethical issues that arise?

Counselors no longer would have to struggle with a conflict between
a concern, on the one hand, that certain uses of their skills, like sex
selection, are wrong and an ideology of nondirectiveness, on the other,
that declares that their moral views are irrelevant. Sex selection, I am
confident, would be banned, as would prenatal testing for other traits
not linked to serious disease or disability. Because we will have prohibited testing for medically trivial conditions, the primary tasks for counselors will be similar to what they are today—a combination of education and supportive counseling.

Difficult moral decisions will remain. Prospective parents will have
to probe the depths of their own character, assess the resources available
to them, and weigh the needs and interests of their children, partners,
and themselves. Anguished deliberations take place, no doubt, in families, between couples, and within individuals as they wrestle with what
is right and what they can bear. Should counselors encourage prospective parents to consider these questions?

There is an important reality here: I expect that many, probably
most, prospective parents regard the decision whether to continue a
pregnancy as a morally serious matter. Counseling sessions that avoid

engaging the moral dimensions of that choice tacitly communicate either that these questions are *not* really important or else that they are merely matters of taste, with no possibility that they might be right or wrong.

We want counselors to be supportive and understanding. We do not want them proselytizing for their own idiosyncratic moral views. But there is a profound difference between trying to impose your moral judgments on choices that already have been judged to be complex and balanced by a fair and informed process and encouraging prospective parents to reflect on the moral substance of their decisions. The latter does not "impose" moral judgments on others. Instead it shows respect for prospective parents as moral agents. It acknowledges the moral dimension of their decisions. And it recognizes that thoughtful people struggle with decisions about prenatal diagnosis and abortion and that it is better for them if we affirm their struggle, rather than deny it. .

This is not a perfect solution, but then there is no perfect solution available for us highly imperfect beings. It would be, however, a considerable improvement over our current practice of unilateral moral disarmament and the fruitless and dangerous pursuit of genetic perfectibilism. It would be a policy based on relevant experience and defensible reasons, one that would support, not undermine, our best understandings of the worth of a child and the meaning of parenthood.

7

Abortion and the Place
of Motherhood

---

*Fetuses are not persons. They are the biological products of
persons.*

    —H. Tristram Engelhardt, *The Foundations
of Bioethics*

*When Susan Smith drove her two babies into a pond, murdering
them . . . it was the moral equivalent to what happens every time
a person has an abortion.*

    —Rev. Dennis Kristof, "Orthodox Speak
against 22 Years of a Barbarity"

*[T]his round of the abortion debate is so passionate and hard-
fought because it is a referendum on the place and meaning of
motherhood.*

    —Kristin Luker, *Abortion and the Politics of
Motherhood*

    Imagine that someone introduced an argument into the
debate over whether fetuses are persons that persuaded virtually everyone. People on the opposing side abandoned their position and con-
ceded that their opponents were, in fact, right. Abortion ceased to be a
divisive political issue. Both pro-life and pro-choice groups disbanded
because there was nothing left to fight about.

  This is an unlikely scenario, for at least two powerful reasons. First,
there is little or no prospect of some important new argument in the
debate about fetal personhood. So many arguments have been tried

out, without success, that the chance that one will appear which addresses fetal personhood in an utterly novel yet compelling way is exceedingly remote. If we follow the conventional wisdom—that differences over the ethics of abortion are best explained by different beliefs about whether fetuses are persons—there is little hope for accommodation or social peace.

Second, it is not at all certain that even a terrifically creative, pertinent argument would convince anyone who has strong feelings about abortion—whether pro-life or pro-choice. We could dismiss those who do not respond to this marvelous new hypothetical argument as ornery, stupid, or both. But consider another possibility: that people's beliefs about fetal personhood are neither decided on purely philosophical or religious grounds nor readily isolated from other beliefs and commitments that are central to our culture's differences over abortion.

If we take fetal personhood to be the principal and decisive question, we do not have many promising choices about what to do next. We could abandon serious moral dialogue, the effort to persuade those who do not agree with us, and resort either to raw political battles or, as some have now done, to violence. We could persist in the struggle to invent some new argument that would prove conclusively that fetuses are—or are not—moral persons, a struggle that has proven futile thus far despite the enormous investment of energy and intelligence devoted to it. Or we could look for some other avenue that might not be the blind alley fetal personhood has proven to be. Simple prudence and a desire to avoid further bloodshed ought to be sufficient motivations to look for alternatives. But we have additional reasons to doubt whether metaphysical disputes about fetal personhood are actually at the heart of the conflict. We need to consider why activists focus on the moral status of fetuses. Is it because this is *the* fundamental philosophical question, with all other morally relevant considerations secondary to or derivative from it? Or is it possible that this metaphysical belief is part and parcel of a network of beliefs and commitments and that there are other explanations of why it, rather than other components of that network, plays such a prominent role in the American debate over abortion?

In this chapter I want to take seriously the possibility that metaphysical beliefs about the personhood of fetuses do not drive the abortion debate; that, instead, they are carried along with a complex of other beliefs and commitments, especially with profoundly important views about what gives meaning and shape to the lives of women. Our beliefs about the metaphysical status of fetuses do not determine our views about what constitutes human flourishing for women. At most, they are concurrent with them. It is even possible that our commitments about moral personhood and fetuses are as much the product of these other commitments as the cause. Our customary way of thinking about moral disagreements prompts us to look up—to the highly abstract and general concepts and beliefs that presumably determine our everyday moral decisions. But this top-down approach is not the only way to think about our practical moral reasoning. Employing the metaphor of tapestry and web yields quite a different view of the abortion debate and of the place of fetal personhood within it.

Understanding Abortion: Tapestry and Web versus Top-Down Ethics

The conventional wisdom about abortion assumes that the crux of the dispute is over a single issue, whether the fetus is a person. All other important commitments—whether abortion is murder, whether it should be illegal, whether women should or should not be permitted to choose whether to have an abortion—follow from this central premise. That, at least, is the conventional wisdom. It implicitly assumes a "top-down" model of moral reasoning. Top-down ethics stresses the importance of supposedly fundamental theoretical considerations. All that is important flows downward from the high perch of our most general commitments and theory. Particular facts about the problem are relevant in determining what general theoretical considerations are pertinent, but that is their sole function. From the perspective of top-down ethics, a focus on the social context of a moral controversy is more likely to be a distraction than an illumination.

Consider an alternative view: that our attitudes toward abortion, including our beliefs about fetal personhood, are part of an interrelated network of beliefs including images portrayed on the tapestry that depicts the good and the bad in human lives. To be sure, there are threads in the tapestry representing our convictions about the moral status of fetuses, but they are woven in among other threads to make up pictures of individuals and families—of children, women, and men—of their flourishing, as well as of their withering and suffering. The threads that carry our conceptions of human flourishing are every bit as important in determining the pictures that appear on the tapestry as our metaphysical beliefs about when personhood begins. Our views about gender differences, about what gives meaning to the lives of women that might differ from what structures the lives of men, make an enormous differ ence in what images appear on the tapestry.

We know that this difference is not merely hypothetical. In an insightful and groundbreaking study of activists on both sides of the abortion issue, Kristin Luker found that they differed dramatically on several matters. Above all else, they disagreed about women's nature, about what constituted flourishing for women, and most especially about the place of motherhood in women's lives. Abortion opponents believed that women were largely defined by their capacity for motherhood and that flourishing for women was to be found in an openness to motherhood. Activists who favored legal abortion believed that women's flourishing depended on their having a choice whether to compete in the job market with men. They also believed that uncontrolled fertility was the single greatest threat to successful economic competition.[1]

Those views were every bit as central and clear in the two camps as any metaphysical convictions about fetal personhood. Indeed, views about women's flourishing, which implied views about men's nature and the differences between the genders, touch directly more vital parts of our daily lives and social institutions than any abstract dispute about when personhood begins. What happens if we take seriously the possibility that the metaphysical arguments about personhood are no more central, indeed perhaps less so, than disagreements about what images of women's flourishing belong on the tapestry?

Look for a moment at how we justify our conclusions in practical, everyday moral discourse. The top-down approach instructs us first to identify and defend our most abstract theoretical premises. From those general presumptions, we can then deduce our conclusions about what to do in particular practical situations.

In the top-down view, the reasoning of abortion opponents would look something like this:

1. Fetuses are persons who deserve the same moral concern and protection as all other persons. (The thesis about fetal personhood.)

2. Intentionally killing a person is wrong, in the absence of compelling reasons to justify it (such as killing in a just war, or to protect innocent life).

3. Abortion is the intentional killing of a person, deserving exactly the same level of moral concern and outrage as any other intentional killing of a person.

In this view, the biological fact that fetuses are inside women's bodies is not especially important. Fetal personhood and the wrongness of intentional killing are the central moral considerations; everything else is secondary.

The moral reasoning of those who defend legalized abortion is not so easy to represent. Probably the most common strategy is to attack the first premise, that is, to deny that fetuses are persons in the moral sense. This strategy joins the battle on the ground of metaphysics, and it is the strategy I want to question. It should be noted that other strategies have also been tried. Some have asked what happens if we grant that a fetus might be a person and argued that, under some circumstances, a pregnant woman has no greater moral obligation to provide the use of her body to keep that fetus alive than we would be obliged to give the use of our body to maintain a stranger's life.[2] Another strategy has been to argue that even if some or all abortions are *morally* wrong, nevertheless there are compelling reasons why it should remain legal. Former Governor of New York Mario Cuomo offered a widely reported version of this defense of legal abortion.[3]

Each of these analyses of the abortion debate accepts explicitly or implicitly that a top-down model of moral reasoning is the appropriate one. It is certainly true that we can usually reconstruct our moral reasoning to resemble top-down arguments. That is, we can look for and find quite abstract premises to buttress our practical conclusions. But top-down ethics may be neither a particularly good description of how practical moral reasoning actually proceeds nor a guide to how to do good—by which I mean insightful as well as nondefective—practical moral reasoning.[4] Examining the relation between our theoretical, abstract commitments and our practical moral judgments helps ensure that we are not being inconsistent. But those commitments do not provide a detailed map for practical decisions.

Conceiving of practical moral reasoning as relying on tapestries and webs affords a useful perspective. When we try to reason about complex practical problems, we construct webs made up of many kinds of considerations, including threads borrowed from the tapestry. We want to build as sturdy and regular a web as we can. Fetal personhood is only one strand in the web holding our moral judgments about abortion.

The threads representing our convictions about good lives for women, men, and children constitute most of the web. I also believe that those threads and the images on the tapestry from which they are borrowed give a more powerful account of both the content of our differences over abortion and the stunning emotional power those differences carry.

The Metaphysics of Personhood: H. Tristram Engelhardt and Paul Hill

What happens when you begin with the presumption that the metaphysical question of fetal personhood is the essential issue? You could go in either of two directions. You could deny that fetuses are persons, and follow through the implications of that conclusion. This is the road taken by H. Tristram Engelhardt and some other theorists. Or you could assert that fetuses are morally protectable persons, and trace the implications of that position, as abortion opponents do, including the claim that physicians who perform abortions are murderers. Some take the further step of arguing that violence against abortion providers is morally justified. And a few, such as Paul Hill, act on that conclusion.

Engelhardt's magnum opus is titled *The Foundations of Bioethics*. It is clever and thorough and based on a concept of personhood that makes the capacity for reason the central attribute. Having captured what he thinks is the essence of personhood, Engelhardt develops his theory around what he calls "persons in the strict sense," that is, autonomous, competent, rational adults. What moral consideration is due others—the demented, young children, fetuses, and all others who are not rational, autonomous, and competent—is entirely dependent on their relevance to true persons. In other words, embryos and fetuses, as well as children, are objects of moral concern only secondarily; their welfare is hostage to the interests and whims of "persons in the strict sense."

For Engelhardt, then, it follows that "abortion is not a serious moral issue. It is not possible to justify, in general secular terms, holding embryos and fetuses to be persons. At the beginning of human life, as at the end of life, one will need emotionally to come to terms with the intellectual realization that human biological life is not coincident with the life of persons."[5] He makes his stance clear: "Fetuses are not persons. They are the biological products of persons."[6] The connotation of "product" as property is not accidental. For Engelhardt, as it was for the philosopher John Locke, the object we own most unequivocally is our body. It is no surprise then that he believes "next to one's own body, the sperm, ova, zygotes, and fetuses one produces are most primordially one's own."[7] The commercial implications are straightforward: "Privately produced embryos and fetuses are private property."[8] Thus we may do just as we like with them, as long as we do not violate Engelhardt's supreme commandment: thou shalt not impose thy will on unconsenting "persons in the strict sense." As for embryos, fetuses, and young children, there are no strictly moral barriers to whatever we want to do with them. We may destroy them, sell them, exhibit them, or experiment on them.

Given the way Engelhardt has framed the issue—his views on personhood, property, and the sovereignty of the individual will—justifying any limitations on what persons do with their embryos and fetuses will be nigh impossible. The only beings that count morally are his "persons in the strict sense." For him the moral authority of any constraints on those he regards as real persons will be weak and derivative. We would have to justify restrictions on the grounds that his "persons in the strict sense" somehow consented to them.

Not surprisingly, Engelhardt would give parents of impaired infants enormous leeway in deciding whether to authorize their children's deaths. Infants, like fetuses and embryos, are not persons according to Engelhardt. Not just severely impaired infants; all infants. If it is all right to kill or sell or experiment on fetuses, is it also all right to do the same with infants? The answer seems to be yes. Engelhardt writes, "It is difficult to mount a plausible, nonculturally biased, strong argument against infanticide."[9] Though he allows that particular communities can create rules limiting infanticide, his own account of the centrality of persons and property, and of the severely limited authority of the state, would seem to bar almost all interference with the "owners' "— that is, parents or those to whom they have transferred ownership— alleged rights to do whatever they want with their "property." He grants that we may be in for some surprising results if we accept his theory: "The more one takes the freedom of individuals seriously, the more one will need to take seriously as well the moral standing of the family as a free association of persons who have rights to judge regarding those of its members who are not persons in the strict sense."[10]

Engelhardt carries the notion of family autonomy as far as it can go. Within the terms of Engelhardt's ethics, it is impossible to find any compelling moral reasons to ban such practices as the sale of children and infants or, for that matter, using newborns and young children as organ repositories to be harvested for the benefit of his "persons in the strict sense," as long as we made sure they were dead before they became full persons. I cannot even find in Engelhardt's moral theory any compelling reason to object to selling one's baby to a person who wished to kill it painlessly and use it for fertilizer. What is crucial to Engelhardt is that the transaction take place with full consent between the "strict sense" persons involved. Everything else is secondary, weak, and derivative.

The problems with Engelhardt's ideas on abortion are typical of strategies that take personhood to be the centrally relevant question in the abortion debate, and then proceed to deny the status of personhood to fetuses and embryos. If we accept this version of the top-down approach as the proper way to frame the problem, one urgent question immediately arises: What distinguishes infants and young children from fetuses and embryos? We must then try to discern what are the distinctive, essential moral qualities that make a person a person. The search for some essence of personhood has a great deal of difficulty making the case that a late-stage fetus is radically different in its capacities from a newborn infant. If it denies the honored status of personhood to fetuses, it denies it to babies as well. Engelhardt and a few other theorists do not seem to be bothered by this implication of their quest to define personhood. Many other people would find in such a conclusion good reason to doubt or to reject completely his entire account of ethics.[11]

In contrast to Engelhardt's strict—dare we say stingy?—reservation of the elevated moral status of personhood to rational, mature adults stands the unqualified ascription of personhood to embryos and fetuses by abortion opponents. One of the favored rhetorical tactics is to refer to abortion at all stages of embryonic and fetal development as killing an "unborn baby." Methods of contraception that prevent fertilized embryos from implanting in the uterus, to be consistent, also would have to be regarded as killing unborn children. Some pro-life advocates accept this implication of their position. The movement as a whole, however, recognizes that making opposition to contraception a featured part of their public platform would be unpalatable to many people. So groups such as the National Right to Life Committee (NRLC) that are not exclusively tied to one religious group that opposes contraception like the Roman Catholic church take no public stand against contraception. Nonetheless, the claim that embryos as well as fetuses are full moral persons remains a crucial part of the pro-life movement's scholarship [12] and its lay rhetoric. [13]

In an article arguing against abortion, the Reverend Dennis Kristof referred to a story that was gripping the nation at the time. A young mother had reported to police that her car with her two young children inside had been stolen by a carjacker. A nationwide search failed to find the boys. Finally, she admitted that she had sent her car into a lake with her children inside strapped in their car seats. To the horror of millions of Americans, the car, with the two bodies in it, was pulled from the water. For Kristof, the murder of those children was nothing less than "the moral equivalent to what happens every time a person has an abortion." [14] In the same brief article he uses words like *barbarity* and *atrocity* and makes the analogy to Nazi genocide.

Kristof's choice of language and analogies is well within the mainstream of pro-life writings. Wanda Franz, president of the National Right to Life Committee, refers to "the horrific reality of privatized killing by abortion," arguing that "pro-abortionists speak of 'terminating a pregnancy' in order to obscure what they really want: a dead child." She urges her readers to "unmask this chilling pro-abortion rhetoric and remind our fellow citizens again and again that abortion kills, and that the victim is a beautiful human being in the womb." [15] Franz asserts that being human is inseparable from being a person and that arguments otherwise are just "pseudophilosophical assertions." In the same publication, its editor, Dave Andrusko, argues that we need to be reminded that people who perform abortions "do evil, inhuman acts to real, human babies. That the act of tearing precious preborn children limb from limb has evolved from what was once billed as a 'tragic dilemma' to a routine act of stomach-turning violence which literally knows no bounds. . . . In short, of the utter necessity to be outraged by this systematic campaign of torture and gross abuse of human rights." [16]

The same issue that featured these denunciations of abortion with graphic language about mutilation, torture, and dead children also featured a condemnation of the murder of Dr. David Gunn, who performed abortions at a clinic in Florida. To be sure, the NRLC also condemned in the same sentence what it called "the violence of abortion that has killed 30 million unborn children in the last 20 years." [17] When John Salvi murdered two receptionists at abortion clinics in

Brookline, Massachusetts, on 30 December 1994, some leaders of the pro-life movement felt compelled once again to distance themselves from violence and those who would defend it.[18]

Pro-life leaders have a stance—official opposition to violence—and an argument—that legalized abortion itself contributes to an atmosphere of disrespect for life and hence to a climate that encourages violence. But they also have a problem. The language and images on which they rely lead irrevocably to the conclusion that they regard legal abortion in the United States to be organized mass murder—not just any mass murder, but the systematic murder of babies, the most innocent and helpless among us.

Their problem is this. Once one accepts their premise that abortion in the United States constitutes the unquestioned evil of mass murder, then one is compelled to reflect on the appropriate means to combat this evil. Mainstream pro-life leaders reject violence as both wrong in itself and as counterproductive for their movement. It is counterproductive because the overwhelming majority of Americans are horrified by it. But, and here is where the problem has its bite, for people who sincerely believe that abortion is the equivalent of an American holocaust, nonviolent resistance is not the only plausible response. Take pro-life rhetoric at its word: If David Gunn and other physicians who perform abortions are equivalent to the Nazis who murdered by the millions, then would not people, like Paul Hill, who kill abortion providers be equivalent to courageous individuals who tried to stop the death camps by killing the executioners?

I am not arguing that all pro-life people accept this line of reasoning. Without question, many who hold that all human life is sacred sincerely oppose violence against abortion providers and clinics. They would, presumably, also have opposed violence against those who operated the Nazi death camps. But many people, I expect, would be willing to defend violence against Nazi executioners, both because they view them as murderers who have forfeited their own right to live and because they hope it would slow down or stop the killing of innocents. For the Paul Hills of the pro-life movement, the analogy probably seems very close between violence to stop the Nazi Holocaust and violence to stop what they view as an evil at least as massive—the one-and-a-half million abortions that take place in the United States each year. If it would have been morally justifiable to kill Nazi mass murderers, would it not be similarly justifiable to kill the perpetrators of what they view as the contemporary American holocaust?

There is no simple cause-and-effect relationship between pro-life rhetoric and violence against abortion providers and clinics. Pro-life leaders have a right to defend themselves against charges that they have incited violence, particularly where they have consistently and forcefully condemned it. But there can be little doubt that the rhetoric and images they use place abortion on the same plane of immorality as child murder and the Nazi Holocaust. This follows from the top-down logic of their position that fetuses and embryos are persons and that abortion is therefore the intentional killing of a person. It appears that the vast majority of pro-life people agree with other Americans that violence against abortion providers is immoral and repugnant. But those who do not agree, who believe that violence is a proportionate response to what they fervently believe is the egregious and immoral violence of abortion, are accepting the same characterization of the situation. They disagree only on what is a justified and productive response. Given their shared picture of abortion-as-holocaust, it cannot be a great surprise when a few decide that counterviolence might be justified. The Paul Hills of the world are taking fetal personhood deadly seriously.

A Closer Look at the Rhetoric of Personhood in the Abortion Debate

The image of abortion as child murder is consistent with the metaphysical position that personhood begins at conception. But its more important function in debate seems to be to capture our deep-seated moral revulsion to hurting and killing babies, and to transfer that revulsion to abortion. Most people, I suspect, do not pay much attention to the abstract philosophical arguments. They *just know* certain things. Luker found that the pro-life activists she interviewed just knew, in that sense, that embryos and fetuses were people like everyone else. They were often shocked to learn that many others did not share their view of the fetus.[19] Similarly, people who support abortifacient contraceptives are probably puzzled when that is equated with infanticide. They just know that not allowing an undifferentiated embryo to implant in a uterus is nothing at all like killing a baby. What is more interesting for us is how the images used by both sides attempt to evoke other things that most Americans presumably "just know" to be true.

Much of the rhetoric used by organizations opposed to abortion stresses the resemblances between fetuses and babies—in appearance, physiology, behavior. There are lapel pins in the shape of fetal foot-

prints, graphic representations of fetal heartbeats, and pictures of fetuses sucking their thumbs. In one famous film, a visual image of a fetus
said to be in the process of being aborted is interpreted as a "silent
scream." Along with these go bloody photos of dismembered fetuses,
claimed to be from abortions performed late in pregnancy and looking
like nothing so much as cruelly tortured infants; rituals such as mock
funeral processions; and symbols, such as the white crosses used to mark
graves. Even the vocabulary of the anti-abortion movement emphasizes
the continuity between infants and the fetuses and embryos that are the
movement's concern: these are all "unborn" or "preborn" babies.

We do not find those same abortion opponents carrying placards on
which embryos are represented life-size. Nor are they likely to flaunt
life-size representations of very early fetuses—before they look like babies. Imagine a demonstration against a contraceptive that prevents implantation in which the protesters held up placards with pinhead-sized
dots on them with the slogan "Prevent the murder of these unborn
babies!" Such a demonstration would evoke a good deal of head-
scratching, but it is unlikely to win many converts to their cause or to
inspire much moral indignation.[20]

For their part, those who want to permit women to have abortions
display pictures of bloody coat hangers, hoping to evoke sympathy with
women who seek abortions even when the risk is great and anger
against those who would deprive women of safe and legal abortions.
Supporters of women's choice avoid representations of fetal remains,
especially from late abortions, as fervently as abortion opponents parade
them. Presumably they too recognize the power of such pictures to
provoke moral disquiet.

The rhetoric and images of both sides are intended to evoke responses based on what most of us "just know" to be true. Pro-life advocates hope to evoke against abortion the same moral response as the
one we have toward harming and killing infants. That response—repugnance and horror—is widely shared and properly taken as a mark of
one's moral character. (A person who remained unmoved by the suffering and death of a baby would be suspected of moral insensitivity, at
the least.) The question here is whether abortion opponents can transfer our moral responses legitimately from infants to fetuses and thence
to embryos, or whether there is a sleight of hand involved—a sort of
ethics shell game. The answer will depend on a more careful analysis of
what we find offensive and repugnant about causing pain and death to
babies.[21]

Different analyses are possible. Many of them would give an

important place to the pain caused to the child. Empirical evidence, such as facts about neurological development and fetal responses to noxious stimuli, would clearly be pertinent. Reasonable people might draw different conclusions based on the same evidence. But not all conclusions would be equally reasonable. If, as we believe, newborn infants experience pain, then it seems likely that late-stage fetuses do likewise. Preventing pain and suffering is morally important and would become a morally relevant consideration at whatever stage fetuses develop the capacity to experience it. But not before. It would not be reasonable to conclude that embryos and early fetuses, before they develop nervous systems and brains that form the necessary conditions for experiencing pain, suffer in this sense from abortion.

If we take repugnance at inflicting suffering on babies as part of the basic equipment of morally perceptive people and as a sign of a morally vital community, what can we say about the effort to enlist that natural and commendable repugnance in the service of opposition to abortion? First, it helps to explain why there are virtually no voices defending very late abortions, when the similarities between fetuses and infants are most pronounced. Whatever sympathies we may feel for women who do not wish to be pregnant, however important we think the moral case for controlling what goes on inside one's body, and however adamant we are about limiting the state's power to compel us to do what others believe to be right, the possibly painful destruction of a late gestational age fetus strikes most of us as just too similar to the killing of an infant to be morally justifiable in all but the most extreme circumstances.

Second, and as important, we can see what makes it so difficult to muster that same repugnance against very early abortions or methods that prevent the implantation of embryos. The plain fact is that at its early stages, the developing human organism neither looks nor functions like an infant, and does not, without a considerable leap of imagination or logic, evoke the kind of moral outrage that flows readily from the specter of badly treated infants.

Anyone who wishes to argue that all abortions, from the moment of conception, are equally immoral must persuade us that what most people "just know" here is wrong; that, for example, preventing implantation is the precise moral equivalent of infanticide. To make this case, the abortion opponent has two strategies available. He or she can either take the route of abstract argument, from philosophy or theology, to attempt to prove that this is so. The top-down strategy that emphasizes fetal personhood, as I have argued, may end up justifying too much, for example, violence against abortion providers. Or the pro-life advocate can try to show that related strong, well-considered, clear moral judgments, with their accompanying social practices, are consistent with his or her claim.

Most of the debate has taken place over the first battleground. Abortion opponents have a tough job here; they must overcome the general perception that embryos are quite different from infants, that a concept such as "torturing" an embryo is incoherent because the capacity to be tortured requires the capacity to suffer. They have offered a host of arguments about the moral significance of potentiality, or the importance and timing of ensoulment, or the connection of genetic identity with personhood, or of the moral imperative of drawing a line at the time of conception.[22] What abortion opponents cannot do is enlist our immediate and unforced sympathies for infants and children.

It is very important to understand what I am *not* saying here. I am not claiming that preventing pain and suffering is the only or most important factor to be weighed against permitting abortion. I am not saying that there are no counterbalancing factors that should be weighed in favor of permitting abortion. Nor am I saying that the capacity to suffer is all that people mean when they claim that fetuses are persons. Indeed, most pro-life writers would argue that an actual, current capacity for suffering is not required in order to declare that embryos and fetuses are persons. What I *am* trying to say is that using the concept of personhood to elucidate what we believe is at stake in the arguments for and against permitting abortion is a mistake. It introduces simplification and obliterates crucial distinctions precisely where we need to consider issues in their full complexity and particularity. Do not rely on the shorthand when you most need the full text. In seeking metaphysical purity and elegance, both sides of the personhood debate lose touch with what grounds our firmest and most reliable moral judgments.

In practical moral reasoning, the concept of personhood serves as a kind of moral shorthand, as an umbrella term that summarizes a large number of sound, reliable ideas about morality. To say that someone is a person describes certain capacities the individual has, makes sense out of morally relevant ascriptions like praise and blame, and sets out certain obligations we have to him or her. Persons are the sort of entities that reason, feel, make plans, have preferences, form attachments, love, and are loved. We can ascribe moral responsibility and agency to persons;

they can be blamed for immoral actions, and praised for courageous, generous, and wise ones. Without good reason we should not cause persons to suffer pain or emotional distress; we should treat them with respect, not lie to or deceive them; we should take seriously their choices and seek their consent in matters that concern them.

Problems arise when we want to call certain beings persons for some purposes, but where the label fits poorly for others. Nature does not package consistently together all of the attributes we are inclined to bundle into our notion of persons. When, for example, someone is profoundly demented we want to protect them from suffering, and perhaps to honor commitments made to them prior to the onset of their dementia. But when their dementia is far advanced, we know better than to take a "yes" from them as having anything near the moral force their assent would have had when they were fully competent. Likewise, the more their dementia severed the connection between their reason and their behavior, the less we would ascribe moral praise or blame to them.

At any point along the continuum from rationally capable actor to demented, arational reactor, we could ask the question, Is this still a person? Much philosophical debate certainly treats this as a cogent and coherent question. But the general notion of personhood provides little help in answering specific moral questions. Why should we not permit this individual to be tortured or to suffer from untreated bedsores? We could say because he or she is a person; but we could say just as well, because it is wrong to permit suffering when it can be avoided. I add little if anything to that explanation by invoking the concept of personhood. Why should we not ignore the considered wishes of a rational agent? Again, I could say, because this is a person. But I could give a multitude of more specific reasons as well: because we would want our own wishes respected, and we should be consistent; because the individual is likely to have a clearer idea of what he or she wants than an outsider could have; because whether they choose foolishly or wisely, they will have to live with the consequences. Do we add anything to the force of our justification by adding that the agent happens to be a person?

The concept of personhood may be very helpful in clarifying certain questions in the philosophy of mind, for example. It may also be useful in thinking about the relationship between the capacity to reason and the conditions under which ascriptions of moral agency, of credit and blame, are intelligible. The concept of personhood may or may not be useful in elucidating a particular problem; its helpfulness is not guaranteed. Efforts to nail down a particular conception of personhood, and then to use that to try to answer specific, substantive moral questions about abortion may have it backward.[23] The quest to discover the essence of personhood may help us to clarify which attributes are relevant across a wide range of moral questions and which only narrowly, but each time we ask a specific moral question, we should be able to give specific, relevant reasons to justify our actions. As Wittgenstein showed for the concept of "games," we should not expect to uncover some fundamental essence for a natural language concept as rich and flexible as "personhood." Whenever someone attempts to answer a moral query by saying "because this is a person," we can always ask what it is about this person that makes your answer persuasive.

Engelhardt and those like him who claim that fetuses are not persons because they lack the essential qualities of personhood show the same insensitivity to how we use the concept as do those who declare that embryos are persons from the instant of conception. They take a complex set of moral ideas and lump them together under a single simple umbrella, rather than attend to the nuances of how the many insights that coexist under the umbrella are actually used in our most sensitive and insightful practical moral reasoning.

If Not Personhood, Then What? An Alternative to Metaphysical Perseveration

I have given several reasons for not wanting to place the dispute over fetal personhood at the center of the abortion conflict. First, as a metaphysical disagreement about the nature of a fetus, it has resisted all efforts at resolution. It seems likely to remain irresolvable for the foreseeable future. Second, because for pro-life people abortion is child murder, there is little or no room for compromise or accommodation. It is hard to imagine pro-life people agreeing to give up their movement if the number of abortions each year was reduced from 1.5 million to 0.5 million, or even 10,000. From their perspective, that would still be 10,000 innocent children killed. Third, efforts to put fetal personhood at the top and work downward to practical moral decisions lead too readily either to absurdity or to violence. Fourth, a careful examination of how personhood is used in practical moral reasoning suggests that it actually functions as a kind of umbrella or shorthand for a variety of related but distinguishable moral ideas, and that we can usually identify a more precise and specific moral idea that explains our considered moral judgments. The concept of personhood per se does little of the useful work in practical moral reasoning.

Despite the enormous efforts and intellect devoted to persuading the other side, arguments that embryos and fetuses are or are not persons have failed completely to persuade those not already disposed to agree. Despite this resounding failure, both sides continue to flail one another with arguments old and new, with no evidence of success. When animals (or people) persist in behavior that fails repeatedly to achieve its goal, scientists call it "perseveration" and consider it a sign of organismic dysfunction. Insisting that the public debate over abortion be framed as a dispute over personhood is as dysfunctional as any rat's futile bar pressings, so much so that it might be called "metaphysical perseveration." Is there any reason to hope that we might find an alternative?

Indeed, there are several reasons for hope. First, most Americans do not fall neatly into either the pro-life or pro-choice camp. A review of over one hundred public opinion surveys conducted between 1962 and 1993 reveals a remarkable complexity in Americans' opinions about abortion.[24] Many believe that abortion is morally wrong but want it to remain legal. They view abortion as a personal decision, best kept between a woman and her physician. They would support some restrictions on abortion such as requiring adolescents to notify their parents and married women their husbands. They object to government prohibitions on what doctors can tell their women patients about abortion, but they also object to government funding of abortions, except perhaps for those deemed "medically necessary." This complex mix of positions does not fit neatly into either the pro-life or the pro-choice agenda. The same review indicates that people with this middle position have little electoral influence. Abortion is much more likely to affect the votes of those at either end of the spectrum, with pro-life people roughly twice as likely to say that the candidate's stand on abortion affected their vote as pro-choice people. Nonetheless, neither pro-life nor pro-choice activists can achieve their full agendas without at least the passive cooperation of the majority of American voters. Thus both sides must continue to appeal to the many Americans who hold complex, mixed opinions about abortion.

Second, there is reason to believe that even advocates on both sides hold positions that are not entirely circumscribed by their views on fetal personhood. Ronald Dworkin relies in part on the complexities in public opinion to argue that the apparent contradictions—that most people regard abortion as wrong, even a form of murder, but want it to remain legal—can be resolved by appreciating that the disagreement is not in fact over personhood but over differing views of what gives human life its intrinsic value. Dworkin's argument will receive more detailed consideration shortly. For now, I want to agree with him that fetal personhood does not provide a very useful description of Americans' views about abortion.

Third, the metaphor of tapestry and web suggests that no single thread such as fetal personhood, or, for that matter, Dworkin's notion of the intrinsic value or sacredness of human life, is likely to be able to account for why people hold the beliefs they do. In particular, disagreements about fetal personhood explain at most only half of the passion in the conflict. For pro-life advocates, preventing the murder of innocent children could well arouse the level of passion we have witnessed. But even for them, more is at stake. We cannot begin to explain the passionate commitment of pro-choice activists from their views on fetal personhood. Their energy is better understood as an expression of their views about what women need to achieve justice and to flourish. But then again, it turns out that deeply held ideas about women's nature and women's flourishing are equally important to pro-life activists. We will turn to those contrasting tapestries after we look at the most interesting recent reinterpretation of the abortion conflict—the one offered by Ronald Dworkin.

Ronald Dworkin and the Intrinsic Value of Human Life

Dworkin states his case forcefully. He distinguishes between *derivative* and *detached* objections to abortion. The former are based on the claim that "abortion violates someone's right not to be killed[;] . . . it presupposes and is derived from rights and interests that it assumes all human beings, including fetuses, have." The latter make no presumptions about what rights or interests fetuses may have. Instead, they declare abortion wrong because "it disregards and insults the intrinsic value, the sacred character, of any stage or form of human life." [25]

His hypothesis is that "very few people—even those who belong to the most vehemently anti-abortion groups—actually believe" the derivative objection, that fetuses have rights and interests against being killed. Instead, he claims that the real division is "a markedly less polar disagreement about how best to respect a fundamental idea we almost all share in some form: that individual human life is sacred." [26]

Personhood is too ambiguous a concept to be of much use in answering the questions that genuinely count, in his judgment. He proposes two: "Does a fetus have interests that should be protected by rights, including a right to life? Should we treat the life of a fetus as sacred, whether a fetus has interests or not?" [27]

He argues that we can best understand the positions of all of the disputants—pro-life as well as pro-choice—as efforts to answer the second question rather than the first; about detached objections based on convictions about the intrinsic value of individual human lives rather than objections derived from rights to continued existence held by embryos and fetuses. The Roman Catholic church has historically opposed abortion, regarding it as an insult to the sanctity of life, even when it regarded ensoulment as occurring only at quickening. It was enough to show disrespect for the sacredness of human life and the God that created it, even if the fetus was not yet a person. Most pro-choice feminists, in contrast, do not dismiss the fetus as morally inconsequential. Dworkin writes, "They emphasize not the woman's right suggested by the rhetoric of privacy, but a woman's responsibility to make a complex decision she is best placed to make." The decision is a morally serious one. "Abortion wastes the intrinsic value—the sanctity, the inviolability—of a human life and is therefore a grave moral wrong unless the intrinsic value of other human lives would be wasted in a decision *against* abortion." [28]

Dworkin develops an account of how and why we believe that something is sacred or has intrinsic value. He argues that intrinsic value always reflects our respect for the investment made, whether by God, or people, or nature. Our differences over abortion, he concludes, can best be understood as differences "about the relative moral importance of the natural and human contributions to the inviolability of individual human lives." [29] Pro-life people are likely to have strong religious faith and to believe that every fetus reflects God's handiwork. Pro-choice people are likely to emphasize the human contribution to fetal life.

Both of these positions, and all of the intermediate ones, Dworkin argues, deserve to be understood as spiritual, religious beliefs. This step in his argument turns out to be crucial. Dworkin wants to declare that we do not have to reconcile our different views about the intrinsic value of life in order to settle the question of what our laws ought to be. The First Amendment to the Constitution guarantees freedom of religious belief. And our differences over abortion, Dworkin concludes, are at heart religious differences. Hence the government may not enact laws that significantly interfere with a woman's choice to obtain an abortion:

A state may not curtail liberty, in order to protect an intrinsic value, when the effect on one group of citizens would be special and grave, when the community is seriously divided about what respect for that value requires, and when people's opinions about the nature of that value reflect essentially religious convictions that are fundamental to moral personality.[30]

Dworkin's argument, if accepted, would indeed solve the public policy problem. We would have to live with our differences about the sanctity of life, permit legal abortion, but also accept limitations designed to underscore the moral gravity of abortion decisions. He effectively concedes that there is little hope for agreement on the underlying morality of abortion. Those who oppose it will continue to find it morally repugnant, a profound violation of the sanctity of human life. But by designating our differences as essentially religious in nature, he offers us a way out of our policy conundrum.

Dworkin's analysis of abortion, like those who declare it a dispute about fetal personhood, treats one strand—our interpretation of the sanctity of human life—in isolation. He does not attempt to tie it to a larger pattern of beliefs about the nature and destiny of human life. He does not reflect on why differences in social position (except for religious beliefs) are reflected so sharply in different beliefs about whether abortion should be legal. Although his account does much better than the fetal personhood approach at explaining the complex patterns of attitudes and beliefs around abortion, it is not much more successful at explaining the tenacity and emotional intensity of the conflict. One passage exhibits why I believe he misses these things. In it he tries to explain that the dispute is deeper than an argument over fetal personhood. It is, he writes, about "different conceptions of the value and point of human life and of the meaning and character of human death."[31] Kristin Luker's work demonstrates that it is not human life generically that is at stake. It is the significance of motherhood in women's flourishing.

Abortion, Motherhood,
and Women's Flourishing

In her study of pro-life and pro-choice activists, Luker learned "that each side of the abortion debate has an internally coherent and mutually shared view of the world that is tacit, never fully articulated, and, most importantly, completely at odds with the world view held by their opponents." [32] They differed on how to understand the moral significance of fetuses and embryos, of course. But they held contrasting views on other issues as well. They made very different life choices that both expressed and reinforced their beliefs. And it is not much of an exaggeration to say that they lived in quite different worlds, in which their respective views were rarely challenged.

The U.S. Supreme Court decision in 1973, which declared constitutional support for women's access to abortion, brought new recruits into the pro-life movement. Called the "housewives" by the previous generation of anti-abortion activists, Luker found them to be married women with children, not in the job market, with a high school education or perhaps some college. Their views on abortion were clear, and they were shocked that the Supreme Court, and many other Americans, could think otherwise: "Their values and life circumstances made it unlikely that they themselves would need abortions, and they were surrounded by people who shared these values. Moreover, since they were known to be devout, traditional women who valued motherhood highly, they were not likely to be on the receiving end of confidences from women who did not share these values." [33]

Pro-life and pro-choice people held different attitudes toward several crucial issues. Pro-life people emphasized the reproductive aspect of sexuality, in the belief that this was in harmony with the nature and purpose of human sexuality and that this understanding of sexuality enriched the relationship between husband and wife. Pro-choice people were more likely to emphasize sexuality's contribution to emotional intimacy. They did not think sex morally inferior when reproduction was avoided.

They differed on their view about the efficacy and desirability of human control of events. Pro-life people tended to be deeply religious, to trust in God, and to see human efforts to manage lives as arrogant and futile. Pro-choice people, in contrast, strongly valued rationality, con-

trol, and planning. They were more likely to have faith in human interventions.

Even their views on the nature of morality were different. Pro-life
people tended to "subscribe to explicit and well-articulated moral
codes. . . . Morality, for them, is a straightforward and unambiguous
set of rules that specify what is moral behavior. Since they believe these
rules originate in a Divine Plan, they see them as transcendent principles, eternally valid regardless of time, cultural setting, and individual
belief." [34] Pro-choice people were more likely to see morality as the
sensitive application of moral principles to complex situations, rather
than something determined by inflexible rules.

The life choices made by activists on both sides are neatly summed
up in Luker's profiles. The typical pro-choice activist was a forty-four-
year-old woman, who had married at twenty-two and had one or two
children. Her father was a college graduate. She had some graduate or
professional education. She worked, as did her husband, who was a
professional. Religion was not particularly important in her life. The
typical pro-life activist was also a forty-four-year-old woman. She had
married at seventeen and now had three or more children. She may
have gone to college, though her father was a high school graduate.
Her husband was likely to be a small businessman or to hold a low-level
white-collar job. She was most likely a Catholic, possibly a convert to
that faith, and religion was very important in her life. She attended
church once a week or more. Her family income was only about 60
percent of the income of a pro-choice activist's family. [35]

For activists on both sides, Luker describes their beliefs about abortion as the " 'tip of the iceberg,' a shorthand way of supporting and
proclaiming not only a complex set of values but a given set of social
resources as well." [36] Each group had its distinctive set of resources.
Pro-life activists tended to count among their assets their stable marriages, skill and dedication as parents, and supportive communities. For
pro-choice activists, their jobs, education, and income distinguished
them. The life paths that led the respective groups to gather these resources were also characterized by divergent views about gender differences and about what was most important in women's lives.

Pro-life people saw the human world divided into two spheres—
male and female. Men and women are fundamentally different, they
believe, and those differences are to be celebrated rather than regretted.
Women are best suited by nature to raise children, men to work.
Women provide what tenderness, feeling, caring, and self-sacrifice the

world knows. If women become like men, all that may be lost. And the way they will become like men is by competing toe-to-toe with men in the brutal and uncaring world of work.

Pro-choice activists do not reject motherhood or its satisfactions. But they are inclined to see men and women as fundamentally equal, their natures more similar than dissimilar. For them, "motherhood, so long as it is involuntary, is potentially always a low-status, unrewarding role to which women can be banished at any time. Thus, from their point of view, *control* over reproduction is essential for women to be able to live up to their full human potential."[37] Abortion becomes a means both to achieve competitive equality with men in the labor market and to assure that children are born to parents ready and able to give them what they need.

One of the ironies Luker found in her study was that pro-life activists, while willing to accept "career women" who had forsaken family for work, were less forgiving of working women with children. They regarded such women as "selfish"—able to work only because other women, the homemakers, "carried the load for them in Boy and Girl Scouts, PTA and after school, for which their reward was to be treated by the workers as less competent and less interesting persons."[38] Ironically, the pro-choice women in Luker's study were more active in such community activities than the pro-life women.

More than any other factor, the differences between pro-life and pro-choice activists centered around their views of motherhood in women's flourishing. I could not summarize it better than Luker does:

Women come to be pro-life and pro-choice activists as the end result of lives that center around different definitions of motherhood . . . that motherhood is the most important and satisfying role open to a woman, or that motherhood is only one of several roles, a burden when defined as the only role. These beliefs and values are rooted in the concrete circumstances of women's lives—their educations, incomes, occupations, and the different marital and family choices they have made along the way—and they work simultaneously to shape those circumstances in turn.[39]

The clash, that is, between pro-life and pro-choice forces is not primarily a metaphysical dispute that could possibly be settled by better arguments. It is an existential struggle over the meaning of women's lives, over the differences between men and women, over the place of motherhood in women's flourishing. In that sense, it is equally a struggle over the place of fatherhood in men's flourishing—over men's fitness to be nurturing, tender parents, and the importance of that kind of parenting to men's flourishing.

The Bad News and the Good News

First, the bad news. Clever new arguments, particularly the sort that philosophers and theologians specialize in, will be little or no help in promoting social peace or persuading either side to abandon their cause. Indeed, I believe that as long as we act as though metaphysical disagreements about fetal personhood are at the center of the conflict, we are conducting a sideshow that distracts people from more important disagreements.

There is more bad news. Those other disagreements, about the value of control, the significance of sexuality, the nature of morality, and especially about women, men, and the place of motherhood, are no less profound and no more loosely held.

Now the good news. These other disagreements, while they will not easily be resolved, are at least open to different kinds of considerations than the metaphysics of fetal personhood, considerations that perhaps both sides can see as valid. Evidence about how well children do in families where fathers take on equal or major responsibility for their nurturance would be relevant to the presumptions about differences between men's and women's nature, for example. Furthermore, because they do not require flat yes or no answers, questions about the meaning of motherhood and women's flourishing are open to nuances of understanding, and hence to accommodation and compromise.

There is one more source of hope. As social conditions change, the lives of men and women change as well. More women with children have entered the labor force; the pressures of work may also make both women and men more grateful for the values and experiences found in family life, especially in nurturing children. As the resources available to men and women evolve, and parenting becomes more valued by more men, perhaps the social circumstances that energize the abortion struggle will alter. It is even possible that those changes will allow, in time, some of the passion to ebb. But peace is not guaranteed; the conflict may intensify instead.

Seeing the debate as about the substance of good lives for women and men prompts us to ask a different set of questions. What makes a good life for a woman? What does it mean for a woman to cultivate the virtues appropriate to her humanity? Should women have a different set of life goals and virtues than men? What place does nurturing parenting play in men's flourishing? We can go further and ask what social and political institutions must exist to promote the flourishing of women, and men, and children. These would be more fruitful questions to ask, and we have some hope that even if no definitive or final answers may be expected, at least the contours of disagreement would alter and perhaps the ferocity of the battle subside. Reframing the debate over abortion in this way has another salutary effect: it directs our attention to the images of women's and men's roles, and the worth of children in the lives of both, that enliven our tapestry and animate our culture.

8

Tapestry and Web

*I am sitting with a philosopher in the garden; he says again and
again "I know that that's a tree," pointing to a tree that is near
us. Someone else arrives and hears this, and I tell him: "This
fellow isn't insane. We are only doing philosophy."*
—Ludwig Wittgenstein, *On Certainty*

The world is full of moral disagreement. At times, no
doubt, those disagreements reflect very deep differences in core beliefs
and values. But the task of someone committed to work in practical
ethics must be more than showing in an intellectually clever way how
different premises lead to different conclusions. Practical moral reasoning must make an honest effort to confront culturally significant moral
disputes, not as opportunities to show off its own ingenuity, but to
make whatever contribution it can to illuminating and, if possible, set-
tling them.

Rarely, I suspect, does good practical moral reasoning resolve a disagreement rapidly and permanently. But from time to time it does show
problems in a new light that allows most of the parties to a dispute to
agree on an acceptable response. Consider such well-settled issues as
physicians' obligation to tell their patients the truth about their condition, the importance of informed consent in human subjects research,
and the permissibility of somatic cell gene therapy. In each of these
disputes, consensus was achieved after vigorous and extensive debate.
Once physicians' reasons for withholding bad news from their patients

were examined, they appeared to have more to do with physicians' re-luctance to deal with patients' reactions to bad news than with any defensible account of the physician-patient relationship. The case for informed consent in research grew slowly but inexorably in the after-math of the horrors revealed at Nuremberg. Before somatic cell gene therapy could be accepted, it had to be distinguished from germ cell gene therapy; once that was accomplished, somatic cell gene therapy could be seen as essentially similar to other novel therapies for which the risks were poorly understood.

There would be no need for ethicists and no field of bioethics if there were no great moral disagreements. We might still want painters and poets and novelists to illuminate the beauty of our shared values. But we would have no use for those professional analysts of moral conflict—the ethicists. Moral disagreement makes the field of practical ethics nec-essary. Moral agreement makes it possible. Practical ethics, in turn, needs to be responsive to the concrete moral disputes that are its raison d'être. In light of the goals of practical ethics, I want to suggest several requirements for a useful method in practical moral reasoning:

1. It should be able to identify the moral considerations relevant to a problem.

2. It should help identify potential areas of agreement as well as areas of disagreement.

3. It should distinguish disagreements that are superficial or resolv-able from those that reflect deep differences in core values and commitments, especially beliefs about human flourishing.

4. It should be alert to false trails and to claims that fundamental disputes must be resolved before any agreement is possible in a practical moral disagreement. Such claims have two parts, and both must be true before practical moral agreement is impossible. First, the area of deep disagreement must be unresolvable; sec-ond, it must be central and inseparable from the practical moral dispute in question. Both conditions sometimes hold—as in the controversy over abortion, where central differences persist, al-though commentators disagree about *which* differences are really central. But circumstances in which both of these are true are the exception rather than the rule.

Scholars in ethics have engaged in a vigorous recent debate about how to do good reasoning in ethics. A key dispute has been over two intertwined issues: the relation of the specific to the general and the sources of reliable moral knowledge. If what we know with the greatest certainty are general principles, then moral reasoning should proceed from the general to the specific: to answer a moral question, we must first determine under what general principle it falls, and then deduce from that principle what the right answer is for the particular case. If reliable moral knowledge comes from more diverse sources, including considered judgments in specific cases, then sound moral reasoning is a more complex enterprise that relies on gathering morally relevant considerations and weighing and sorting among multiple and diverse sources of moral knowledge. This latter pattern of reasoning is what I have in mind with the metaphor of a tapestry: a rich collection of images and threads.

Out of threads borrowed from the tapestry we construct webs to support our practical moral judgments. The web is the metaphor I employ for justification in practical moral reasoning. Webs can be flimsy, consisting of only a few thin strands. They can be narrow, woven around one strong central thread, but weak on either side. They can be irregular, with many holes and weak spots. The best webs have many strong strands woven harmoniously together with few gaps. Strong webs provide good support for our practical moral judgments.

My strategy in the remainder of this chapter will be to contrast the models of top-down and tapestry ethics. I will give particular attention to a powerful critique of any method in ethics, including the tapestry and web approach, that relies on something other than appeals to abstract principles. The claim is that some of the essential raw materials of these methods, materials like considered judgments and shared understandings, are inevitably and fatally laden with ideology and therefore cannot be satisfactory sources of moral insight or critique. I want to look in particular at one version of the critique—the claim that relying on shared social meanings effectively reinforces the existing patterns of dominance and injustice and deprives ethics of any grounds for incisive critiques of existing arrangements. The chapter ends with a brief recapitulation of my approach.

Ethics: Top-Down or Tapestry?

Contemporary philosophers are traditionally trained to be contemptuous of tradition. Our moral judgments are supposed to rest solely on what can be established by uncontaminated reason. Reason alone must provide the premises from which our particular practical moral judgments are derived. From whatever first principles reason yields, we are then supposed to deduce what is to be done in practice.

This is close to a parody, although we can find influential examples of work in bioethics that come awfully near in their approach. This way of viewing how we know in ethics—moral epistemology—and how we justify moral judgments has been dubbed "deductivism." The term "deductivism" nicely conveys both the commitment to deductive logic that is presumed to be the cornerstone of good ethical reasoning and the analogy with reasoning from fundamental premises, axioms and definitions, characteristic of deductive systems like geometry. This way of conceiving of moral epistemology and moral justification places the crucial elements at the top and works downward to messy particulars and practical moral judgments—a "top-down" ethics.

In top-down ethics, the author selects a highly general and abstract idea or small set of ideas and churns an assortment of substantive moral questions through them, spitting out one normative conclusion after another. This method is an excellent way of showing what follows from a set of theoretical propositions and assumptions, but it has difficulty being generally persuasive. To be persuasive, a top-down ethical theory has two possible strategies. Either it must speak to the already converted, or else the conclusions it reaches must strike the reader as eminently sensible despite the fact that he or she disagrees with the supposedly foundational theoretical views presumed to justify them. The first strategy works well enough, but only for those who already share those foundational commitments. The second results in an uncomfortable quandary for the top-downer: people may agree with me, but not for reasons I can recognize as sound ones. If people do not accept my starting point, which I regard as critical to all that follows in my reasoning, then what moral significance can there be if they find my conclusion sensible? To a top-downer, such a lack of disagreement on practice is at best a happy accident, happy because it precludes the political conflict that might otherwise follow on disagreement.

A crucial disadvantage of the top-down approach is that it has no idea of what to do with refractory disagreement, except to return to its theoretical starting points and attempt to drub the recalcitrant disbeliever into submission. This take-it-or-leave-it quality limits severely its usefulness in fostering dialogue among those who disagree. At its worst, it sponsors a kind of moral-theoretic fundamentalism that declares, if you disagree with my basic premises, we have nothing further to discuss. The "top-down" method of nailing one's fundamental principles high on the wall and trying to derive every substantive conclusion from them is not well suited to the task of fostering nuanced consideration of particulars and compromise.

Top-down ethics does have its distinct virtues. The first is simplicity or economy; one always knows what its fundamental commitments are. The second is its clear ties to particular moral theories, permitting a critique and defense of the fundamental commitments in terms familiar to moral theorists. The third is its supposed independence from any specific culture's moral beliefs and practices. This relative independence allegedly gives such theories a sharp critical edge with which to cut into a culture's accepted acts, practices, and institutions where it finds them wanting.

Not surprisingly, top-down ethics has vices that are mirror images of its virtues. The emphasis on simplicity or economy of principles leaves the top-downer with an unhappy choice: either we retain simplicity and generality, but at the price of insensitivity to particular circumstances, or else we sacrifice simplicity for attentiveness to the messy particulars of actual practical moral disputes. The closeness to moral theory tends to push disagreements up rather than down, to fundamental commitments rather than to subtleties of interpretation or potentially resolvable differences over facts. When the disputants cannot find agreement on the particulars of the problem, their only resort is to question the premises on which their opponent's judgment is based. Last, the ability to offer radical moral critiques and reinterpretations can lead just as easily to drawing moral conclusions that strike us as foolish, even abhorrent, as to promoting insightful moral critiques.

In an excellent article on the role of cases in bioethics, John Arras offers a concise account of the problems with using top-down ethics to address practical moral problems. For one thing, the person trying to decide which theory to choose has a right to be puzzled. As Arras puts it, "After more than two thousand years of ethical debate among philosophers with rival views, no clear winner has emerged, and clinicians cannot be blamed for doubting that one ever will."[1] Even if a victor appeared, difficulties would remain. Adherents would argue over which account of the theory was the best one. Unambiguous solutions to practical problems would remain elusive, because such solutions typically depend on a variety of factors in addition to moral principles, such as empirical predictions, different views about which entities deserve what kind of moral consideration, and the willingness to accept unintended and undesired consequences of policy decisions. And, as Arras writes, abstract ethical theories are prone to assume "that the chiaroscuro of our moral experience can be reduced to one or two over- arching sources of moral value, such as maximization of happiness or respect for human freedom." This sort of reductionism "will not do justice to the rich diversity inherent in the moral lives of individuals and societies."[2] The result is moral myopia, seeing only what the theory brings into focus.

There are alternatives to top-down ethics. The most popular ap- proach, judging by the success of the primary textbook that embodies it, now in its fourth edition, is a method that focuses on midlevel princi- ples.[3] In its earliest versions, principlism in bioethics seemed to accept the top-down assumption that moral certainty was to be found in gen- eral theory. Principles were derived from theory, which were in turn applied to cases. In its most recent version, the text embraces a dialec- tical conception of practical moral reasoning: moral knowledge is best found at the intersection of considered moral judgments, midlevel prin- ciples, and general theories, an approach with the philosophically re- spectable name "reflective equilibrium."

Reflective equilibrium, as I want to use the concept, holds that no particular component of moral reasoning—grand theory, moral maxim, considered moral judgment—has absolute primacy. Good moral rea- soning takes advantage of all available sources of moral knowledge and insight, giving each whatever weight its reliability and pertinence war- rants, working to and fro, challenging the judgments, reconsidering the theories, seeking always the most plausible and defensible conclusion. Done properly, this process of gathering relevant considerations and playing them against one another helps us arrive at practical moral judg- ments about acts, practices, and institutions that are cogent, critical, and open to further criticism and development.[4]

In the hands of practitioners less sophisticated than its authors, prin- ciplism can still cause concern. It can look like top-down without a real top, now that its proponents have joined the chorus denouncing deductivism in bioethics. Its short list of principles may impoverish our understanding of complex moral situations, especially in the hands of less perceptive practitioners, by dulling sensitivities to cultural nuances that do not fit neatly into the standard list of principles.

Over time, principlism has evolved into a method that is increasingly difficult to distinguish from tapestrylike approaches characterized by their attention to substantive moral problems, to the particulars of place, circumstance, and person, and by the credence they give to considered moral judgments and moral traditions. Any serious effort to come to grips with complex, practical moral problems requires diving into the muck and mire of particulars, where abstract principles must be interpreted and weighed in the light of circumstances and where facts frequently emerge as decisive in particular disputes.

Generalizations about morality are themselves the inevitable product of practical moral reasoning. The search for consistency and inconsistency is a constitutive part of practical reasoning. We want to know what distinguishes case *A* from case *B;* whether that distinction is morally relevant; whether in this particular instance that difference justifies treating the two cases differently. As soon as we begin to compare more than two cases, we find categories of differences, about which we will venture ideas as to why certain groups of cases are similar, what makes these similarities morally important, and how we should weigh the relative importance of one sort of consideration against another. Eventually we will note what appear to be family resemblances of a higher order. In this way we generate ever more abstract and general statements about morality—a process that results in a product that looks more and more like the moral theory of the top-downer.

Top-downers may disdain such messy means of generating ideas about morality. Yet they cannot disdain the checks on intellectual ambition imposed by considered moral judgments and maxims proven by experience to be useful, nor can they provide useful practical guidance without attending to the same aspects of situations that engage those attentive to the tapestry.

Practical Moral Reasoning as Tapestry and Web

Approaching practical moral reasoning through the metaphor of a tapestry offers several advantages. It highlights the importance of images and models in moral reasoning. The crucial role images play is obvious in disputes over abortion where literal images—tiny feet or bloody coat hangers—appear when activists collide. The literal images, though, are less important than the pictures on the tapestry they are meant to evoke. Tiny feet make us think of infants, and how their utter dependency evokes profound feelings of protectiveness in adults.

Bloody coat hangers make us think of women, driven in their desperation to illegal and therefore clandestine and unsafe abortions. The most
important images lie below this level: these are the ones that portray
beliefs about what are good, fulfilling, and meaningful lives for women,
men, and children. Opponents of legal abortion are likely to see a picture there of a woman surrounded by her lovely children and her husband, when he is home from work. The sphere of the family is itself
sharply divided into the mother's and father's portion. Supporters of
legal abortion are likely to include a similar picture in their version of
the tapestry, although it stresses parental love rather than a sharp division into gender-specific spheres. But they are much more likely also to
include a portrait of a woman working at a job that provides satisfaction, economic independence, and hence power within family and society.

The tapestry metaphor alerts us also to look for threads that run
through the tapestry, including threads that might originate in old and
rejected images. If I am correct about the persistence of patriarchy and
the concept of the child-as-property in contemporary adoption controversies, then we should be alert to such threads in other contexts as
well.

Which pictures we choose as the appropriate ones for understanding
an issue frame our thoughts and actions. The unsatisfactory debate over
nontherapeutic research on children shows what can happen when we
confine our gaze to an inappropriate part of the tapestry. Fine scholars
were led astray when they looked at the horrors of Nazi experiments,
and to the rational, informed consent of autonomous adults as the picture they should try to emulate as closely as possible. We are better
served, I argue, by looking to portraits of parents and children in their
daily lives.

HUMAN FLOURISHING AND THE FAMILY

In the context of parent-child relationships we learn
many vitally important things. We learn most of the content of whatever morality we will embrace as adults. We learn some rules, but also
the images that should guide us and the ends we should pursue. Within
families, we also come to adopt our attitude toward morality. We learn,
that is, whether it is worth trying to be moral. If we have been fortunate
enough to have decent parents and favorable circumstances, we will
also acquire the capacity of empathy with others, both as *rationality*,

the ability to take another's point of view, and as *emotion,* the ability to imagine accurately what another person is likely to be feeling. Both of these capacities are crucial to practical moral wisdom. Last, in a family where love survives, we come to understand the centrality of relation-ships in human flourishing.

Any account that takes seriously the notion of human flourishing presupposes that there are some aspects of human nature that are both reasonably knowable and relatively stable. Invoking "human nature" immediately raises suspicion that one is imposing illegitimate and ideo-logically infused conceptions of that nature on people who have good reason to reject it. Mary Midgley offers a strong rejoinder:

The proper response to institutions stained with racism, sexism and other forms of political oppression is to say just what is wrong with them and to point out means by which they can in fact be changed. It is no use trying to shortcut this work by making the wild claim that human beings are infinitely malleable, blank paper at birth—a suggestion that cannot be be-lieved by anyone who has ever seen a baby. That there is *some* underlying human nature—some basic structure indicating what kinds of things can be good and bad for human beings—is a perfectly harmless assumption that we all need to make, and constantly do make, for all kinds of pur-poses. . . . The real source of trouble is the quite different assumption that our own preferred customs are the only ones which suit this nature.[5]

What Midgley calls "a perfectly harmless assumption"—namely, that there is some underlying "human nature" that our understandings about what is good or bad for us must take into account—is often treated as a suspicious, even dangerous presumption. Midgley identifies the most common problem, that people have tended to promote their own preferred notion of what is good and bad for persons as the only possible correct one.

Take that objection seriously. What options do we have? It would be comforting if all of our hard questions about what kind of lives we ought to live had answers that did *not* depend on disputable claims about human nature, if instead they had the firm logical certainty of propositions in geometry. If that were the case, all we would need would be to discover one or a few foundation stones, such as our capac-ity to reason, and build everything else upon them. There are two prob-lems with this strategy, which have already been mentioned but bear repeating. First, we have yet to find the foundation stones that can be established beyond dispute. Second, what we can build on top of the stones fails to reach many of the questions most important to us, questions about good and bad human lives, about families, and about social practices and institutions. Useful answers to the full range of questions we want to ask must assume some substantive account of human nature. This is the meaning of Midgley's claim that we "need to make" such assumptions.

Though we cannot avoid adopting some ideas about human nature, we have reason for caution. Susan Moller Okin argues that basing our conceptions of human nature on traditional or shared understandings is likely to result in bias because "the free, the educated, the wealthy, and men . . . are much more likely to shape them than are the unfree, the uneducated, the poor, and women."[6] Our views about human nature, Okin claims, are likely to be systematically incorrect—erring in ways that favor those with the most influence in shaping those views. The values and practices associated with the less influential are either left out or assigned diminished importance. Okin points out that Alasdair MacIntyre ranks the family alongside playing games and intellectual pursuits and that his list of exemplary virtuous persons contains not one individual actively engaged in rearing children.[7] This, she suggests, is not merely accidental, but a consequence of the dominance of adult males in articulating the traditions MacIntyre admires.

In practice, our presumptions about human nature are always fallible and open to challenge. The source of error may be simple ignorance, uninfluenced by our interests. The more fearsome sources of error, the ones that most concern theorists like Okin, are those that reinforce dominance and injustice. For the former, we must admit the ever-present possibility of error resulting from our imperfect knowledge, and always be open to new evidence and arguments. For the latter, we must be mindful of the likelihood of systematic distortions, vigilant in our search for them, and attentive to the people most likely to be silenced. These considerations argue not for abandoning the quest to understand human nature but for acknowledging the likely ways that search may be misdirected, and for including the voices of the relatively less powerful.

A FOCUS ON PRACTICES AND SPHERES

As I imagine the tapestry, the portraits we find on it represent the most significant human activities and events, the ones most replete with meaning. There would be many scenes of family life including childbirth and portraits of parents (fathers as well as mothers) caring for babies, toddlers, and young children, then adolescents and young adults, on to grandchildren and beyond. We would see love, loyalty, and patience in these scenes, along with joy and mutual laughter. Of course, not all scenes would be happy ones. The tapestry must also represent common sources of strife and suffering, and how families might respond to them with steadfastness, courage, compassion, and solidarity.

Though there are other kinds of portraits on the tapestry, the ones dealing with family life are remarkably numerous, especially in comparison to the relative lack of attention given to them by philosophers until recently. Together they portray a linked set of practices—being a good parent, spouse, grandparent—that constitute a sphere of profoundly important human activities. I have argued that this sphere and the practices within it are characterized by values that stress the good that can come from enduring commitments in human relationships. I have also argued that practical moral disputes, such as whether to permit the buying and selling of babies, are best understood through the values that characterize the sphere—what philosophers refer to as the goods internal to a practice.[8] Not because other moral principles or considerations are irrelevant; but because they may be insensitive to what people value most about that sphere. An ill-fitting moral analysis may impose a moral framework borrowed from another sphere, with the potential to disguise or ultimately corrupt what is genuinely valuable in this realm. A moral framework appropriate to public, market transactions has been imposed on the practice of creating and rearing children. What we need, I propose, are ethical analyses that are attentive to the meaning of the practice of parenting.

METAPHYSICAL DISPUTES AND PRACTICAL MORAL REASONING

The top-down model of moral reasoning inclines us to look upward to the highest, most abstract, and least resolvable disagreements—to metaphysics. Thus the argument between those who oppose and those who favor keeping abortion legal is framed as a disagreement about the personhood of fetuses. Ronald Dworkin claims that few people, even staunch opponents of abortion, really believe that "a fetus is from the moment of conception a full moral person with rights and interests equal in importance to those of any other member of the moral community."[9] He argues that what divides us over abortion cannot be explained by differing views on fetal personhood. When we examine how this belief fits with other related ones, abortion opponents do not appear to agree with all of the implications that reasonably can be drawn from it. Neither do those who favor legal abortion act as if a simple "no" to the question whether the fetus is a person constitutes a satisfactory and complete answer to the ethics of abortion.

I agree with Dworkin that the metaphysical dispute over fetal personhood cannot account for the complexity of the actual beliefs relevant to the abortion debate. But where he wants to argue that the nexus of the dispute is over another, religious issue—the sanctity and meaning of life—I want to bring attention back to the tapestry. If we cannot explain the battle over abortion in terms of the metaphysical dispute over human personhood, I do not believe that we advance our moral understanding greatly by asserting that it is instead over a different metaphysical disagreement. For Dworkin, a legal scholar as well as a philosopher, it offers a neat solution to the legal problem: the First Amendment to the U.S. Constitution protects differences in religious beliefs; if abortion is an expression of religious beliefs, then it falls under the umbrella of a constitutionally protected right.

Dworkin's artful reframing of the abortion debate offers a plausible explanation of why intellectual disagreement persists. But it is less successful at explaining why this, of all intellectual disputes, carries such incredible emotional force in contemporary America. The problem with Dworkin's account is that it is too far removed from the tapestry. By portraying beliefs about the sanctity of human life in highly abstract terms, it fails to notice the centrality of differing views about what gives meaning to women's lives, about the respective life roles of women and men, and about the importance of parenthood in human experience. Differences such as these touch the daily lives of all of us, and concern vitally important sections of the tapestry. These differences are pervasive and powerful enough to supply all of the passion exhibited in the battle over abortion. There is, of course, no guarantee that moving to a debate about what gives meaning to the lives of women and men will provide a resolution to moral or political conflict over abortion. But copious experience demonstrates that the metaphysical dispute leads nowhere. A change of focus, especially one that directs our attention to an issue at least as central as fetal personhood, affords an opportunity to introduce new arguments, new moral considerations, into what has been a fruitless search for accommodation.

Once again, Mary Midgley is a good guide to practical moral reasoning. She affirms that "it is hardly ever sensible to refute any argument just by pointing out an inconsistency within it. What is needed is to trace the considerations on both sides that have led us to hold clashing views, and to rethink them somehow so as to do justice to all these elements."[10] This approach was particularly helpful in understanding what goes on and what is at stake in prenatal testing.

DISTINGUISHING ETHICS
FROM PUBLIC POLICY

Perhaps the most destructive tendency in contemporary moral discourse is to conflate ethics and law. I prefer the term "public policy" to law because public policy conveys the sense of openness,. of many possible public responses ranging from informal moral suasion to state-enforced legal interventions. Even with this broad conception of public policy, the distinction between public policy and ethics remains strong and important. Nowhere was this more clear than in the case of the not-yet-born child. In countless conversations about the issues addressed in that chapter, I have noted again and again how people try to trim their moral judgments to fit whatever public policies they prefer. Once they appreciate that one can believe both that adults have substantial moral obligations to fetuses-likely-to-be-children and that policies that coerce adults—virtually always women—into doing what we believe they ought to do morally may be undesirable, people are freed to do more nuanced thinking about ethics *and* public policy.

The Tapestry, Shared Understandings, and Social Criticism

The most damning criticism of an approach to practical ethics that does not begin with presumably fundamental, unshakable principles, is that it lacks a critical edge. In its strong form, it is the claim that any approach to ethics that relies on a particular culture's considered moral judgments and moral tradition is incapable of making any critique of that culture's predominant acts, practices, and institutions. In its weaker form, the claim is that whatever critique is offered is condemned to be weak and feckless, because it depends so heavily on that which it intends to criticize.

This criticism of a practical ethics that relies substantially on moral traditions and considered moral judgments is misleading for two reasons. It is flawed by a simplistic view of morality; and it fails to recognize the terribly limited critical bite afforded by moral "Esperanto," that is, efforts to find a universal moral language that take no note of the values and practices of a particular culture.[11]

The view that cultures are lacking utterly in resources with which to critique their own practices and institutions is pervasive but false. This is the view behind such notions as the "dead hand" of tradition, or that the received moral views of a culture are nothing more than a collection of groundless prejudices put there by habit, or because they serve the interests of those who dominate the social order.[12]

The main problem with this view is that it presumes a kind of complete and impervious harmony within every culture's morality, coupled with a fantastic flexibility that permits that morality to adapt effortlessly, without a glimmer of conflict, to every twist of the culture's internal development and every turn of outside contact and new ideas. This portrait resembles no culture with which I am familiar, certainly none that has had to grapple with the differing moral perspectives offered by other cultures with which it has come into contact, or that has experienced protest against unequal treatment by any of its members. In no way does it resemble the culture in which I live. Midgley, in her defense of practical moral reasoning, points out that meaningful moral disagreement flourishes. Even apparently small disagreements can result in large-scale change, as their full implications are appreciated over time: "Any culture contains some materials for altering its own value-scheme, and with a very articulate, complex culture like ours, these materials are actually very abundant."[13]

Jeffrey Stout agrees with Midgley: "The ethical heritage of Western culture is not a closed system, a single seamless language, needing only to be received, applied to our situation, and passed on to the next generation. . . . To find oneself in a cultural tradition is the beginning, not the end, of critical thought. There is no simple opposition between tradition and critical reason or between conservatism and reform. Our task is not simply to bring as many possibilities into view as we can but also to judge what is worth preserving, what requires reformulation, and what must be left behind."[14] The contemporary rhetoric of everyday moral and political discourse tries to use "tradition" as a club to beat into submission everyone who disagrees with that person's own, perhaps peculiar, view of what our shared tradition means. But this is a

misappropriation of tradition, a misrepresentation of our shared understandings. Which reading of our tradition is the most valid one is not a
matter of political power, not even of majority vote. Majorities can be
wrong; indeed, there would be no need for prophets or other social
critics if morality were decided by majority vote. Nonetheless, to speak
meaningfully to a culture, we must speak in a moral language it understands; we must speak, that is, from shared understandings. Our social
criticism must connect, as Walzer says, to deeply held values.

Alasdair MacIntyre is probably the most prominent proponent of an
ethics based on tradition. MacIntyre's memorable image of our culture's moral ideas—as a collection of shards from different, incompatible traditions—led him to be pessimistic about the possibility of meaningful moral dialogue in our society. But there is reason to believe that
MacIntyre's pessimism is not entirely warranted. For one thing, consider the multitude of ways in which people do, in fact, engage in moral
conversation that seems, by any reasonable criteria, genuine. They advance considerations, weigh them, offer reinterpretations and other
considerations, make arguments, occasionally persuade others and occasionally alter their own views. Is this all an illusion, or is real moral
dialogue taking place?

Stout detects an interesting conundrum in the narrative structure of
MacIntyre's argument in *After Virtue*. The moral traditions to which
MacIntyre contrasts us unfavorably were not the static, self-contained
systems the story he told there implies. Rather, Stout points out,

New Testament Greek brought several moral languages together, trans-
forming the significance of each. Thomistic Latin was made entirely of borrowed parts, designed to insert Aristotle into a canon intent on excluding
him. These examples suggest that our predicament may not be as distinctive or as bleak as MacIntyre thinks. If premodern language-users have
been able to converse across cultural boundaries, change their minds in
dialogue with strangers, and invent new moral languages out of apparently
incompatible fragments, perhaps we can too.[15]

MacIntyre tells a more complex story about how traditions develop
and change in a later book, *Whose Justice? Which Rationality?* There he
describes factors that challenge traditions of moral inquiry: the discovery of incoherences within a tradition; new circumstances that reveal a
lack of conceptual resources on which to build effective responses; contact with other communities and their contrasting traditions of inquiry.
One possible outcome is what he calls an "epistemological crisis" to

which the tradition must respond by inventing or discovering new concepts and theories.[16] Even with this more dynamic view of traditions, McIntyre remains pessimistic about the possibility of moral coherence in contemporary society. He bemoans the modern self "which has too many half-convictions and too few settled coherent convictions, too many partly formulated alternatives and too few opportunities to evaluate them systematically." This sort of self, he asserts, "brings to its encounters with the claims of rival traditions a fundamental incoherence which is too disturbing to be admitted to self-conscious awareness except on the rarest of occasions."[17]

One possibility, of course, is that even the traditions McIntyre admires were more fractured and less coherent than our contemporary reading of them supposes. Stout suggests as much. In any case, challenge and change within and between traditions is far from a straightforward process in which success is always and immediately apparent.

What are we to make of this untidiness? We could throw up our hands and surrender any hope of meaningful moral dialogue. But we have another option. We can acknowledge the complexity of our moral inheritances and the difficulty of achieving closure on difficult moral questions, but note that our plight is hardly novel and that, over time, agreement often emerges even on issues once regarded as intractable. We can also note that some practices indulged in by earlier cultures have been rejected as morally wrong—that is, that we have made, on some fronts, moral progress.

The view that cultures lack the means in their moral traditions for criticism and change commits one to an odd reading of history. Consider the phenomenon of moral progress. When a culture moves from tolerating slavery to abolishing it, from celebrating human sacrifice to banning it, from treating women as the property of their fathers and husbands to recognizing them as autonomous citizens, from permitting the torture of animals to outlawing it, it seems reasonable to say that this culture exhibits moral progress.

All but the most rabid relativist must accept some notion of moral progress: a state of affairs in which a culture's beliefs, acts, practices, and institutions reflect and support a superior account of morality than what existed prior to that state. Progress is not inevitable; cultures may even lapse into inferior moral states. The claim, though, is modest: that moral progress is possible and that it can be recognized, even if certain changes may be difficult to classify as instances of progress, stasis, or regress.

Once moral progress is acknowledged, the question arises, what prompted it? Here the proponents of top-down ethics or of other views that deny the importance of shared understandings—of tapestry—have a quandary. Either they must admit a crucial role for existing moral practices, ideas, and institutions or they must explain both how the reform-promoting ideas arose independently of existing practices, ideas, and institutions and how those utterly foreign and novel ideas found sufficient resonance within the culture to compel change. Ideas do not arise from nowhere, as studies in the history of ideas repeatedly remind us; the virgin birth of powerful new ideas in ethics seems unlikely. But I want to focus more on the second problem: how a new moral idea can speak forcefully to a culture. A well-developed history of moral change—not merely of ideas, but of actual cultural changes— would strengthen and perhaps correct what follows. Such a history of moral change that gave equal consideration to ideas and social forces would be most welcome, especially a history that looked to the origins of those ideas in moral traditions and practices as well as in leading thinkers, and that counted change as successful only when it permeated the culture's beliefs, practices, and institutions.

Consider the likelihood that a sound moral idea—say, that all people deserve to be treated with equal respect—was introduced into a culture whose beliefs, practices, and institutions worked to quite the opposite effect for most of its population. They kept slaves, practiced torture, treated women and children as the property of male members of the ruling class. It is difficult to imagine that someone who happened along out of the blue extolling radical moral equality and condemning slavery, torture, and the subjugation of women would get a warm welcome. More likely, he or she would be treated to exactly the practices so enthusiastically criticized. Unless, that is, the person making that critique could invoke effectively the central values, the core moral convictions, of that same culture in a way that tied them persuasively to the reforms demanded. This, Michael Walzer reminds us, is the role of the genuine prophet: not to predict marvelous events, but to chide us severely for our failings; to call on us to do honor to our deepest moral commitments. The prophet cannot expect to get a hearing unless he or she can connect powerfully with the deepest values of that culture's existing moral tradition.[18] Prophets can fail for many reasons. They can be ignored or persecuted. But they cannot succeed unless they make their indictment in terms the culture understands. To be able to shame someone, that person must believe at heart that he or she is failing in the way you describe, and that such a failure is a grievous matter.

Moral progress in a culture must take place against the background of shared understandings that permeate the culture's beliefs, practices, and institutions. Unless the new, and better, moral idea can connect with the existing tradition, it is a complete mystery how such an idea could find any hearing or be an effective engine of change. It is not even clear how the culture could find such an idea intelligible.

If we alter our view of a culture's morality from that of a neat and impervious harmony to what seems more realistic, a seething rough-and-tumble, with constant challenge and accommodation, we can give a plausible account of moral progress. Moral criticism that is to penetrate beneath the broadest generalities into the guiding beliefs, practices, and institutions of a particular culture must reach the values of that culture. It will touch, not just moral rules, but forms of life in that culture, ideas about what makes lives worth living—images in the tapestry.

Toward a More Beautiful Tapestry

The time has come to restate my guiding presumptions. First, I believe that the best way to understand many of the debates about conceiving, bearing, and rearing children is by understanding the place of children in the lives of adults. As a corollary, we must consider the possibility that arguments about such matters as the moral status of fetuses are, in an important sense, beside the point.

Second, I believe that a crucial part of the debate is about the differences between men and women: not biology per se, but the place children play in giving meaning and structure to the lives of adults. The images a culture embraces of the lives of women and men will be crucial in framing the debates over conceiving, gestating, and rearing children.

Third, the method appropriate for such an inquiry is not the search for abstract principles that are timeless and contextless. Instead, the result we desire is a complex weighing of interests and values that identifies what is genuinely and deeply at stake for women, men, and children and that achieves perspective not by ignoring but by embracing history and social context. This embrace is necessary to understand what sorts of good lives are available in the culture, and what alternatives might be made available. Attention to history and to context is essential because both yield insight into the presumptions, images, and customs that determine how we frame questions and conflicts, and into the resources available for resolving them.

Our ambitions must remain modest. We are unlikely to offer a radically novel idea about the moral value of children or of the relation of children to adults. But by examining the threads our analysis exposes, we may find some that are gnarled and ugly and some that are beautiful; or sets of fibers that should not coexist in the same tapestry; or some that come from older fabrics we should reject as coarse and inferior. Portions of the tapestry might be found to require extensive repair and reweaving. Other areas that were relatively featureless might now be completed in a way that blends naturally with the rest of the tapestry, without having to distort major strands of warp or weft. In other cases we will have to be content with identifying incompatible major strands, and showing how each of them leads to differences in the design, even as we indicate which one we believe is superior, and why.

However extensive our proposed repairs, filling-ins, and reweavings, the tapestry itself must reveal images recognizable to the culture whose lives it portrays. If our efforts are successful, perhaps they will help to make those images of family life, of children and parents, more beautiful, more true, and more moving.

Notes

Chapter 1. Why Do Adults Have Children?

1. *New York Times*, 17 February 1990, p. 1.

2. Immanuel Kant, *Groundwork of the Metaphysics of Morals* (New York: Harper and Row, 1964), 95–96.

3. Michael Miller, "Teen Who Got Sister's Bone Marrow Looking Forward to Wedding," *Reuters*, 6 June 1991.

4. Ibid.

5. Valerie Kuklenski, "Newborn Holds Key to Life for Teen Sister," *UPI*, 17 February 1990.

6. Richard Saltus, "Conceiving Child for Marrow Termed Ethical; Doctors Say Baby Donor May Save Sister," *Boston Globe*, 18 February 1990.

7. The protagonists in this dispute were Paul Ramsey and Richard McCormick. The details appear in chapter 4.

8. For an enlightening elaboration of the analogy between deductive reasoning in ethics and in geometry, see Albert Jonsen and Stephen Toulmin, *The Abuse of Casuistry: A History of Moral Reasoning* (Berkeley, Los Angeles, and London: University of California Press, 1988).

Chapter 2. Families, the Marketplace, and Values

1. It is difficult to find or invent a phrase that captures concisely and accurately the range of practices included in discussions about what are typically dubbed "new reproductive technologies." Not all of them are new, for example, artificial insemination, and not all of them involve sophisticated technology. One of the most controversial practices, surrogacy for pay, is notable primarily for its legal rather than its technological novelty. To avoid tedious repetition, I will use several variants including the old standby, new reproduc-

tive technologies. They are meant to be taken as synonyms for alternative reproductive practices.

2. Miriam B. Rosenthal, M.D., "Psychiatric Aspects of Infertility and As-
sisted Reproductive Technologies," *Psychological Issues in Infertility* 4, no. 3
(1993): 471.

3. There is a story told about an attorney who set up shop in a small town.
He was starving to death for lack of business until he had a brilliant idea: he
persuaded another lawyer to come to the town; they both prospered.

4. Gina Kolata, "Cloning Human Embryos: Debate Erupts over Ethics,"
New York Times, 27 October 1993, A1, B7.

5. Ibid.

6. In an extraordinary article, Margaret Jane Radin considers the appropriate scope and limits of markets in human affairs. Responding to an economic
analysis of rape, she notes that "for all but the deepest enthusiast, market rhetoric seems intuitively out of place here, so inappropriate that it is either silly or
somehow insulting to the value being discussed." Radin, "Market-Inalienabil-
ity," Harvard Law Review 100 (1987): 1849, 1880. Radin and I agree on
several points:

(1) that a market in surrogacy is problematic;
(2) that the dominant moral language in which the debate is conducted
emphasizes a conception of liberty as negative liberty, a conception of the
person that disguises the significance of nonmarket realms and leads readily
to acceptance of the market as a central expression of human freedom;
(3) that a preferable alternative exists which emphasizes human moral development as essential to the growth of positive liberty and accepts certain
limitations on negative liberty as they contribute to that development;
(4) that, as Radin puts it, "the rhetoric of the market . . . foster(s) an inferior
conception of human flourishing" (pp. 1885–1886); and
(5) that a proper understanding of new reproductive arrangements requires
the best understanding of human flourishing we can achieve.

7. See chapter 3, "Adoption and the Meanings of Parenthood."

8. B. Berger and P. L. Berger, *The War over the Family: Capturing the Middle Ground* (New York: Anchor/Doubleday, 1983).

9. Erik H. Erikson, "Human Strength and the Cycle of Generations," in
Insight and Responsibility (New York: W. W. Norton, 1964).

10. Carol Levine, "AIDS and Changing Concepts of the Family," in *A
Disease of Society: Cultural and Institutional Responses to AIDS,* ed. Dorothy
Nelkin, David P. Willis, and Scott V. Paris (New York: Cambridge University
Press, 1991), 48.

The historian Carl N. Degler suggests that families, across time and culture,
have been typified by five elements: (1) "a ritual between a woman and a man,
a ceremony that we call marriage, and which implies long duration, if not permanence, for the relationship"; (2) "duties and rights of parenthood. . ."; (3)
living together or in close proximity; (4) "reciprocal economic obligations";
and (5) "a means for sexual satisfaction for the partners, though not necessarily
. . . an exclusive one." (Degler, "The Emergence of the Modern American

Family," in *The American Family in Social-Historical Perspective,* 3d ed., ed. Michael Gordon (New York: St. Martin's Press, 1983), 61. Degler's first and fifth elements pertain to families formed and still consisting of husbands and wives. Levine's list encompasses such families but also includes other groupings that provide mutual care, steadfast loyalty, and enduring relationships.

11. See any of the articles about reproduction by the distinguished legal scholar John A. Robertson, e.g., "Embryos, Families and Procreative Liberty: The Legal Structure of the New Reproduction," *Southern California Law Review* 59, no. 5 (1986): 939. For a rejoinder, see Maura A. Ryan, "The Argument for Unlimited Procreative Liberty: A Feminist Critique," *Hastings Center Report* (July–August 1990): 6–12. Ryan writes, "attention to women's experience has taught feminists that there are no 'merely symbolic' harms; we interpret and shape experience through our symbols and therefore how we think about persons, events, and biological processes has a great deal to do with how we behave toward them" (p. 12).

12. See Bernard Wishy, *The Child and the Republic: The Dawn of Modern American Child Nurture* (Philadelphia: University of Pennsylvania Press, 1968), for an analysis of how children were portrayed in American popular culture. For a description of the rise of companionate marriage and the changes in family relations in the first century and a quarter after the Revolutionary War, see Michael Grossberg, *Governing the Hearth: Law and Family in Nineteenth-Century America* (Chapel Hill: University of North Carolina Press, 1985).

13. John Boswell, *The Kindness of Strangers: The Abandonment of Children in Western Europe from Late Antiquity to the Renaissance* (New York: Pantheon Press, 1988).

14. Daniel Blake Smith, "Autonomy and Affection: Parents and Children in Chesapeake Families," in Gordon, *The American Family in Social-Historical Perspective,* 209–228.

15. Letter from Thomas Jefferson to Mary Jefferson Randolph, 31 May 1791, in Sarah N. Randolph, *The Domestic Life of Thomas Jefferson* (New York: Frederick Ungar, 1958), 202.

16. I can still recall an incident from my adolescence that illustrates what happens when this procedure is not followed scrupulously. There was one Tastycake chocolate cupcake left. My sister wanted it. My mother told her to cut it in half and save half for me. She cut in it half—top from bottom—and ate the half with the chocolate icing. One wonders if John Rawls's passion for justice was born under similar circumstances.

17. See Susan Moller Okin for an occasionally scathing view of injustice in family relationships and the failure of moral theorists to confront it effectively. Okin, *Justice, Gender, and the Family* (New York: Basic Books, 1989).

18. Gilbert Ryle, *The Concept of Mind* (New York: Barnes & Noble, 1949).

19. Even incursions of the market as simple as children's allowances must be handled carefully. See Viviana Zelizer, *Pricing the Priceless Child* (New York: Basic Books, 1985)

20. David H. Smith makes a related distinction. In a discussion of surrogacy, he describes alternative "ways of thinking about a woman's relationship to a child she bears and indeed to her own reproductive processes. In one of

these perspectives the relationship between self and reproductive involvement is extrinsic and contingent. Pregnancy is viewed externally and objectively as a temporary state one is in for any one of a number of reasons. The self calculates its reasons for pregnancy, mode and form of personal involvement. . . . Another perspective on body is also possible: I identify myself with my body. I not only control it, but I have to listen to it. . . . I have embodied involvements with others, involvements that are constitutive of me as a self. These constitutive, involving embodiments are clearest in our relations with our parents and our children." Smith, "Wombs for Rent, Selves for Sale?" *Journal of Contemporary Health Law and Policy* 4 (1988): 30–31.

21. John A. Robertson, "The Question of Human Cloning," *Hastings Center Report* (March 1994): 6–14.

22. Robertson, "Embryos, Families and Procreative Liberty," 1031. Robertson's commitment to reproductive liberty is clear in both the title and the text of his book, *Children of Choice: Freedom and the New Reproductive Technologies* (Princeton: Princeton University Press, 1994.) In it he restates his guiding principle: "I propose that procreative liberty be given presumptive priority in all conflicts, with the burden on opponents of any particular technique to show that harmful effects from its use justify limiting procreative choice" (p. 16).

23. Ibid., 1040.

24. Smith, "Wombs for Rent, Selves for Sale?" 33.

25. Ibid, 34.

26. See K. R. Daniels, "Semen Donors: Their Motivations and Attitudes to Their Offspring," *Journal of Reproductive and Infant Psychology* 7 (1989): 121–127, and R. Rowland, "Attitudes and Opinions of Donors on an Artificial Insemination by Donor (AID) Programme," *Clinical Reproduction and Fertility* 2 (1983): 249–259.

27. Paul Lauritzen, *Pursuing Parenthood* (Bloomington: Indiana University Press, 1993).

28. Ken R. Daniels and Karyn Taylor, "Secrecy and Openness in Donor Insemination," *Politics and the Life Sciences* 12, no. 2 (1993): 155–170, confirm that Australia and New Zealand rely on genuine donors. In the same issue of the journal, Jacques Lansac affirms that France uses only sperm donors, not vendors ("One Father Only: Donor Insemination and CECOS in France," pp. 185–186).

29. Alvin W. Drake, Stan N. Finkelstein, and Harvey M. Sapolsky, *The American Blood Supply* (Cambridge: MIT Press, 1982).

30. American Fertility Society, "Guidelines for Gamete Donation: 1993," *Fertility and Sterility, Supplement 1* 59, no. 2 (1993): 5S–9S, 6S; sec. VI.A.

31. Machelle M. Seibel and Ann Kiessling, "Compensating Egg Donors: Equal Pay for Equal Time?" *New England Journal of Medicine* 328, no. 10 (1993): 737.

32. Ibid.

33. Andrea Mechanick Braverman, "Survey Results on the Current Practice of Ovum Donation," *Fertility and Sterility* 59, no. 6 (1993): 1216–1220.

34. In a famous article, Landes and Posner consider "some tentative and

reversible steps toward a free baby market in order to determine experimentally the social costs and benefits of using the market in this area." "The Economics of the Baby Shortage," *Journal of Legal Studies,* 7, no. 2 (1978): 347.

35. John A. Robertson, "Surrogate Mothers: Not So Novel After All," *Hastings Center Report* 13, no. 5 (1983): 28–34.

36. Ibid., 29.

37. Robertson, "Embryos, Families and Procreative Liberty," 1030.

38. Ibid.

39. New York State Task Force on Life and the Law, *Surrogate Parenting: Analysis and Recommendations for Public Policy* (1988). The task force concluded unanimously that public policy ought to discourage surrogate parenting and proposed legislation to ban fees to surrogates or brokers and to void surrogacy contracts. Their response to the argument that children born under surrogacy arrangements are better off because otherwise they would not have been born at all is as follows:

But this argument assumes the very factor under deliberation—the child's conception and birth. The assessment for public policy occurs prior to conception when the surrogate arrangements are made. The issue then is not whether a particular child should be denied life, but whether children should be conceived in circumstances that would place them at risk. The notion that children have an interest in being born prior to their conception and birth is not embraced in other public policies and should not be assumed in the debate on surrogate parenting. (p. 120)

I am grateful to John Arras for pointing out this argument to me.

40. Alexander M. Capron and Margaret J. Radin, "Choosing Family Law over Contract Law as a Paradigm for Surrogate Motherhood," *Law, Medicine & Health Care* 16, nos. 1–2 (1988): 34, 40.

Chapter 3.   Adoption and the Meanings of Parenthood

1. The details of this account are taken from a variety of sources, but rely especially on the excellent article by Lucinda Franks, "Annals of Law: The War for Baby Clausen," *New Yorker,* 22 March 1993, 56–73.

2. Franks, "Annals of Law," 58.

3. Ibid., 72.

4. Isabel Wilkerson, "Couple Is Told to Return Girl to Biological Parents," *New York Times,* 31 March 1993, A10.

5. Joan Biskupic, "Last Hope of Keeping Baby Jessica Lost: High Court Ruling Ends Bitter Adoption Battle," *Atlanta Journal and Constitution,* 31 July 1993, A8.

6. DeBoer v. DeBoer, 114 S. Ct. 11 (1993).

7. Ibid. (Blackmun, J., dissent).

8. Associated Press, "Baby Jessica Adjusting Well as Anna, Aunt Says," *Chicago Tribune,* 31 July 1994, C15. See also Greg Smith, "Baby Jessica Takes to New Life, New Name," *Los Angeles Times,* 7 August 1994, A10.

9. Paul Lauritzen's book, *Pursuing Parenthood* (Bloomington: Indiana University Press, 1993), is a noteworthy exception. See note 17, chapter 2.

10. Franks, "Annals of Law," 73.

11. Jean-Jacques Rousseau, *Confessions*, 2 vols. (New York: J. J. Little and Ives, 1928), 2: 551. Rousseau came to regret abandoning his children. He asked a friend to locate his oldest child, unsuccessfully, and rendered in *Emile* quite a different judgment about fatherhood than his earlier one: "He who cannot fulfill the duties of a father has no right to become one. No poverty, no career, no human consideration can dispense him from caring for his children and bringing them up himself." See John Boswell, *The Kindness of Strangers: The Abandonment of Children in Western Europe from Late Antiquity to the Renaissance* (New York: Pantheon, 1988), 20, n. 42.

12. Boswell, *The Kindness of Strangers*.

13. Sextus Pompeius Festus, *De Verborum Significatu*, ed. W. M. Lindsay (Leipzig, 1913). Cited in Boswell, *The Kindness of Strangers*, 110.

14. Boswell, *The Kindness of Strangers*, 15–16.

15. Ibid., 90 ff.

16. Ibid., 150–152.

17. Ibid., 118.

18. Ibid., 121.

19. Ibid., 37–38.

20. Ibid., 120, citing a declamation, attributed to Quintilian.

21. Ibid., 228 ff.

22. Ibid., 414–417. A tragic irony of the foundling hospital as an institutionalized way of dealing with unwanted children is that the death rates in such hospitals were appalling, with contagious disease probably a significant factor. Contemporary parents sending their young children off to group settings for the first time, whether to a play group, preschool, or kindergarten, are all too familiar with the disease-of-the-month phenomenon, as their children bring home an illness passed around among their schoolmates. Fortunately, with good nutrition and sanitation, nursing and medical care, the diseases our children bring home rarely amount to more than a nuisance; the worst killers have been beaten back through immunization and antibiotic drugs. It is regrettably easy to imagine that many of the infants packed into foundling homes might have perished from those same diseases.

23. Ibid., 424.

24. Michael Grossberg, *Governing the Hearth: Law and Family in Nineteenth-Century America* (Chapel Hill: University of North Carolina Press, 1985).

25. Barry Nicholas, *An Introduction to Roman Law* (Oxford: Clarendon Press, 1962).

26. Ibid., 67.

27. Boswell, *The Kindness of Strangers*, 67.

28. Ibid., 63.

29. Ibid., 65.

30. Ibid., 71. The patria potestas was so encompassing and so central to Roman law that two distinct forms of legal adoption had to be devised, depending on whether the person to be adopted was already in the patria potestas of the adopter or not. The form known as *adoptio* required that the adoptee be

released from one patria potestas and then transferred to a new one. Early Roman law did not recognize a voluntary relinquishment of the patria potestas. But it did have a provision in it probably intended to discourage abuse of the father's right to sell his offspring. After selling his son three times, the father lost his power over him. So early Romans invented a practice in which a male offspring was sold and manumitted three times and thus became eligible to enter the patria potestas of his new father. Women and grandchildren, it should be noted, required only one sale and manumission to escape the patriarch's potestas. Later Roman law streamlined the process considerably.

31. Grossberg, *Governing the Hearth*, 25.

32. Ibid., 235.

33. Ibid. See especially chapter 1, pp. 3–30.

34. Cited in Grossberg, *Governing the Hearth*, 264.

35. Michael Grossberg, "Battling over Motherhood in Philadelphia: A Study of Antebellum American Trial Courts as Arenas of Conflict," in Lazarus-Black and Hirsch, *Contested States: Law, Hegemony and Resistance* (New York: Routledge, 1994), 153–183.

36. Ibid., 166.

37. *Report of the d'Hauteville Case* (Philadelphia, 1840); cited in Grossberg, "Battling over Motherhood," 168 (emphasis in original).

38. Cynthia Eagle Russett, *Sexual Science: The Victorian Construction of Womanhood* (Cambridge: Harvard University Press, 1989).

39. Minot Savage, "The Rights of Children," *Arena* 6 (1892): 13–14; cited in Grossberg, *Governing the Hearth*, 281.

40. Grossberg, *Governing the Hearth*, 272.

41. Ibid., 275.

42. Boswell, *The Kindness of Strangers*, 431.

43. Grossberg, *Governing the Hearth*, 257.

44. Boswell, *The Kindness of Strangers*, esp. pp. 122–126. The Latin word was derived from Greek, meaning "to recognize or discover."

45. Grossberg, *Governing the Hearth*, 25.

46. Cited in Grossberg, *Governing the Hearth*, 258–259.

47. *Compact Edition of the Oxford English Dictionary* (1971), s.v. "steward."

48. Susan Chira, "High Court Call: Father's Right or Child's Interest," *New York Times*, 17 July 1994, 1: 12.

49. Michael Bohman and Sören Sigvardsson, "Outcome in Adoption: Lessons from Longitudinal Studies," in *The Psychology of Adoption*, ed. David M. Brodzinsky and Marshall D. Schechter (New York: Oxford University Press, 1990), 104.

50. David M. Brodzinsky, "Long-Term Outcomes in Adoption," *Future of Children* 3, no. 1 (1993): 153–166.

51. John Triseliotis and Malcolm Hill, "Contrasting Adoption, Foster Care, and Residential Rearing," in Brodzinsky and Schechter, *The Psychology of Adoption*, 107–120.

52. Peter L. Benson, Anu R. Sharma, and Eugene C. Roehlkepartain, *Growing Up Adopted: A Portrait of Adolescents and Their Families* (Minneapo-

lis: Search Institute, 1994). See p. 25 for the percentages reported. Three observations about the study are worth mentioning here. First, one of the reasons it failed to find the incidence of psychological difficulty reported in some other studies is probably due to how this study drew its sample: whereas other studies drew from children seeking assistance for emotional problems, this one used a sample drawn from the population of all adoptive families. The difference in the two sampling techniques may account for the difference in the findings. Second, the families of adoptive children tended to have higher incomes and more education and to remain intact more than the families of the average adolescent. Each of these factors probably supports healthy emotional development. Third, the study does not have a true control group, that is, a group of adolescents raised in nonadoptive families whose emotional development was measured by the same instruments in the same manner at the same time. Instead, the study had to rely on comparisons with a national sample of adolescents and on the data on nonadopted siblings. A true control group would have given us a bit more confidence in the results reported.

53. One facet of Roman law is interesting in this connection. The Romans, up to the time of Constantine, permitted biological parents to reclaim their offspring at almost any time and with few restrictions. They did, however, require that the rearing parents be compensated for the cost of raising the child. It would be interesting to see what impact such a requirement to pay for the expenses of child rearing would have on biological fathers' claims to their offspring. One other virtue of such compensation is that it acknowledges that the adults who raise children have interests that deserve respect. Monetary compensation is not the best way to show such respect, and I would be surprised if many adoptive parents would even accept it, for the same reasons people reject markets in new reproductive technologies.

54. *Uniform Adoption Act* (1994), Chicago.

55. Ibid., sec. 3-707(d).

56. The difference between the two cases is that for Baby Jessica, no final adoption decree was ever issued, whereas for Baby Richard a court did issue such a decree despite the biological father's claim.

57. *Uniform Adoption Act* (1994), sec. 7-105(f).

58. Ibid., sec. 2-104(b).

59. Ibid., sec. 3-301(a)(2).

Chapter 4.   Research on Children and the Scope of Responsible Parenthood

1. Cited in Paul Ramsey, *The Patient as Person* (New Haven: Yale University Press, 1970), 1.

2. Jay Katz, *Experimentation with Human Beings* (New York: Russell Sage Foundation, 1972).

3. Ramsey, *The Patient as Person*, 5, 11–12.

4. Ibid., 14, 13.

5. Ibid., 36.

6. Ibid., 25.

7. Ibid., 34 n. 31.

8. Ibid., 35.

9. Ibid., 28.

10. Ibid., 38–39.

11. Richard A. McCormick, "Proxy Consent in the Experimentation Situation," *Perspectives in Biology and Medicine* 18, no. 1 (Autumn 1974): 9.

12. Ibid.

13. Ibid., 12.

14. Ibid.

15. Ibid., 12–13.

16. Ibid., 14.

17. Ramsey, *The Patient as Person*, 39.

18. Thomas H. Murray, "The Growing Danger from Gene-Spliced Hormones," *Discover*, February 1987, 88–92.

19. Thanks to the reviewer for the University of California Press who pointed out that allowing people to fly is exactly what pixie dust is supposed to do. This is just one example of the many helpful comments I received.

20. National Institutes of Health, *Report of the NIH Human Growth Hormone Protocol Review Committee*, 2 October 1992, 13.

21. Louis E. Underwood, "Growth Hormone Therapy for Short Stature: Yes or No?" *Hospital Practice* (15 April 1992): 192–198.

22. These projected adult heights are two and one half standard deviations below the mean expected heights for adult American men and women. The panel approved these as appropriate cutoffs for determining which children could be admitted into the study.

23. Diane Rothem, Donald J. Cohen, Raymond Hintz, and Myron Genel, "Psychological Sequelae of Relative 'Treatment Failure' for Children Receiving Human Growth Hormone Replacement," *Journal of the American Academy of Child Psychiatry* 18 (1979): 505–520.

24. Gladys B. White shares my reservations about defining short stature per se as a disorder. She also employs the analogy with skin color. See White, "Human Growth Hormone: The Dilemma of Expanded Use in Children," *Kennedy Institute of Ethics Journal* 3, no. 4 (1993): 401–409.

25. Ad Hoc Committee on Growth Hormone Usage, the Lawson Wilkins Pediatric Endocrine Society, and Committee on Drugs, "Growth Hormone in the Treatment of Children with Short Stature," *Pediatrics* 72, no. 6 (1983): 891–894.

26. Carol A. Tauer offers a penetrating critique of the NIH panel's reasoning with respect to the rules governing research with children. She concludes that revising the regulations is preferable to bending the rules to make them fit ideas about what is morally acceptable. I agree with Tauer, but I would urge that we revisit our understandings of the ethics of research with children before revising the rules. See Tauer, "The NIH Trials of Growth Hormone for Short Stature," *IRB: A Review of Human Subjects Research* 16, no. 3 (1994): 1–9.

Chapter 5.   Moral Obligations to the Not-Yet-Born Child

1. Eric P. Finamore, "*Jefferson v. Griffin Spalding County Hospital Authority:* Court-ordered Surgery to Protect the Life of an Unborn Child," *American Journal of Law and Medicine* 9, no. 1 (1983): 83–101.

2. Nancy K. Rhoden, "The Judge in the Delivery Room: The Emergence of Court-ordered Cesareans," *California Law Review* 74, no. 6 (1986): 1951–2030.

3. Automobile Workers v. Johnson Controls, 499 U.S. 187 (1991).

4. The Missouri Supreme Court recently ruled that parents could sue for harms caused by actions taken several years prior to conception. A woman had given birth to a child with Rh-positive blood. If her own Rh-negative blood type had been entered correctly in her medical records, she could have been given a drug known as RhoGAM that would have prevented her from developing antibodies to Rh-positive blood. Her Rh type was entered incorrectly by a lab technician, Kathy Jadwin, she developed antibodies against Rh-positive blood, and, as can happen in such cases, her antibodies attacked the Rh-positive blood of a fetus conceived years later. The child, Tyler, was born alive, but suffered severe damage. The majority decision allowing the parents to sue included the following hypothetical:

> Assume a balcony is negligently constructed. Two years later, a mother and her one-year-old child step onto the balcony and it gives way, causing serious injuries to both the mother and the child. It would be ludicrous to suggest that only the mother would have a cause of action against the builder but, because the infant was not conceived at the time of the negligent conduct, no duty of care existed toward the child. It is unjust and arbitrary to deny recovery to Tyler simply because he had not been conceived at the time of Kathy Jadwin's negligence.

The case is Lough v. Rolla Women's Clinic, Inc., 866 S.W.2d 851 (Mo. 1993) ¶23, 105.

5. Ronald Dworkin, *Life's Dominion: An Argument about Abortion, Euthanasia, and Individual Freedom* (New York: Vintage Books, 1994).

6. W. L. Prosser and W. Page Keeton, *Handbook of the Law of Torts,* 5th ed. (St. Paul, Minn.: West Publishing Co., 1984), 368.

7. D. E. Johnsen, "The Creation of Fetal Rights: Conflicts with Women's Constitutional Rights to Liberty, Privacy, and Equal Protection," *Yale Law Journal* 95 (1986): 599–625.

8. Prosser, *Handbook of the Law of Torts,* 369.

9. *Johnson Controls,* 5.

10. Men, of course, become parents too. This is relevant both biologically—to the extent that exposures to workplace toxins affect men's ability to conceive a healthy child—and morally. The moral analogy between pregnant women and their not-yet-born children and fathers and their born children is a crucial part of my argument. For the *Johnson Controls* case, including a male worker showed that the company's policies treated men and women differently.

11. *Johnson Controls,* 7.

12. Ibid., 8.

13. Ibid., 11.

14. Ibid., 13.

15. The case known as *McFall v. Shimp* provides an interesting analogy. Robert McFall suffered from aplastic anemia. His cousin, David Shimp, was the only member of McFall's family to have possibly compatible bone marrow. After preliminary tests for compatibility, Shimp refused to undergo further testing, effectively eliminating him as a potential marrow donor to his cousin, McFall. McFall asked the court to order Shimp to complete the immunological testing and, if he was found to be compatible, to donate his marrow. The court refused, although it indicated that Shimp's refusal to do what might save his cousin's life was morally reprehensible. There is little reason to think that a closer degree of relationship—from father to child—would prompt judges to overthrow a legal tradition that refuses to force individuals to permit their bodies to be significantly invaded in order to aid another. The Shimp decision is reported at 10 Pa. D. & C.3d 90 (1978).

16. J. R. Leiberman, M. Mazor, W. Chaim, and A. Cohen, "The Fetal Right to Live," *Obstetrics and Gynecology* 53, no. 4 (1989): 515–517.

17. To this point, we have limited discussion to children who will be born alive. The fetus in this case was stillborn. Nonetheless, the father-child analogy is useful here, along with the concept of obligations to born children as the upper limit of obligations to not-yet-born children. If we can show that under roughly comparable circumstances public policy should not compel a father to bear similar burdens for similar benefits to his born child, then consistency requires that we not compel a pregnant woman to bear comparable burdens for comparable benefits to her not-yet-born child. In addition, most people, including people who support women's freedom to choose abortion, see the full-term healthy fetus as morally equivalent to the newborn baby. We do not need to settle precisely when the full-term-fetus-about-to-be-delivered becomes morally similar to a newly delivered baby to address forced cesarean sections; only that a few days or hours prior to delivery do not seem to make a monumental difference when dealing with a full-term, viable fetus.

18. Scholars in bioethics are split over whether forced cesareans should ever be permitted. Two of the best articles taking a firm stance against them are Rhoden, "The Judge in the Delivery Room," and George Annas, "Forced Cesareans: The Most Unkindest Cut of All," *Hastings Center Report* 12, no. 3 (1982): 16–17, 45. Frank A. Chervenak and Lawrence B. McCullough argue that court-ordered cesarean sections "are not unjustified" in some cases, though they offer this conclusion with what they note is "considerable trepidation." See their article "Justified Limits on Refusing Intervention," *Hastings Center Report* 21, no. 2 (1991): 12–18. Bonnie Steinbock takes a dim view of forced cesareans, but she does not close the door on other possible interventions "where the risk to the woman is very low and the benefit to the baby very great." She adds, however, that "such cases are virtually nonexistent." See her book *Life Before Birth: The Moral and Legal Status of Embryos and Fetuses* (New York: Oxford University Press, 1992), esp. chap. 4, pp. 162–163.

Chapter 6.   Prenatal Testing and the Quest for the
Perfect Child

1. Ruth Schwartz Cowan, "Aspects of the History of Prenatal Diagnosis," *Fetal Diagnosis and Therapy* 8, supplement 1 (1993): 10–17.

2. Dorothy C. Wertz and John C. Fletcher, "Prenatal Diagnosis and Sex Selection in 19 Nations," *Social Science and Medicine* 37, no. 11 (1993): 1359–1366.

3. Troy Duster, *Backdoor to Eugenics* (New York: Routledge, 1990).

4. Thanks to Adrienne Asch for first pointing out this distinction to me.

5. Sheldon C. Reed, *Counseling in Medical Genetics*, 3d ed. (New York: Alan R. Liss, 1980), 11.

6. F. C. Fraser, "Genetic Counseling," *American Journal of Human Genetics* 26 (1974): 636–659.

7. James R. Sorenson, "Genetic Counseling: Values that Have Mattered," in *Prescribing Our Future: Ethical Challenges in Genetic Counseling*, ed. Dianne M. Bartels, Bonnie S. LeRoy, and Arthur L. Caplan (New York: Aldine de Gruyter, 1993), 6.

8. Joan H. Marks, "The Training of Genetic Counselors: Origins of a Psychosocial Model," in Bartels et al., *Prescribing Our Future*, 15–24.

9. Dorothy C. Wertz, "Providers' Gender and Moral Reasoning: A Proposed Agenda for Research on Providers and Patients," *Fetal Diagnosis and Therapy* 8, supplement 1 (1993): 81–89.

10. Bonnie S. LeRoy, "When Theory Meets Practice: Challenges to the Field of Genetic Counseling," in Bartels et al., *Prescribing Our Future*, 41.

11. Robert Proctor, *Racial Hygiene: Medicine under the Nazis* (Cambridge: Harvard University Press, 1988).

12. Charles Bosk, *All God's Mistakes: Genetic Counseling in a Pediatric Hospital* (Chicago: University of Chicago Press, 1992), 171.

13. Charles Bosk, "The Workplace Ideology of Genetic Counselors," in Bartels et al., *Prescribing Our Future*, 28.

14. Wertz, "Providers' Gender and Moral Reasoning."

15. If the demand for genetic services accelerates as predicted, there will not be nearly enough trained genetic counselors available. Primary care physicians may have to pick up the slack, which will raise problems about adequacy of genetic knowledge among physicians and about their skill and comfort with counseling.

16. Wertz and Fletcher, "Prenatal Diagnosis and Sex Selection."

17. CIOMS, "Group B: Genetic Screening and Testing," in Z. Bankowski and A. M. Capron, *Genetics, Ethics, and Human Values: Human Genome Mapping, Genetic Screening and Therapy* (Geneva: WHO, 1991), 184.

18. Wertz and Fletcher, "Prenatal Diagnosis and Sex Selection," 1363.

19. Ibid., 1365.

20. I use sex selection here to mean avoiding having a child of the unwanted sex in the absence of good medical reasons. There are genetic disorders linked to the X chromosome that affect only males, some of them severe. Cases

like this are comparable to other instances of testing in order to avoid having a child with a genetic disorder.

21. Dan W. Brock, "The Ideal of Shared Decision Making between Physicians and Patients," *Kennedy Institute of Ethics Journal* (March 1991): 28–47, 31.

22. Ibid.

23. Ibid., 32.

24. Ibid.

25. Brock's article does an excellent job of showing the difficulties with what he calls "the incorrigibility thesis."

26. This quotation and the others from Asch in this section may be found in Adrienne Asch, "Reproductive Technology and Disability," in *Reproductive Law for the 1990s*, ed. Sherrill Cohen and Nadine Taub (Clifton, N.J.: Humana Press, 1989), 86.

27. Adrienne Asch, "The Human Genome and Disability Rights," *Disability Rag and ReSource* (January–February 1994): 12–15, on p. 13.

28. Lisa Blumberg, "Eugenics vs. Reproductive Choice," *Disability Rag and ReSource* (January–February 1994): 3–11, on p. 4.

29. Asch, "The Human Genome and Disability Rights."

30. For a sensitive discussion of the notion of a life that would be burdensome to the child living it, see John D. Arras, "AIDS and Reproductive Decisions: Having Children in Fear and Trembling," *Milbank Quarterly* 68, no. 3 (1990): 353–382.

31. Marsha Saxton, "Prenatal Screening and Discriminatory Attitudes about Disability," *GeneWATCH* (January–February 1987): 8–10.

32. John Passmore, *The Perfectibility of Man* (New York: Scribners, 1970), 208.

33. Cited in Passmore, *The Perfectibility of Man*, 187.

34. Ibid., 22.

35. Diogenes Laertius, cited in Passmore, *The Perfectibility of Man*, 58.

36. Passmore, *The Perfectibility of Man*, 324.

37. Ibid., 323.

38. Ibid., 325.

39. Asch, "Reproductive Technology and Disability."

Chapter 7.   Abortion and the Place of Motherhood

1. Kristin Luker, *Abortion and the Politics of Motherhood* (Berkeley, Los Angeles, and London: University of California Press, 1984), 193.

2. Judith Jarvis Thomson's article is the most famous example of this approach. See her "A Defense of Abortion," *Philosophy and Public Affairs* 1, no. 1 (1971): 47–66. Many writers, including staunch defenders of choice, have been critical of Thomson for failing to appreciate the special nature of a pregnant woman's relationship with her fetus.

3. Mario Matthew Cuomo, *More than Words: The Speeches of Mario Cuomo* (New York: St. Martin's Press, 1993).

4. For a more thorough discussion of top-down ethics and the implications of a tapestry approach, see chapter 8, "Tapestry and Web."

5. H. Tristram Engelhardt, *The Foundations of Bioethics* (Oxford: Oxford University Press, 1986), 242.

6. Ibid., 237.

7. Ibid., 219.

8. Ibid.

9. Ibid., 229.

10. Ibid., 118.

11. There are other, more nuanced, philosophical approaches that do not take personhood to be the central issue in abortion. Bonnie Steinbock, for example, in *Life Before Birth: The Moral and Legal Status of Embryos and Fetuses* (New York: Oxford University Press, 1992), asks what sorts of interests fetuses have at various stages of development, and how such interests affect a fetus's right not be killed. Such an approach to the ethics of abortion is an improvement over personhood approaches, I believe, for reasons soon to be made clear. But, by focusing attention on the moral status of the fetus, it may distract us nonetheless from other morally relevant issues that are at least, if not more, central to the public controversy.

12. John F. Crosby, "The Personhood of the Human Embryo," *Journal of Medicine and Philosophy* 18 (1993): 399–417.

13. The instances of this are numberless. See virtually any issue of the *National Right to Life News* or any other pro-life publication.

14. Rev. Dennis Kristof, "Orthodox Speak Against 22 Years of a Barbarity," *Cleveland Plain Dealer*, 25 January 1995, B: 13.

15. Wanda Franz, "Arguing the Pro-Life Case—Part II," *National Right to Life News* 20, no. 6 (30 March 1993): 3.

16. Dave Andrusko, "A New Way of Seeing," *National Right to Life News* 20, no. 6 (30 March 1993): 2.

17. Anonymous, "NRLC Condemns Shooting of Abortionist Dr. Gunn," *National Right to Life News* 20, no. 6 (30 March 1993): 1.

18. See, e.g., Wanda Franz, "Violence Is Not Pro-Life," *National Right to Life News* 22, nos. 1–2 (January 1995): 3.

19. Luker, *Politics of Motherhood*, 141.

20. When my colleague and friend, Paul Lauritzen, read this passage he informed me that someone else had already thought of this possibility. Garry Trudeau, the creator of "Doonesbury," had composed and then withdrawn a series of six comic strips in reaction to the right-to-life film *The Silent Scream*. In Trudeau's version, a follow-up has been made called *Silent Scream II: The Prequel* in which a 12-minute-old embryo is aborted. The narrator claims that the embryo can be seen uttering as its final words, "Repeal *Roe v. Wade*." The strips appeared in the 10 June 1985 issue of the *New Republic*.

21. In fairness, supporters of legal abortion should also be called to defend their symbols: Will restrictions on abortion such as waiting periods in fact lead to more illegal abortions and to more mutilations and deaths of women? I will not pursue this here because my focus is on the consequences of making a metaphysical construct like personhood the crux of a policy debate.

22. See chapter 2, "Abortion," of Steinbock, *Life Before Birth*, for a thoughtful analysis of pro-life defenses of fetal personhood.

23. See Ruth Macklin, "Personhood in the Bioethics Literature," *Milbank Quarterly* 61, no. 1 (1983): 35–57.

24. Robert J. Blendon, John M. Benson, and Karen Donelan, "The Public and the Controversy over Abortion," *JAMA* 270, no. 23 (15 December 1993): 2871–2875.

25. Ronald Dworkin, *Life's Dominion: An Argument about Abortion, Euthanasia, and Individual Freedom* (New York: Vintage Books, 1994), 11.

26. Ibid., 13.

27. Ibid., 23.

28. Ibid., 57, 60.

29. Ibid., 91.

30. Ibid., 157.

31. Ibid., 67.

32. Luker, *Politics of Motherhood*, 159.

33. Ibid., 138.

34. Ibid., 174.

35. Ibid., 197.

36. Ibid., 200.

37. Ibid., 176.

38. Ibid., 204.

39. Ibid., 214.

Chapter 8.   Tapestry and Web

1. John D. Arras, "Principles and Particularity: The Roles of Cases in Bioethics," *Indiana Law Journal* 69 (1994): 983, 989.

2. Ibid., 990.

3. Tom L. Beauchamp and James F. Childress, *Principles of Biomedical Ethics*, 4th ed. (New York: Oxford University Press, 1994).

4. Jeffrey Stout, *Ethics after Babel: The Languages of Morals and Their Discontents* (Boston: Beacon Press, 1988). Stout suggests that creative moral thought involves a process he calls "bricolage," in which we "start off by taking stock of problems that need solving and available conceptual resources for solving them. Then [we] proceed by taking apart, putting together, reordering, weighting, weeding out, and filling in." He goes on to accuse contemporary moral philosophy of favoring "a particular kind of *bricolage*—the kind that draws sharp lines around a secularized moral language, dismissing all else as inessential, and then reducing what is left to a single principle employing a single essential concept" (p. 75).

5. Mary Midgley, *Can't We Make Moral Judgments?* (New York: St. Martin's Press, 1993), 92.

6. Susan Moller Okin, *Justice, Gender, and the Family* (New York: Basic Books, 1989), 69.

7. Ibid., 56.

8. To Michael Walzer's *Spheres of Justice* (New York: Basic Books, 1983) I owe my use of the concept of spheres of human life. The concept of goods internal to a practice is taken from Alasdair McIntyre's *After Virtue*, 2d ed. (Notre Dame, Ind.: University of Notre Dame Press, 1984).

9. Ronald Dworkin, *Life's Dominion: An Argument about Abortion, Euthanasia, and Individual Freedom* (New York: Vintage Books, 1994), 13.

10. Midgley, *Can't We Make Moral Judgments?* 14.

11. Stout, *Ethics after Babel.*

12. Jaroslav Pelikan, *The Vindication of Tradition* (New Haven: Yale University Press, 1984). See also Michael Walzer, *Interpretation and Social Criticism* (Cambridge: Harvard University Press, 1987).

13. Midgley, *Can't We Make Moral Judgments?* 76.

14. Stout, *Ethics after Babel,* 73.

15. Ibid., 218–219.

16. Alasdair McIntyre, *Whose Justice? Which Rationality?* (Notre Dame, Ind.: University of Notre Dame Press, 1988). See especially chapter 18, "The Rationality of Traditions."

17. Ibid, 397.

18. Walzer, *Interpretation and Social Criticism.*

Index

Printed in the United States
152867LV00004B/3/A